CONFESSIONS OF A PhD

Tales of Struggle and Success in the Ivory Tower

VOLUME I

by D. Anthony Miles

The contents of this work, including, but not limited to, the accuracy of events, people, and places depicted; opinions expressed; permission to use previously published materials included; and any advice given, or actions advocated are solely the responsibility of the author, who assumes all liability for said work and indemnifies the publisher against any claims stemming from publication of the work.

All Rights Reserved
Copyright © 2023 by D. Anthony Miles

No part of this book may be reproduced or transmitted, downloaded, distributed, reverse engineered, or stored in or introduced into any information storage and retrieval system, in any form or by any means, including photocopying and recording, whether electronic or mechanical, now known or hereinafter invented without permission in writing from the publisher.

Dorrance Publishing Co
585 Alpha Drive
Pittsburgh, PA 15238
Visit our website at *www.dorrancebookstore.com*

ISBN: 978-1-6491-3224-6
eISBN: 978-1-6491-3731-9

CONFESSIONS
OF A
PhD

Tales of Struggle and Success in the Ivory Tower

VOLUME I

ACKNOWLEGEMENTS

There are so many people we want to thank for the publication of this book. This book could not have been completed without the assistance and input of many people. It is the people behind the scenes that made this book successful. First and foremost, we are grateful to the twelve authors that contributed to this book. We are incredibly grateful.

The authors have written their stories in hopes that it will inspire others. First, we want to thank these authors that put their confidence in me to publish their stories with excellence. They share their hearts with their stories. We do not take that lightly. Without your contribution this book would not be possible. We thank you so much.

Second, we would like to thank the many colleges and universities from which we have graduated. Those schools provided us with a doctorate to get to this point in our careers. Those colleges and universities provided the foundation for all of us to pursue our education endeavors. Those schools provided the basis for our philosophies, ideologies, and critical thinking. We appreciate your undying support.

Third, we would like to thank our students from the many colleges and universities which we have taught, as well as organizations we serve in a leadership role. We thank you for not only inspiring us to write this book but inspiring us the be better scholars of our prospective fields of study. In addition, we would like to thank the Black Doctoral Network (BDN) for providing an academic platform for meeting black academics and scholars.

Fourth, we would like to thank our publisher, Dorrance Publishers. Your guidance with publishing this literary work is invaluable. We appreciate the editors, artists, and staff at Dorrance for making this book a reality. We appreciate you so much for publishing this literary work. We thank you so much.

Fifth, we would like to thank Ms. Jill Twist, editor of the book. She provided a critical eye for details that were vital in the success of publishing this book. We appreciate her editing skill for completing this book. She is invaluable.

Lastly, but not least, we want to thank our families for their support. We want to thank the many mothers, fathers, children, uncles, aunts, spouses, cousins, and other family that supported us. We really appreciate your support. We could not have done this without you and your support. There were many struggles and pitfalls that occurred with the publication of this book. We thank you so much!

I want to dedicate this book to the late Dr. Tonjalyn R. Ford. She was one of my former students. She was awarded her doctorate degree posthumously. I will never forget you and your drive to complete your doctorate. I will always remember you. God bless you.

Dr. D. Anthony Miles, Managing Editor

FOREWORD

Foreword by the Honorable Dr. Ivy Taylor, President, Rust College

This volume contains stories of Black Americans that are not often told. As a child growing up with parents who did not advance beyond high school, I never thought about pursuing education beyond a bachelor's degree. There was no one in our family's circle who had attained the highestacademic degree possible. It was not until later in life that I met many black individuals who hadobtained the Ph.D. At a certain point, I thought that it was too late for me to pursue that goal. After leaving San Antonio's City Hall where I served as mayor for three years, God opened the door for me at age 48 to continue my education. In 2020, I completed a Doctor of Education (Ed.D.) at the University of Pennsylvania.

The Bible says in Proverbs 29:18, "Where there is no vision, the people perish," and I current times and in current times, we are apt to say that our children, "can't be what they can't see." That is why collecting and publishing these stories is so important. These stories allow people to see themselves and the full range of possibilities for their lives.

In reviewing them, I noted common threads as most of these Black academics began with very humble beginnings. In the 21st century, many disadvantaged young people see very limited options for their futures due to the challenges they currently face. The contributors to this volume encountered challenges in achieving their goals and their perseverance is admirable. The practical advice they offer should be heeded by those considering academia as a career. In addition, I hope all will take away the message that lifelong learning is essential.

Currently I am serving as president of Rust College, an HBCU in Mississippi, which allows me to fulfill my personal goal of connecting people to opportunity. I realized long ago that education is the best way to make that happen. Rust College has taken many from humble beginnings and provided the platform for them to rise to heights in a variety of careers. Several of the writers contained in this volume also got their start and were nurtured at institutions like Rust College. I am so glad they are sharing their stories to encourage others to live up to their full potential.

Thank you to the individuals who participated in this incredible and inspiring project.

Dr. Ivy Taylor, President
Rust College
2023

Foreword by
Dr. Brenya Twumasi, Academic Scholar and Practitioner

My people perish from the lack of knowledge; we are all versed in the meaning and sentiment of this statement.

We must share our journey to support those coming on up. We share not to discourage not to defuse hope but rather to share we can do this – we can make it through despite the interference we face and the hurdles we must jump.

With knowledge passed on to us by our elders and by our ancestors we are thus strengthened. We are strengthened despite the smoke screens to comprehend our individual and collective strength. Our strength is of diverse natures; coming together as the fabric of a marvelous quilt. Our success is birthed from perseverance; perseverance stitched with hands that are knobbed and knuckles that are bruised. The journey has not been easy – it has been tedious; we acknowledge that. With communal support we do flow with lessened impediments.

Dr. D. Anthony Miles has done us proud. My Dad would say to us as children (age appropriate) this that I took fully to heart:

As you study - take a pause – look behind you; do you see the queue of people behind you – the queue is so very long you cannot see the end of such. It is so long it is more than a mile and curves around the block.

Listen to the voices – the voices are in unison stating go keep studying because we do not have the possibility to study as you have had. Keep studying keep studying so you can open each door that we can then follow you through.

Dr. D. Anthony Miles thank you for keeping on studying and opening the door for all others to follow through.

Dr. Brenya Twumasi, Academic Scholar and Practitioner

Fields of Law, Psychology, Criminal Justice, Academic Innovation and Artificial Intelligence

2023

TABLE OF CONTENTS

***Disclaimer:** *Disclaimer: The stories in this book reflect the authors' recollection of events. Some names, locations, and identifying characteristics have been changed to protect the privacy of those depicted. Dialogue has been recreated from memory.

CHAPTER 1

Dr. Willie Black, Jr.

Educator and Administrator, and Judson Independent School District

BIOGRAPHY

Dr. Willie Black is an educator and administrator. He has twenty years of experience in K-12 education. He has had a successful career in K-12 education. He has vast experience as a K-12 educator. He has been a coach, teacher, administrator, principal, and assistant superintendent.

Dr. Black was born in Big Lake, Texas. He is the oldest of three children. He has won numerous awards for his hard work and community involvement.

He is a member of the *Talented Tenth Scholars of San Antonio* and was part of documentary with the group. He has traveled around the country and spearheads programs improving K-12 schools in his district. Dr. Black is well-known in the media for his research on African American male principals in Texas.

CREDENTIALS:

- EdD in Educational Leadership, *University of Texas at San Antonio*
- MA in Sports Management, *Southwest Texas State University*
- BA in Exercise and Sports, *Southwest Texas State University*

And whatsoever ye do, do it heartily, as to the Lord
and not unto men

~ *Colossians 3:2*

***Disclaimer:** The stories in this chapter reflect the author's recollection of events. Some names, locations, and identifying characteristics have been changed to protect the privacy of those depicted. Dialogue has been re-created from the author's memory.

A New Beginning

Personal Background

The world could be perceived as unforgiving and cruel; however, this perception may lie within the eyes of the beholder. The lens that we possess will be adopted and molded by those who have been placed in our path to lead and direct us. These people come in many forms, such as parents, leaders of the community, mentors, and family members. It is those who intervene and provide the guidance necessary to mold and create productive citizens. To be contributors of society and not takers is the goal of the community of African American people. After careful reflection of my life and how far I have come, I cannot help but acknowledge those who have been placed in my path to help guide me to where I am today. This place is not of status or prestige but of spiritual connectedness. My life, as many others, is full of memories: the good, bad, and not so happy moments. These moments are what have helped ground me into who I am as a person.

I came from a humble upbringing. My father and mother instilled in me a sense of moral and ethical perceptions that doing the right thing all the time and respecting others is the way of life. My father was, and still is, a deacon of the church. My parents raised God-fearing children and loved us per biblical standards. I am grateful that my parents molded me into being the man I am today, withstanding the test of the world and all that it consists of.

My childhood was a normal one. I took part in the activities of an average child. I came from a time when we enjoyed the simple things, like playing outside with friends, filling my time with sticks, and acting like cops and robbers. The small town from which I came from provided me with a nurturing and wholesome environment. Where the ubiquitous phrase "It takes a village to raise a child" was used at its height. Everyone in the community knew where Willie was and where he was going. I do miss those times, where riding down the street didn't cause the stress and worry that consumes me now that I am a parent myself. Growing up in west Texas was a great time. These young men, the Standly brothers, were much older than my brother and I, attributed to my advancement in sports by playing with the older kids. This helped me to be better. The field of sports, both baseball and football, filled our spare time. Living the dream and goal of being a professional football player consumed me during my adolescent years.

I was the oldest of three children. I had the opportunity to establish the tempo as the older sibling regarding behavior and the fact of "towing the line." I was the most curious during this time and would rather take disciplinary action by my father than forgo a good football game at the field. My strong will got the best of me most of the time. I would weigh my options: "to stay and have fun" or "sustain the punishment of not reporting home on time." I, usually, choose the latter of the two and had my fun. My rationalization consisted of convincing myself that I could take the punishment, which lasted only a few minutes, compared to the hour of fun I had had.

I had a rude awakening during high school. I loved the social part of high school football games and dances, but I didn't pour energy into academics. I participated in every extracurricular activity except for golf. I would have participated but couldn't fit it into my schedule. Being a typical student, I enjoyed band and playing the alto saxophone. It was a blast. I had to drop out of band the last two years of high school to take Spanish, but that was a great experience.

I wasn't fully aware of what was needed in order to matriculate in higher education.

In retrospect, I have come to the realization that those responsible for educating me on how to navigate this arena may not have been completely interested in assisting me. When my friends were called into the guidance counselor's office to discuss their plans for college, little Willie was not summoned. I began to question why. I did not know that ACTs and SATs were prerequisite for the application process. I was ignorant about the process of applying for college. To compound my ignorance, I totally believed that my athletic ability would be my ticket into higher education. I had already received a few letters of interest from a few universities, and I believed that I was on my way to a full scholarship. Needless to say, I believed that if I worked hard enough on the football field, a scout from some university would notice me and offer me a scholarship. *Boy, was I wrong!*

During my junior year in high school, I had a huge shift in my life. I was injured during a game that landed me on the sideline for a few games. I was totally determined to get back on the field to showcase my abilities. I made it back from my knee injury and finished the last three games of the season. I believed everything was just fine, until I was called into the coach's office for a meeting. Coach proceeded to tell me that I was not healed and that surgery would be required for me to return next season. I was dumbfounded. I felt fine; what was he talking about? However, those who coached me knew from observing me that I wasn't 100 percent. Eventually a trip to the doctor made me realize. I needed knee surgery. My anterior cruciate ligament (ACL) was completely torn and needed replacement.

I concluded that my chances of going to college on an athletic scholarship were now slim, but my strong will and character would not allow me to acquiesce. I went through a short bout of depression, although I didn't realize it at the time. I withdrew from friends and family; I couldn't cope with being injured. I had always been healthy and capable of carrying out my athletic responsibilities. I then engaged in a very rigorous therapy program. I was determined to return to the football field healthy and in full force. I had one of the best sport medicine trainers in the country, and I knew when I completed his rehab program, I would be ready for the next football season.

My junior year soon passed, and I felt better than ever! I continued to work hard throughout the summer in preparation for my senior year of high school. As football season began, I was ready for an outstanding return to the field; however, tragedy struck again. During practice, I suffered another knee injury. My right knee, this time, a teammate landed on it during drills. I remember that day very well; it was as if my whole world ended. I knew for certain that my football career was over. I did not know it then, but I believe everything happens for a reason. I can vividly recall my close walk with the Lord during my freshman and sophomore years of high school; however, I did not know that God was speaking to me, and I had not turned my thoughts into glorifying Him but to my selfish thoughts of getting what I wanted. See, sometimes in our lives we believe that all things come from what we think to be hard work and perseverance; however, I believe that God orchestrates all that we have and the path we walk. Just like a child who disobeys his parents, consequences befall those who disobey the Lord. I truly believe that turning our eyes from our Father in heaven is the worst travesty that a man can experience. Nevertheless, I had to accept the fact; I sought entrance to higher education the traditional and expected way, through academics. I followed friends and enrolled to take the ACT and SAT. I felt somewhat academically inadequate due to what I now think was the misguidance of some key players in my path; however, to this day I consider this to be a blessing. Proverbs 16:9 states: "The mind of man plans his way, but the Lord direct his steps."

College Educational Experiences

When I finally got accepted into college, it was on a probationary basis due to low test scores, and I ended up taking a few remedial classes for Math and Science. My father and I attended orientation together, which seemed a blur to me. I was in another world, totally different from which I came. I came from a small west Texas town with a population of around four thousand to a college town with a population of roughly forty thousand when school was not in session. I felt as if I were in the big city and embarking upon on a new journey.

I've often been asked why did I not choose the military, and my response was "Why would I leave the army to go to the army?" My father was a Vietnam veteran and ran the household just as if he were still in the army. I made that statement jokingly; however, there were many times when my father's discipline felt like boot camp. We had strict guidelines, and his expectations were high. I understand now, as a father and husband, why my father had such high standards for his children. In December, my father would always tell me that I was a leader. It never clicked until later in life that my father saw something in me that I did not see in myself. I would always seek permission to socialize with certain individuals; however, I found myself befriending those with a mischievous personality. It wasn't until my adulthood that my father revealed to me his rationale behind his decision making regarding this matter. He knew that allowing me to fraternize with the nonconforming students, I would be able to enhance my leadership qualities. He believed that if allowed to socialize with those with similar qualities, my leadership would be diminished. I still wonder, had I known the rationales then, what kind of impact would that made on me today?

My father also taught me the value of the dollar at an early age. My two younger siblings and I did not want anything. My father always provided what we needed, when we needed. I can remember the times my father taught me a valuable lesson. We would always shop for school clothes and my father explicitly stated, "You need to make these shoes last until January." I didn't heed my father's request and abused my tennis shoes and boldly asked my father for more shoes in December. His response was "Boy, what did tell you? I told you to make those shoes last until January. You had better get a job!" I was crushed. I realized, at that time, my father was serious, and I needed to explore my resources in obtaining work. I was thirteen years of age, looking for odd jobs here and there, mustering up enough money to purchase shoes. After approximately a month had passed, I found myself in the mall, shopping a little differently, since the money I was spending was mine. I needed to spend frugally and mindfully. I ended up with shoes half the cost of the original selection, a new shirt, and the purchase of a meal. I did that all on my own! My father was a genius. I know that now was a calculated effort by my father to educate me once again.

As I navigated the academic world, I found myself acclimating to the party scene rather than making schooling my priority. I joined a fraternity and was living the good life. I purposely did not have Friday classes so I could extend my weekend. My weekend typically began on Thursday and did not conclude until Sunday evening. This behavior was not conducive to that of a productive college experience, academically. I found myself on academic probation more than twice, but I seemed to pick up the slack just at the right time to be removed from the list.

I was a sophomore before I finally declared a major. In the beginning, I thought I would coach the sport I loved, football, but due too poor guidance in high school, I didn't realize that the university didn't offer a coaching degree. When I was forced to declare a major, I learned that I would need a teaching certificate to coach. That's when I decided to become a teacher. I declared exercise sports science as my major and health as a minor, which is somewhat typical of a coach. I needed these courses to coach in related teaching positions.

I realized that my independence was worth fighting for. I felt like I needed to be my own person and began to cement my identity in the real world. I resented the lectures my father gave me when I requested more money. Although I'm sure the feeling was mutual, I applied for a job at Arby's. That was an interesting change of pace, considering all that I had done in the past consisted of manual labor, whether on the oil field or the cotton field; I worked at an early age and would not have changed it for the world. I felt more like an adult being away from home and no longer felt like enduring lectures given by my father. The Arby's job lasted a month. Then a friend turned my interest into a position dealing with challenging young adults. I landed a position with Gary Job Corp. This was a vocational facility that awarded technical certifications in the area for electricians, brick masonry, business office technicians, dental assistants, etc. My job was a recreational position dealing with the running a weight room and grooming athletes to compete in power-line events. This experience was priceless and prepared me for the positions of a coach and teacher for the future. I was in contact with students from all over the world. There were students from third and fifth ward from Houston, students from China, Mexico, Cuba, and New York. I encountered many walks of life at Gary Job Corps and learned a valuable lesson: there is a ghetto in every race, and no matter where the location may be, there is an economically disadvantaged demographic; however, it is only in America that we focus on this one area. I make this statement to underscore the fact that we are driven and we live by how others perceive us. I learned that no matter what I do in America, I will be perceived as different. At this point, I turned that energy into my favor. I would not allow myself to judge others and began to measure a person by their merit and character as human beings.

During my work and continued schooling, I prayed that my life would find direction. I now reflect on my life and realized I needed to slow the pace and focus on my education while planning. I had one of the best things happen to me at that time! God answered my prayers and I met my wife. She struck me as a person who was determined and focused on finishing school; this was something I needed at that time. Her determination was infectious. I found myself more focused on my studies, and my passion for learning grew. The social scene was now in my rearview, and a meaningful future was full steam ahead. I proposed to her the day of graduation. That was the best decision I had made in my life. I can vividly remember that point in my life and how much it has changed.

Everything was so clear, and I was focused on what God had in store for our future. A month after I proposed, I landed my first teaching and coaching position in the same community I conducted my student teaching. I had no idea how hard it was to come by health teaching positions, due to fact that that these positions were usually guaranteed to coaches who were brought on by head coaches. My cooperating teacher approached me with an offer to stay on staff after graduating. The position would be as a middle school health instructor, mid-year, with a possible coaching position for the upcoming school year. I replied, "No, I think I'm going to take a break." After a mini lecture from my cooperating teacher, along with a few other coaches, I took the job. This decision proved to be one of the best decisions I had ever made, obviously, the work of God himself. God has his hand in everything we do; our paths are forged before time; often we are spiritually unaware how great he is.

I finished the school year teaching and landed the coaching position for the next year. I taught for approximately seven years and felt as if I was ready for the next move, which was, clearly, high school coaching. At that time, I aspired to be an athletic director. I then met with the current head coach and expressed an interest in a freshman football position and informed him of my intent to enroll in a master's program and obtain another degree in sports management. I had put a great deal of work into my current position and felt I needed to move. I had a rude awakening and learned something about the political aspect of upward mobility that I wasn't aware of. A recent college graduate from that hometown was awarded the freshman position. I was infuriated that my position was given to someone with less experience. At that point, I went through a moment of grieving; I reflected on my position as a coach and leader on the campus and began to hear all the recalled discussions with supervisors and peers encouraging me to seek the position as principal.

I didn't give it a second thought since I was on the administrative track. I believed that administrators spent their day meting out discipline behind a desk throughout the day. I received my master's in sport management and promptly enrolled into an alternative principal certification program.

Shortly after enrolling, and apprising my administrator about my intentions of becoming an administrator, upper-management began utilizing me in the front office as a substitute administrator whenever other administrators were out of the office. What an invaluable experience for me; I spent a lot of time in the office learning firsthand how to become an assistant principal. This process continued throughout the school year, and I became very comfortable in the position. After completing a year in the program, the group could apply for positions with an endorsement from the program. We gained experience while practicing in the assistant principal position and principals under the auspices of the program. From this process, the staff received a probationary certification status.

My campus administrators continued to utilize my skills and made me aware of a promotion that had become available in the district. I was to replace the newly promoted person. It seemed that the job was as good as mine. I, coincidently, turned down two interviews in neighboring districts, placing all my trust in the current administrators that I would be placed in the position. I was under the impression that the interview process would be another formality. With school about to begin, I had already devoted two weeks of my time during the summer, acclimating to the position I knew was mine. I went into the interview confident that everything was already decided; all I had to do was move into the office.

I remember that day vividly; it was a professional development day on the Thursday before school began, and I had returned from my interview at central office. My wife, coincidently, was working at the same school as a special education teacher. We both waited in anticipation to hear the formal offer for the position. I was pumped and ready to embark on this new position, hoping to make the impact I knew I could. I was summoned to the principal's office, confident that the job was mine, only to be blindsided by the news that I was not chosen for the position after all. I found out shortly that the political-social capital played a part in the hiring of the new assistant principal. Basically, I didn't have the social pull; to say I was devastated was an understatement. My disappointment fueled me to aggressively search for positions in the neighboring area. I interviewed eleven times that spring before I landed my first assistant principal position at a high school in a rural community southeast of Austin, Texas. I remained an assistant principal for three years before becoming a principal at the junior high school of that same district. I was the first African American principal in that community.

Doctoral Study Experiences

As a principal, I attended many professional conferences and activities. I became more aware that I was the only African American principal in the audience. I did not give it a second thought; I was now accustomed and felt indifferent about being the only minority in the building. As I began my second year of principalship, my desire to lead as a superintendent weighed heavily on me. I began to realize that I would need to further my education to be a part of the top 1 percent of the applicant pool. I felt that, being Black and in educational leadership, my abilities and education would have to be above average. I would have to stand out in such a way that hiring committees could not turn my application away. I considered myself to be a God-fearing man and would turn to spiritual guidance my decision to pursue my doctorate. I began researching institutions online and gathered facts to assist my decision to further my education. My wife and I felt that pursuing a terminal degree would take much time and commitment from everyone in the family.

The process of deciding about where to attend school was very challenging. I quickly discovered that the monetary demands of pursuing a terminal degree would require from twenty-six thousand to fifty-six thousand dollars, depending on the program. Although online programs seemed to fit the convenience of my work schedule and family life, I decided to seek information from local institutions, known as "backyard universities." If leaving the state were an option for employment after receiving a doctorate, then an online program would be acceptable; however, if I planned on residing in the state, then obtaining a terminal degree from a local institution would be best. There also seemed to be a negative connotation from receiving a degree from online programs. Additionally, the traditional educational setting suited my learning style better. Consequently, I applied to two universities, one of them being my alma mater, Southwest Texas State University and The University of Texas at San Antonio.

During researching online versus traditional setting classrooms, research revealed that receiving education to include all degrees attained from university did not fare well if the professorate was a consideration. Research also revealed that obtaining degrees from multiple institutions displayed diversity in learning and allowed for greater marketability if I were to consider teaching higher education. I decided to pursue my doctorate at The University of Texas San Antonio; however, I did apply to both, to increase my chances of being admitted. Southwest Texas had a PhD (Doctorate of Philosophy) program versus UTSA's EdD (Doctorate of Education).

There seemed to be a perception in the academic world regarding the rigor of both doctorates. The EdD was a terminal degree of choice for me, as it was created for and designed to meet the needs of the practitioner. Both universities had the usual requirements; however, SWT did not require a GRE for the application process. That factor appealed me because my GRE scores had lapsed, being outside of the five-year window for current scores. UTSA did accept one of two tests, the GRE scores and MAT (Miller's Analogy Test) scores. I had taken the MAT test and was in the last year of current available scores. I submitted both applications to each institution along with a writing sample detailing my educational statement and rationale for obtaining a terminal degree. It was not long before UTSA contacted me for an interview with the committee. I was extremely nervous and anxious about embarking upon this journey. I knew that this was the path laid for me, and I wanted to matriculate here as a student, seeking a terminal degree. I knew that, pursuing a doctorate, I was establishing an expectation not only for my two children but for my entire family. I would be the first-generation doctoral student and, possibly, doctoral recipient in my family.

The day of the interview with UTSA is another memorable day, which I vividly remember. As I made my way to the designated room, I noticed a few people waiting in the hallway. After a few minutes, I started a conversation with the adults and inquired whether they were there for interviews as well. Two of the three had recently finished an impromptu educational writing sample. I was a bit confused and wondered if I had missed a step in the process. This information only exacerbated my nervousness and raised doubt.

I was called into the assigned room, filled with approximately six people seated in boardroom fashion. I met them with a smile and greeted all with warm energy. This interview was a bit different from the principal positions; the university was seeking to establish a fit for both the student and the university. The most obvious concern was how I would deal with the commute from workplace and school. The university was approximately one and a half hours away, one way. I explained that my commitment to this program far outweighed my commute. It was apparent that the committee sought students that would contribute and grow within the program. The interview was an exhilarating experience. I came out feeling like I was truly headed in the right direction. The university had established a seamless process regarding the application process. The original writing sample had been accepted by the university with the application, and they did not require me to produce an additional impromptu educational writing sample. I received my acceptance approximately two weeks later.

Lessons Learned

I had a preconceived notion that doctoral studies were very rigorous and demanding. However, as my first semester as a doctoral student began, I must admit that classes were very like the master's program in that professional discourse was embedded within the curriculum. Of course, there was much reading and writing to do; however, the program quickly guided me through the process of acclimating to doctoral studies. I can remember the first day of class where introductions were conducted and lifelong relationships began. We were all educators with varied backgrounds and levels of leadership. There were teachers, counselors, assistant superintendents, and principals who were part of the cohort (cohort, an associate, colleague, or supporter). Readings were assigned along with warranted group work. This approach was very like the studies conducted at the master's level.

We were taught to begin searching for a topic that could be dissertation worthy. This approach would assist later in the coursework. I had to consider whether I wanted to conduct a quantitative or qualitative study. The professors ensured the cohort that we had time to work out the topic. However, during the coursework, our writing a specific topic of interest would be helpful in the future. I learned a great deal during my coursework and formed a few alliances along the way. I used the word alliances because that is exactly what I felt at that time. Engaging in group work consisted of someone not contributing and everyone else picking up the slack. Aligning myself with those of exceptional work ethic and perseverance was beneficial both to myself and to the team. I learned that having a strong support system while in the program not only elevated the participation level but also created a sense of community among colleagues.

Another integral part of navigating the doctoral program successfully was having the appropriate advisor. One who would guide and assist with the concerns regarding schedules and the demands of the program. Initially, I had an advisor that did not work out for me. I had concerns regarding the direction of my research and needed my questions answered, but my questions were not answered in a timely manner. I do not fault that particular person, but I must admit, that experience was quite frustrating. There were times I did not receive a response for a few weeks. I continued with my course work, but I was to have an experience that would shift my thoughts to another level.

I was in my second year of coursework when I participated in a culture leadership class. This class changed my perception of how leaders lead in schools today. I quickly gravitated to the professor's leadership style. His name was Encarnacion Garza. He is a retired superintendent and now a tenured professor. He had practitioner experience and could attest firsthand to the travails of educators in the field. It is rare to have a practitioner with superintendent experience in the professorate. Dr. Garza operated through the lens of a social justice advocate. I was not familiar with that term at the time; however, it would not be long before I gravitated to this theme. This is what I have lived all my life. I did not have the platform to express how I have felt for so long; obtaining a doctorate would assist my quest to provide the marginalized a voice, and it is now my charge to do so. After being inspired by one of his lectures, I approached Dr. Garza after class and asked if he would consider taking me on as his mentee. Thankfully, he accepted, and I spent the last two years of the program growing under his stewardship. I consider him my mentor to this day.

It was not my last class that I realized I had reached a milestone. Research reveals that the coursework is the most manageable portion of the doctoral program. Traditionally, we have been conditioned to attend class, engage in discourse, and write. Usually, a syllabus is issued at the onset of the class and a detailed lecture about expectations ensues. Although the program does its best to prepare each student as it pertains to expectations, it does not, nor will it, prepare you enough to write the dissertation. I will expound further. The book *Good to Great*, written by Jim Collins, best illustrates how I felt during this time. As a leader, we acquire many skills that assist us in the positions we currently hold; however, those skills will never be diminished at the next level; we flounder for a moment until we acquire new skills. Jim Collins refers to this as the ten levels of leadership. Each level carries with it a skillset inherent to the position. I would equate my skillset as a number seven moving up to an eight, academically speaking. During the time of acquiring this new skillset, frustration and doubt permeate our comfort zone. However, once this period passes, we then become experts until the next transitions or professional promotion.

UTSA required a qualifying exam which consisted of questions presented by the committee. The rationale was to hone in on the topic proposal. Our topics were being developed during our coursework in the program, and the rationale would be to focus on the research and possibly fine-tune the first three chapters of the dissertation. These questions could take if a semester or as little as one month to complete. However, it was now where isolation began to kick in. Once you enter this phase of the program, it would behoove the candidate to find a strong network of recent or past graduates with doctoral degrees to keep in touch with for continued support. Not knowing what to expect or how to navigate the process promotes a high level of anxiety. Fortunately, at this point, Dr. Garza also accepted to chair my dissertation committee. I consulted with him, and he assisted me by providing resources and advice, which curbed some of the stress. But I still felt alone at times; I would often reflect on many of those who came before me who did not finish and are still to this day ABD (All but Dissertation). Was it at this point of the journey they decided they couldn't continue? I had to lean on my God more closely during this part of my walk or, too, may have been a static. I have seen applicants who claim ABD on their resume when applying for positions in the school districts, with no intention of completing their terminal degree. I vowed not to be that person.

Dr. Garza also assisted me in choosing the committee members. I quickly found that this was a vital segment of the proposal and doctoral defense process. There were four members on my committee to include: my chair, Dr. Garza, and three other professors from the program. The day of my defense is yet another vivid memory, etched in my mind as if it were yesterday. I asked my wife to attend the defense with me for support. I was well prepared for the defense as I delivered my presentation. At the end of my defense, I was escorted to a room where my wife had already been waiting. And only five minutes later, my chair returned with the news. I'll never forget the first time I heard my new title, "Congratulations, Dr. Black."

Final Thoughts

My doctoral research revolved around minority principal leadership and the obstacles or characteristics that contributed to their ascension to the position. The study revealed that demographics of students in the United States are vastly changing. There are growing numbers of children of color in US public schools. Statics have shown that African Americans are significantly underrepresented in the principalship as compared to their European American counterparts. As the number of minority students continues to increase, the racial and ethnic representation of administration does not reflect this shift.

Principals that promote a mainstream education are not prepared to meet the needs of an ever-changing student population. As fewer minority leaders enter the field, schools with diverse demographics are largely impacted. A need for a multicultural curriculum is paramount to meet the needs of this population. As African American leaders enter the field, there may be many obstacles and barriers preventing a successful evolution of learning for the students whom they serve. It is imperative that the training received in principal certification programs infuses a belief in a culturally stimulating curriculum. The knowledge of how to meet the needs of all students is essential for the principal's success.

The historical context of African American leadership has provided a platform for misperceptions and stereotypes of how these leaders are perceived in education. African American leaders encounter many obstacles in the principalship and have overcome adversity to lead multicultural schools to success. These obstacles, as presented in my doctoral research, have not prevented African American male leaders from attaining success but rather served as motivation in overcoming hardship. The principalship is no small task; however, increasing the diversity among educational professionals is probably the greatest challenge that schools face.

Being in a leadership position and reflecting on the research has been a stimulating experience. I have lived through and shared sentiments with my participants within the study. Being an African American male in the leadership position has allowed me to analyze the participants' experiences through a lens of leadership, which has inspired me to encourage others who aspire to the position. It all began with assimilating the idea that I could affect more students by entering the leadership position. As an educator and coach, I witnessed the transformation of students within the schools in which I've worked. Colleagues and supervisors encouraged me to matriculate administration; as an African American male in education, I was initially doubtful and questioned whether administration was for me. Being a first-generation college graduate, the experience of teaching was a positive experience, but I personally had not seen many African Americans in such leadership roles. Thus, I had not conceived of going past my bachelor's degree or doing anything other than teaching and coaching.

Once I committed to the idea of entering the leadership role, supervisors placed me into positions in the school in which I could develop my skills. I began to see myself the way others saw me, as a leader people would respond favorably to. I felt that the impact would be much greater on a school in this position compared in that of the classroom. Colleagues, parents, and supervisors accepted me, and my influence was evident during the internship. However, as reflected in this study's findings, lessons are to be learned regarding politics, social perceptions, and barriers faced when ascending to the position. But as an African American principal, no other experience has compared to the resistance experienced as a minority in the leadership position.

I realized that African Americans have been marginalized for quite some time. Until my research, I was not aware of the extent to which administrators and educators had been dispersed throughout the integration era and how this was to impact the future of education for s. The most salient aspect of my dissertation research was the realization that mainstream education has created disconnection between public education and the marginalized students it serves. Also, although African Americans have been unfairly scrutinized in the past, that mindset must be completely dissolved. The form of scrutiny may be subtler, disguised by politics and bureaucracy, but is still ever present.

Through my research, I also began to appreciate that sharing the same ethnic background does not necessarily enable a leader to meet the needs of their students. It behooves the educational process to have a multicultural leader, whether minority or not. Leaders who enter the field must be culturally sensitive to the needs of various students. Leaders must build a school community. My research served to magnify the need for programs that qualify aspiring principals academically and culturally, so they, in turn, can meet the needs of an ever-changing demographic in the school population of America.

• • •

CHAPTER 2

Dr. Michael J. Laney

Provost and Vice President for Academic Affairs, Savannah State University

BIOGRAPHY

Dr. Michael Laney recently accepted a position a provost and vice president for Academic Affairs at *Savannah State University* (SSU). He came from *Our Lady of the Lake University* in where he has served as dean and professor over the *College of Arts and Sciences* since 2012. He was responsible for the oversight and management of an annual $3.8 million budget in support of thirty-nine full-time faculty, fifty-three adjunct faculty, five staff members, and over five hundred students.

Upon college graduation, he accepted a commission in the *United States Army Signal Corps* as a second lieutenant and entered active duty. He held command and deputy command responsibilities at the captain and major level and was responsible for one thousand soldiers and civilians and the command and control of assets in excess of $110 million. He retired as a major on October 1, 1995, with twenty years of federal service. He is a member of the *Talented Tenth Scholars of San Antonio* (TTSA).

CREDENTIALS:

- PhD in Communications, *University of Tennessee*
- MA in Telecommunication, *Michigan State University*
- BA in Political Science, *Southeastern Massachusetts University*.

"If you know from whence you came there is really no limit to where you can go."

~ *James Baldwin*

***Disclaimer:** The stories in this chapter reflect the author's recollection of events. Some names, locations, and identifying characteristics have been changed to protect the privacy of those depicted. Dialogue has been re-created from the author's memory.

My Journey from Student, to Soldier, to Servant, to Scholar

Personal Background: The Life of an Army Brat

"God sure has an incredible sense of humor, just look at how my life turned out!" (MJ. Laney, May 23, 2014) If you had told Michael J. Laney when he was eighteen years of age, a skinny, black , 145-poundshrimp, that one day he would inspire every family member in his house to go to college, that, like his father, he would serve his country as a soldier in a time of war and peace, that he would accept the calling of God in the role of servant and rise to the rank of a bishop in the church, and that he would earn a doctorate and become a college professor and rise to become the first person of color in the position of dean of the College of Arts and Sciences at Our Lady of the Lake University, San Antonio, Texas, he would have laughed out loud in your face and shouted, "That's impossible—you must be pulling my leg!"

Michael Jerome Laney was born in Flushing, New York, on April 26, 1955. The oldest son of four children, born to the late James Laney and Celestine Burr Laney, Michael grew up in a loving and supportive home, but a disciplined one as well. His parents had left their southern roots of Raeford, North Carolina, (Dad) and Jacksonville, Florida, (Mom) in the early 1950s in the exodus that author Isabel Wilkerson (2010) in her work *The Warmth of Other Suns* described as the "great migration" and headed north, riding that great train to the "promised land" on the coattails of the US army. James Laney would rise from the ranks of a private to retire from the military after twenty years of distinguished service as a chief warrant officer. James Laney's service would carry Michael and his "army brat" siblings to Ft. Hamilton, New York; Ft. Bliss, Texas; West Germany (during the height of the Cold War); and, eventually, home ownership in Bridgewater, Massachusetts, were the Laney family would settle into a traditional nuclear family model, with Celestine Laney staying at home and then only working part time once the children grew older. James Laney held several jobs, Boston Naval Shipyard and General Dynamics Corporation, before landing a position with the Department of Interior and the National Park Service. Following his military pattern for success and upward mobility, Laney was quickly promoted and moved from field positions as a park ranger into management and supervisory positions with the National Park Service system. His father was a pioneer for civil rights in the 1960s and 1970s, breaking the color barrier by becoming one of a handful of African Americans nationwide to hold management and, eventually, superintendent-level positions at Gateway National Park, New York; Yosemite National Park, California; Sequoia and Kings Canyon National Park, California; and the Southern Arizona Region, Phoenix, Arizona, where he eventually passed away through an illness contracted in the line of duty in 1989.

The Challenges of Integration

Raised in a strict Catholic home, faith would play a seminal role in Michael's life and shape his career path and destiny. At the age of ten, while an altar boy and an acolyte in the Pattonville Chapel Parish in Ludwigsburg, Germany, Michael kneeled at an altar and said, "Lord, when I grow up, I want to be a priest and serve you and your people all the days of my life." More than two decades would pass before this promise would be realized, but the journey would not be without some challenges. While his parents' thought that fleeing the South would mean escaping the South's Jim Crow and racial prejudice, vestiges of race prejudice refused to die. Bridgewater, MA, like many small towns in the north, also had its struggles with racial tolerance, in housing and employment. Unlike the rural south, the number of African Americans in these suburbs in the north was so small that they did not represent a threat to the majority. In most cases, instances of overt racism were rarely on display in this small town of ten thousand people, nestled between Boston and Cape Cod, comprised of third and fourth generation of Portuguese, Italian, Irish, and Catholics. Michael was one of only three students (Leonard Montgomery and Yvonne Dukes) in the graduating class of 1973 at Bridgewater-Raynham. Regional High School. He was an avid writer and an extrovert. While he excelled in most subjects in high school, he had to always study harder than most. Mathematics was his nemesis and a constant source of stress and tears as he frequently made "Ds" through middle school and high school and, on one occasion ,an "F." Such poor academic performances resulted in a severe dressing down and the inevitable encounter with "the belt," which was swiftly meted out by James Laney with all the efficiency and power an army officer could muster.

Despite those times of having his bottom set on fire, Michael enjoyed his experience in school and found some friends while working on the newspaper staff. He would pave the path for his younger siblings, who would later excel at "B-R" as well. Sister Michelle would become a standout athlete in basketball and track, and younger brother Mark would become the first student of color to become the president of his class as a freshman. Michael would graduate and go on to college as the first in his family and set the example for the family to follow but not without a major confrontation between a former guidance counselor, Mrs. Lillian Carter, and his mom. Early in Michael's high school career, his guidance counselor had told Michael, then a rising sophomore, to switch his career path to a vocational track. "I think that you will find the college track too challenging, and you are probably much better suited to work with your hands. You'll be happier in the vocational track." When Michael shared this news with his mother, Celestine Laney, a petite but determined woman, his mother marched into the office and faced down the towering and bulky guidance counselor and informed her, in no uncertain terms, that "her son and her four children would all be taking the college preparatory track, and that was the end of the discussion." Michael would later discover that the other students of color were also being provided with similar career counseling from this guidance counselor, but their moms did not have the modern-day version of a showdown at "OK Corral" with Mrs. Carter. After that day, Celestine Laney became Michael's heroine and inspiration for success, and she has remained so to this very day.

An Enterprising Youth

Michael credits both of his parents with instilling in him a strong work ethic and sense of discipline at an early age. His father's favorite refrain was "Michael, you are the oldest, and I expect you to set a good example for your brothers and sister." By the time he was twelve, Michael was a budding entrepreneur with a growing newspaper route, delivering the evening edition of the *Brockton Enterprise* throughout his neighborhood on his bicycle. At its height, his newspaper route served over one hundred families, and Michael employed his siblings, Anthony and Michelle, to assist with deliveries along the three-mile route. At the age of fourteen, he secured his mom's permission to work a "real job." He had been washing dishes at home since he could remember and had mastered the skill. He picked up a part-time job at Howard Johnson's Restaurant on I-75, heading towards Cape Cod. He was washing dishes and working his way up the ladder to short order cook; he would, eventually, recruit all his siblings to work with him at "HoJo's." However, early on, he turned his newspaper route over to his younger brother, Anthony, but while just sixteen months younger, his brother lacked the self-discipline, which would later plague him into adulthood, to consistently deliver the newspaper, and he lost the business. Upon reflection, Michael would offer that delivering newspapers matured him and developed critical thinking skills, delayed gratification, and mental toughness: "You had to deliver those papers in the rain, snow, and scorching summer heat. When your friends were going to the movies, you had a job to do, and you had to take care of those customers. You had to fight off angry dogs and patiently work with deadbeat customers, and if you were short on your money, you had to take it out of your salary—which was twenty-five dollars a week. I grew up fast being a paperboy!"

His parents, James and Celestine Laney, were early social justice activists and community organizers, working for desegregation in housing, urban renewal, and pressing for equal employment opportunities for women and people of color. Active in the Democratic Party, the family campaigned for progressives such as Sen. Ted Kennedy, Rep. Gerry Studds, Rep. Tip O'Neil, and Shirley Chisolm, in her bid to become the first woman of color to run for president. While Martin Luther King Jr. and Malcom X were making headlines, in sleepy New England College towns (home of Bridgewater State University), the real mentors and folk heroes were the Kennedys. It would be Senator Ted Kennedy who would provide a senatorial appointment for the United States Military Academy at West Point for young Mark Laney and fulfill their father's dream of having a son attend and, eventually, graduate from West Point.

College: The New Frontier

When Michael stepped onto the Frank Lloyd Wright cement and futuristic award-winning campus of the University of Massachusetts in North Dartmouth (formerly Southeastern Massachusetts University-SMU), unbeknownst to him, this was the "new frontier" of higher education. His great adventure of becoming a lifelong learner and developing a love for education would begin. He passionately attacked his political science and journalism courses with the dream of becoming either an attorney or an investigative journalist. The crusading journalism of Carl Bernstein and Bob Woodward would inspire many in his generation to become politically active and aware. Laney continued writing and worked on the campus newspaper as a staff reporter/photographer as well as an on-air personality, "The Sundance Kid," on WUSM 90.5 FM and took to electronic media with passion and zeal. However, it was the mentorship of African American faculty members, the first he had ever seen, with PhD's that would change his life. The Upward Bound program would provide necessary financial aid and tutorial structural support. The mentorship of Dr. Will Tate (Sociology), Dr. Hazel McPherson (Political Science), and Dr. Everett Hoagland (English) would inspire him by saying, "Mr. Laney, you are smart, and I expect you to keep up the good work in my class." Apart from his parents, Michael could not recall any teachers ever calling him "smart." He was "funny," "outgoing," had a "nice smile," a "good kid" but never "smart." So powerful were those three words, "You are smart," that Laney took every course that Dr. Tate offered just to win his approval.

Jungle Fever and Cross-Cultural Exchanges

SMU's nurturing environment, with an enrollment hovering around five thousand in the mid-1970s, would allow Michael to become a "big fish in a small pond" and provide opportunities for him to explore previous taboos, such as interracial dating, alcohol, recreational marijuana use (yes, he did inhale), and Black consciousness raising through the Black Student Union. Peers like Loretta Blake of New Bedford, fellow resident assistants, Eddie Velasquez, and campus leaders like Manny "Tiny" Fernandez, who would become community organizers, made a powerful impression upon him and were pivotal in shaping his emerging Black identity.

While the campus climate helped to shape his growing Black identity, popular culture and media did as much, if not more. ABC premiered the miniseries *Roots* while he was a student and involved in an interracial relationship with his first love, "Tina" (not her real name), a petite, feisty, young brunette with a great smile and light brown eyes from Seekonk, MA, with a passion for social justice and an engaging mind. Tina loved to talk about social justice and politics, subjects that, up to that point, had not interested the black girls, who had no interest in Michael with his "nerdy ways" and beanpole physique. But Tina became his best friend, and Michael was smitten. This was his first love. They savored the sweet nectar of young, intense love. While Tina was comfortable in the relationship, and comfortable in her own skin, Michael was less so. Tina would become defiant and combative or oblivious to the stares and whispers they would invariably encounter as an interracial couple when they would venture outside of the safe bubble of the campus into the "real world" of New Bedford or Block Island. In retrospect, they must have been a sight. Michael had finally begun to experience a delayed growth spurt that would take him from five feet to six feet tall and gangly with his "afro" and mustache. Tina was just barely five feet with heels, light brown hair, and pale skin with freckles. Michael became increasingly uncomfortable with the comments and lack of social acceptance from both blacks and whites.

Still, this was not enough to derail the relationship; surprisingly, it would be something as innocuous as a television program. It was during the viewing of *Roots* that the weeds of discontent would bloom in their relationship. During the first night, Michael and Tina were cuddling on the sofa watching the program in the suite with other residents; however, by the time the credits had rolled, Michael had pulled away from Tina and was sitting by himself, angry, confused, hurt, and unable to explain or understand why he was rejecting his girlfriend, who had done nothing but attempt to sit beside him. By the time the *Roots* series had run its course, the relationship had descended into a downward spiral, with Michael fleeing and Tina not understanding and wanting him to stand up and fight for the relationship, but he simply could not and felt that he needed to be with a black girl. A couple of years would pass, and Michael would find himself again in a similar relationship with a very creative and beautiful young artist from Long Island, NY, named "Lee" (not her real name). Once again, they would start out as friends, drawn by similar interests, art, politics, photography, social justice, intense debate, and eventually fall in love. While Lee was ready to commit herself to the relationship, Michael struggled with his old demons of "What will people say; what will people think?" Lee always had a sharp retort, and her gray eyes would flash, her white teeth glinting, "F—-k them—who gives a s—-t what they think!" Like Tina, she, too, was a fighter. Like Spike Lee's African American male character in *Jungle Fever*, Michael did not either possess the energy to fight for their love against what he perceived as the "whole world" nor had come to the realization that their love could not endure the pressures of society once they emerged from the safe and warm cocoon of the university campus and the company of their classmates and suitemates. Off campus, color mattered, issues of race were real, and in 1977, depending on where a black man lived in this country, if caught in the company of a white woman, they were matters of life and death. Yet these encounters would serve to strengthen his Black identity and gird his resolve when seeking a life partner years later.

Angels to the Rescue

For Michael, it must have seemed as if God was watching over him; even if he had detoured and strayed from the path of faith and was pursuing the pleasures of sin, God kept the angels watching over him. Often other "angels of another color" would step in to provide guidance and support as Michael worked his way through college in his role as a resident hall assistant in the form of Manny Correrio, Director of Residence Life. Being a resident assistant (RA) provided him with free room and board and tuition and tremendous leadership experience that he would build upon in later years. Michael embraced mentors of all ages, genders, and races, and one of his favorites was the late Dean Don Howard, the beloved dean of students at SMU. Dean Howard challenged Michael to pursue campus leadership opportunities, get involved, and become comfortable with being out in front; he also demanded academic excellence. It would be Dean Howard (along with Dr. Will Tate) who would write the strong letters of recommendation for admission to graduate school that would land Michael a spot in the incoming class of 1977 at Michigan State University. He was admitted into the MA program for Telecommunications as a teaching assistant for the late great television producer Colby Lewis. He additionally landed a staff position as a residence hall director over a group of one hundred freshmen.

Although SMU, like any public university setting, provided numerous opportunities for exploring the forbidden, it also provided a pathway for success as well. His contact through work in radio and newspapers gave him access to interviews with celebrities such as actress Cicely Tyson, poetess Gwendolyn Brooks, and Gov. Jimmy Carter on the presidential trail. SMU exposed him to scuba diving, world class speakers, the arts, and the world of politics. When he graduated with honors, a "Who's Who in American Colleges and Universities" full scholarship to MSU, and the first in his family to earn a college degree, Michael made sure that he mailed a graduation announcement to his old high school guidance counselor, Lillian Carter—"Yep, he actually was college material, and he was on his way to becoming graduate material!"

Graduate School: "Go Spartans!"

The entire Laney family was elated and profoundly proud when Michael made the decision to attend Michigan State University. He had just achieved a historic milestone in the family by graduating from college, and now he was about to do what had never been attempted by a member of the family, graduate school. Michael had the good fortune of having a close friend from SMU and fellow RA Lester "Chip" Yensan (who went on to become the Assistant Vice President for Student Life and Director of Housing at the University of Rhode Island), who had also been accepted to MSU in another graduate program. Chip convoyed with him on the long and boring drive from Bridgewater, MA, to East Lansing, MI. When Michael and Chip pulled off the interstate into East Lansing and onto the sprawling campus of MSU, they were in awe. The campus population would swell to over fifty thousand that fall, more than five times the size of their hometowns, and there were more black people on the campus than Michael had ever seen in his life! The best part of being a Spartan was that these students were just as smart, if not smarter than, he was.

Army ROTC

Living on campus as a residence hall director in a freshman complex supervising twelve resident assistants (RAs) and one hundred freshmen, all males, was a new adventure, but he loved the challenge. He made friends quickly as a graduate student and enjoyed his teaching duties in the Introduction to Mass Communication course. Some of his marquee students were also members of the legendary Spartan basketball squad that would go on to win the 1978–1979

NCAA Championship (Earvin "Magic" Johnson [LA Lakers], Greg Keesler [Detroit Pistons[, and Jay Vincent [Dallas Mavericks]). In the first weeks after arriving on campus, Michael headed directly to the offices of the Army Reserve Officer Training Corps program (ROTC) to sign up. Major Lee, Assistant Professor of Military Service and LTC Brokaw, Professor of Military Service, were excited about the prospect of having a mature graduate student enter the program, especially one seeking a master's degree in telecommunications. Michael wanted to earn some spending money as well as his commission as a second lieutenant and serve in the Signal Corps. By this time, his youngest brother, Mark, had made family history by being accepted at the United States Military Academy at West Point. Michael knew that his advanced degree would allow him to become an officer, and he also hoped to gain practical experience as a military broadcaster and communicator and make himself employable when he was discharged. His plan was to only do four years and then return to the civilian sector as a news reporter or news anchor in a medium-sized market, but once again, God had other plans.

Michael enjoyed the challenge of managing a full-time course load in graduate school, full-time job as a residence hall director, and full-time schedule as a scholarship ROTC cadet. He was in school, debt-free, had his own apartment, car was paid for, money in his pocket, and life was great. MSU provided tremendous support to their graduate students, and Michael turned to that support network when he took his statistics course. Stats was his lowest grade during his graduate school experience. He made a "C," and it resulted in a warning letter from the dean of the graduate school. This frightened him so much that he went into hyper drive for the next three semesters and finished with a 3.75 GPA; he also vowed that he would never make a "C" in statistics again! MSU had a slew of black role models to emulate, from President Clifton Wharton to numerous vice presidents and deans. Michael selected as his mentor, a wise and savvy administrator, Dr. Betty Floyd, who astutely shared with him that the young lady he was currently engaged to would not make a "good army wife" and that he had better cut "that heifer loose." It would take another six months for Dr. Floyd's wisdom to settle in, but eventually, Michael broke the engagement, ended the relationship, picked up his commission, skipped graduation, and headed on to Ft. Gordon, Augusta, Georgia, for the Signal Officer Basic Training Course. It was a sweltering summer in 1979, and a "Yankee" was in the place he had feared the most and never wanted to be living in, "the deep South."

From Soldier to Servant

Upon graduation, he accepted a commission in the United States Army Signal Corps as a second lieutenant and entered active duty, following in the footsteps of his father, and continuing a tradition of military service blazed by his father and his uncle and emulated by his brothers. Laney loved the life of being a soldier, and the army was a good fit for him, even "issuing him a wife" in the form of First Lieutenant Leonora Suggs, who he met in his role as her sponsor in South Korea in 1981. They married in 1982 and became a service couple, spending eight years overseas and giving birth to all their children in military hospitals while stationed overseas in Germany and South Korea. Laney served in a variety of communications and information management related positions with the army. He held command and deputy command responsibilities at the captain and major level and was responsible for assets more than $110 million dollars and command and control assets of more than one thousand soldiers and civilians. Additionally, he served temporary duty as an Aide-de-Camp to the Deputy Commanding General, 7th US Corps in Stuttgart, Germany, and was assigned in a joint command role with the Combined Field Army as a liaison officer to the Republic of Korea Army in South Korea. His military awards and decorations include Overseas Service ribbon (five awards), Korea Defense Service Medal, Army Service Ribbon, National Defense Service Medal, Army Achievement Medal (four awards), Army Commendation Medal (two awards), Meritorious Service Medal (three awards), and the Joint Defense Meritorious Service Medal. He retired as a major on October 1, 1995, with twenty years of federal service.

While in the military, on September 15, 1981, at Kino Chapel, Ft. Huachuca, AZ (Sierra Vista), Laney had a dramatic religious conversion experience, accepted Jesus Christ as his personal Lord and Savior, was baptized, and was called to serve God. He was later ordained into the ministry as a servant of God in 1987. He served as senior and associate pastor of churches in Germany, Korea, Arizona, and Tennessee. In 1993 he was credentialed as an ordained bishop in the Church of God, Cleveland, Tennessee. The vow of a little boy to "serve the Lord, when I grow up, to be a priest and serve Him and His people, all the days of my life" had truly come to pass.

In 2002 he and Leonora later went on to become the founders and CEOs of Faith House International Ministries Inc. (2002), a 501c3 ministry that provides educational funding for the next generation of Christian leaders in Kenya.

Doctoral Experiences: Dissertation Survival of the Fittest (Or So You Want to Be a PhD)

Laney's doctoral experience at the University of Tennessee-Knoxville turned out to eventually be positive, after all. He did complete the process but not without picking up some battle scars in the process. Early on, he was offered sage advice by the late Dr. Cliff Schimmels, an education professor and former coach at Lee University. When he heard that his colleague was starting a PhD, he said, "Would you like some advice that will cut off a couple of years on your program? Pray about your dissertation topic!" Was that it, just pray about the topic? However, that is what Michael did, and it proved to be prophetic. In retrospect, Michael would offer that one "research your passion, because this is what you will be known for in most cases for the rest of your academic life, and you'll be seeing it a lot, so you had better love it!"

However, before he had this conversation with Dr. Schimmels, Michael almost did not get into a PhD program at all. His MA grades were solid, but his Graduate Record Exam scores were mediocre at best; he has always struggled on standardized tests on the math and analytical components, and he worried about this being a factor. The first time he applied, in 1995, he was interviewed by the former dean of the graduate school. The dean asked Michael, "What is your research agenda?" To which he replied, "Media and Religion." After a couple of minutes of silence on the line, he responded, "I think you would be better off at Regent University; that's not our area." Disappointed, he applied to Regent University and was accepted. However, Regent University, in Virginia Beach, Virginia, used an online model, and tuition was almost six hundred dollars a credit hour. Since this was not the type of educational experience Michael was suited , he declined admission. The next year he applied again at UTK and was interviewed by the exact same dean. The dean asked Michael, "What is your research agenda?" To which he replied, "I would like to explore the intersection of media and religion in America." Immediately the dean responded, "I think that you would be an excellent fit for our program." The late Dr. Herbert Howard, a noted broadcast communication historical researcher, would eventually become a valuable committee member and mentor to Michael during his time at UTK and when he returned to his parent institution. So, what was the difference in Dr. Howard's response this time? Laney believed that perhaps it was the size of the doctoral cohort for the year he was accepted. The incoming class in 1995 had a cohort of ten, but the incoming class of 1996 had a cohort of fifteen, and he believes that those five extra seats, as well as a tough economy in 1996, may have made the difference in his being admitted. The lesson here is do not quit if you get rejected, continue to be positive, ask questions, and keep applying.

Age Is Just a Number

Michael noticed that while he was not the oldest person in his cohort, at age forty-one (the oldest was fifty-five), neither was he the youngest (she was twenty-six); the average age in his cohort was about thirty-five. Once inside the classroom, with many eighteen- to twenty-one-year-old undergraduate students, Michael began to succeed academically. Much of this could be attributed to his maturity and the discipline he had learned in the military over the years. He had learned to set aside the distractions that proved dangerous and destructive for many of the young undergraduates in his classes. He also found that his doctoral cohort peers did very well in the classroom because, like him, they were focused on their goals and understood why they were in school.

To give himself a boost, Laney enrolled in summer courses, commuting daily the 160 miles, round trip, and took nine hours (a full load) in summer to prepare. He initially struggled with academic writing, having been out of the classroom since 1979, almost seventeen years. However, he recognized the need for a tutor, joined a study group, and began sharing his research topic with the members of his cohort. During this sharing process, an amazing thing began to occur since he was the only one doing any research connected to media and religion: his peers began providing him with source material that they came across in their journal assignments and readings, and he began to build an annotated bibliography. He also put to practice the advice given by Dr. Schimmels and started writing and researching about "Media and Religion" in every class he took: psychology, law, economics, history, quantitative research methods, qualitative research, broadcasting, religious studies, and statistics. By using this approach, he quickly developed a thirty-page bibliography and content for the future five chapters of the dissertation.

The Birth of a Scholar

Michael came alive in the classroom. He would later discover that when he took the Gallup Strength Finder Inventory, his number one strength was *Learner*, which is someone who absorbs information and thrives on obtaining knowledge. He discovered that knowledge was powerful and very seductive. He enjoyed gathering with both his African American doctoral peers, like Reggie Murphy and Kadesha Washington, as well as other graduate students, over a beverage after class in the student lounge. He noted, "My peers and I were having conversations on levels of abstraction and philosophical planes that I had never encountered before. It was pretty heady stuff, and it had the unintended effect of bonding me to the people I was relating to. It really was a form of escapism, almost like a very powerful drug."

He also observed that if allowed to remain unchecked, this escapism created tension and stress in his marriage, as he returned home late in the evening to his spouse, who had struggled with raising three young children, ages seven, nine, and eleven. One time, Leonora spied a mouse in the house and demanded that Michael get home as soon as possible to take care of the problem. He reflected, "There I was, in my mind, solving the problems of the world with my doctoral peers, and she wanted me to drop that weighty stuff and come home to kill a mouse?" As his studies intensified and his knowledge of theories, statistics, and research methods increased, he had to work hard to improve his communication and his relationship with Leonora, who was also a college graduate but was challenged to remain grounded in the realities of home life. Her role as "Mom-In-Chief" back in small town, Cleveland, TN, did not allow her the luxury of escaping into the abstractions of esoteric philosophy and theories. Michael also observed that some of his peers' marriages could not take the strain of doctoral studies and crumbled. He watched in amazement as some of his graduate peers in other colleges and schools, seemingly liberated and free for the first time in decades, began to explore other relationships with people outside of their marriage. In many ways, they resembled the eighteen-year-old freshmen in terms of their lifestyle choices or middle-aged men and women trying to recapture lost youth. For those who fell prey to this snare, the trap was baited through the seductive aphrodisiac of knowledge, and then, over the course of the semester, they drifted into illicit sexual relationships with members of their cohort or classmates. Michael even recalled that one of his peers, who was doing online research, met his wife in an internet chat room and married her in less than three months. The results later proved to be a disastrous distraction for him, and he did not complete the program. In many cases, these "hook-ups" amongst "mature adults" had all started with these powerful conversations.

Paying for the PhD

Despite what folks say about all the free money for education, doctoral education is terribly expensive. It requires plenty of research to find the money, and much of it may come with strings attached. While Michael was fortunate that his institution was willing to pay for one course, many graduate students are not as blessed. For him, much of his graduate education was an exercise in "walking by faith for the finances." "I remember that first fall of 1996, and the bill for the tuition was due, and no financial aid had come through yet. It was rough." Friends told Michael to take loans or use his credit card, but he refused and believed that God would supply his needs. He decided to skip some meals and pray and trust God for a miracle. The deadline was a Friday afternoon at 5:00 p.m. for payment, or his schedule would be purged. He waited by the phone all day for a call from the financial aid office at UTK but heard nothing. At 4:55 p.m., he received a call from the Office of the Chancellor; it seemed that a graduate student who had been previously awarded a Tennessee minority scholarship for that semester would be unable to attend. They asked him, "Would you be interested in accepting this seven-thousand-dollar scholarship? No teaching is required, but you must maintain a 3.5 GPA." Michael exclaimed with joy, "Praise God, yes, please, I will accept the scholarship; thank you so very much!" To his additional surprise, the scholarship was extended each additional semester he was enrolled due to his strong academic performance and in the absence of the original recipient. This meant that Michael's only expenses for school were his gas and meals.

After the first year of classes, Michael was adjusting to the rhythm of being a commuter student. He often joked that one of the biggest hurdles in his doctoral program was "finding a parking spot at UTK; we had parking permits, but they were just a hunting license!" His routine consisted of teaching a 5/5 full time load in the Communication Arts Department. He had arranged with his chair to teach early classes on Monday, Wednesday, and Friday at Lee University so that he could finish his last class at 2:00 p.m. and then drive the eighty miles to Knoxville for a 4:00 p.m. class and usually finish the last class by 9:00 p.m. Since he did not teach on Tuesday and Thursday, he could take morning and afternoon courses at UTK to complete his schedule. Throughout this time, and while taking a full load, he missed only a single class over six semesters, and that one absence came because of a chemical spill on I-75, and he pleaded with the statistics teacher not to drop his average. She considered the absence as excused and extended him grace.

Networking 101: Essentially for Minorities on a Majority Campus

Successfully navigating a doctoral program requires one to develop an extensive support network. No one who completes a doctorate does it alone. While PhDs may not admit it publicly, more than likely, they had a strong support network upon which they relied to varying degrees. Michael worked diligently to secure a wide web of support within his church community, academic community, and graduate school community. The church community helped to sustain him spiritually, as he often asked for prayers from his faith community as he was doing course work, and, later, when collecting data for his dissertation. One church member from his Sunday School class, Kevin "Bud" Chinn, was instrumental in distributing Michael's online survey, which had previously suffered from a poor response rate of under 450 respondent thresholds in his first data collection attempt. Leonora reached out and made an appeal to Bud who was in Physician Assistant School at the time in the Pacific Northwest. With the help of Kevin's vast church contacts and the prayers of the class, Laney's "University of Tennessee, College of Communications, Religious Web Site Survey" went from being hosted on a handful of minor church sites during the period June 12, 1998–July 18, 1998. He contacted 1,061 sites; eighty-five webmasters agreed to participate, and forty Christian websites around the nation hosted the survey on sites in the Northeast, South, East, and West, as well as two sites in Toronto, Canada. Ultimately, the survey generated 912 usable responses, with respondents from forty-ninety states, Puerto Rico, Guam, the District of Columbia, as well as twenty-one countries. For Michael, the role of divine intervention in answer to his prayers cannot be underestimated.

His contacts in the academic community at his parent institution and at UTK informed him about scholarships, grants, and fellowship opportunities. He researched financial aid options at UTK and made sure that Dr. Linda Painter and the personnel in the administrative staff were aware of who he was and to apprise him of any possibilities. The plum jewel scholarship was the thirty-thousand-dollar Appalachian College Association Mellon fellowship, which was being administered at that time by Mr. Andrew Baskin of Berea College, Kentucky. Baskin was keen to improve the number of African American doctoral-prepared faculty members at Appalachian College schools, of which both Lee University and the University of Tennessee were member institutions in this consortium. Laney worked to secure the support of Dr. C.W. "Bud" Minkel, Associate Vice Chancellor at UTK, as well as his chief academic officer at Lee University, Dr. Carolyn Dirksen, and the president of Lee University, Dr. Paul Conn, to earn the fellowship. This financial support provided the income that allowed him to take a one-year paid leave of absence from his teaching position, cover tuition costs, and become a full-time student, carry a twelve to fifteen graduate credit course overload and support his stay-at-home spouse and their three young children, ages five, seven, and nine. Without this level of financial support, it would not have been possible for him to complete the degree without student loan debt.

While it is essential to have the support of the faith community, as well as the academic community, many doctoral students underestimate the necessity for cultivating their network of graduate students, particularly for students of color on a majority campus. Without the emotional support provided by like-minded peers such as Kadesha Washington and Reginald Murphy, whose camaraderie as well as academic support in reading notes, bouncing ideas, or understanding the additional "black tax" that minorities face at the hands of some white students, staff, and faculty, success would not be possible.

Course Work - Navigating the Maze

A common pitfall of some doctoral students is taking too many "exploratory" graduate-level courses. No doubt some of my colleagues will disagree with me on this point and encourage students to take a wide array and breadth of course work while they are a doctoral student. Laney would argue that the time to have done this was in the bachelor or master's programs. Often you would hear professor's pleading with students to sign up for their pet elective course, which invariably fell outside of the required degree map. As intriguing as they sounded, Michael chose to avoid these "bunny trails." He would speak with his major professor, chair, or mentor and determine "Is this a must have course for me?" If the mentor's response was "It would be nice, but it is not necessary," he would let it go.

Michael observed that the students in his cohort, and in the cohort that started a year before him, who explored too many of these advertised "pet" courses and did not focus on the course material for their discipline and their cognate area of concentration (which is outside of the discipline—his was religious studies), struggled to get to all but dissertation status (ABD) with their cohort peers. These students also tended to struggle in getting their proposals approved by their committee in a timely manner.

He recalls that one member of his cohort, a kind, gentile, middle-aged, Southern faculty member, had battled depression after she had attempted three times to get her proposals past three different committees a few years after he had left the university. Michael was informed by a former cohort member that, tragically, sometime after being notified that her proposal had not been approved for the third time, she again slipped into depression. Her brother found her body in her apartment; she had committed suicide by hanging and had left a note. This is clearly an extreme but tragic case. We may never know with certainty what caused this dear, sensitive soul to feel the need to take her life. For Michael, her case highlights the frustration and dangers of drifting through your program and not having a strong support network. Once the doctoral candidate has completed residency, they return home, and their graduate student support network begins to quickly erode. In his mind, the key for the doctoral student to be successful is to focus on the essentials such as "What does the eighty-eight-hour program require?" and "What does one need to take to complete?" Michael considered anything else as an expensive and wasteful distraction to be avoided if he was to complete his course work in six semesters. One only need considers the financial implications, with doctoral credit hours today exceeding eight hundred to nine hundred dollars per credit in private universities, opting for a focused approach is much more cost efficient.

Committee Member Selection - Who Gets Booted Off the Island

Apart from developing your research agenda, the most important decision a doctoral student will ever make is selecting the advisor and the members of their committee. Having spent time with several friends who are still ABD (all but dissertation, aka—"all but dead") because of committee member disruption, attention to this aspect of your doctoral studies is critical. If your committee is too large, the logistics of managing faculty schedules can get out of hand. Finding the member who is outside of your college to serve on your committee can also become a major challenge; you must be diligent in this area as well. If your committee is too small, you may not have enough points of view or subject matter experts to adequately address the topic. Most doctoral programs have guidelines as to minimum composition for the committee and the required rank of the faculty. In Michael's situation, four proved to be the ideal number.

Michael recalls that a former colleague was unable to complete because two committee members who were married to one another divorced, and both left the committee. In another instance, the chair left the university. This could have occurred with Michael's committee, but he had selected a great chair, and she had prepared him in advance of her pending departure to Florida A&M University in 1997. She went on to continue her distinguished academic career. Dr. Lady Dhyana Ziegler, DCJ, joined FAMU as the Garth Reeves Eminent Scholar in journalism. She went on to hold several administrative positions, including Assistant Vice President for Instructional Technology, Acting Vice President for Research, Interim Director for the Office of International Education and Development, and Interim Director for University Planning and Analysis. Dr. Ziegler has received numerous awards, including being knighted as a Dame of Justice in 2008. Her research interests are new technologies, ethics, multimedia, and diversity in the media.

Ideally, each committee member should bring a degree of expertise to your dissertation that is essential for your research project. The major professor, or chair, directs the dissertation and the committee. When looking for your chair, seek out someone who is well respected in the institution. Dr. Ziegler had an impeccable reputation at UTK and was the sole faculty member of color in the College of Communications at that time; she was also a minister, and Michael felt that they would make a strong advocate for him and that she would help him to successfully navigate the political and academic minefield of doctoral education. Find out how many dissertations the person has directed either at that institution or at another school. In a perfect world, you would have taken a course with the faculty member and you know their style and temperament. In Michael's case, this did not happen because she was not teaching in his area at the time. Whenever possible, if the prospect is chairing a dissertation defense, go and observe them in action as they support their candidate. Michael had seen his chair do this, but it was after she was already his chair. Ideally, the person you select would be your mentor and your support system. Again, this does not have to be the case, but it is wonderful when it happens and beautiful to behold. Michael observed Dr. Dorothy Bowles, a renowned constitutional communication law professor, defending for Linda Lyle. The respect and affection between the two was obvious, and Dr. Bowles had prepared Linda well. Linda did an outstanding job in her defense presentation. Dr. Bowles did not broker any foolishness from members of the committee or from those in the gallery asking questions she felt were out of bounds. Dr. Linda Lyle successfully defended her dissertation the first time around.

While Michael had also hoped to extend his research with his major professor beyond the dissertation; it did not happen. Sometimes logistics, strong personalities, and life changes can prevent this, and when it happens, just let it go. There are no perfect chairs or perfect doctoral candidates. It is successful when you have a powerful ally and advocate whose presence ensures success by securing the signatures of the committee members on the dissertation, and that's the role Dr. Ziegler played for him in that board room on that Friday afternoon, Labor Day weekend, in 1998.

In Michael's case, since he was doing a quantitative dissertation, he selected someone on the committee with a strong statistics background to guide his thoughts in the conceptualization and methodology of the dissertation. While Dr. Benjamin Bates, a Fulbright Scholar, proved to be the most challenging member of the committee to deal with, the man was brilliant. It was Dr. Bates' expertise in statistics, particularly, factor analysis, that strengthened the dissertation and produced solid research that allowed Michael to publish from this work several years later. His outside area or cognate consisted of twelve hours in religious studies. He chose the faculty member in that department who had the strongest interest at the time in looking at how media and the internet were supportive of religious expression. Dr. Rosalind Hackett, formerly of Leeds University, was a noted researcher and scholar. Dr. Hackett's encouragement and insightful suggestions regarding various religious perspectives in the development of the dissertation were tremendously beneficial. Dr. Hackett, the outside committee member, influenced Michael to push to the edge of the technology boundary to explore what motivates individuals to use religious websites; she was excited about mediated religion, and her passion influenced him as well. His fourth committee member was selected to be "the referee" and bring balance, editorial skills, and harmony to the committee. As the dean of the Graduate School, Dr. Herbert Howard was intimately familiar with the process and how to successfully navigate the university, and Michael felt that he would need that level of expertise on his committee to succeed. Dr. Howard was gracious with his time, provided helpful suggestions and words of encouragement throughout his coursework in the graduate program.

Successfully working with the committee means that it is your responsibility to keep everyone informed and updated on your progress. Always make sure that everyone has the latest copies of your proposal or your dissertation drafts. A painful lesson learned by Michael was that he had placed his document on the university desktop in the computer lab. His media picked up a virus and wiped out his first three chapters of the proposal he was to present to the committee. The backup copy, which was located on the university server, was also corrupted. All his research and documentation would have been lost except for the fact that he had printed out a single hard copy of 120 of the 150 pages. He had to reconstruct the remaining thirty pages from memory. Additionally, since he had to provide electronic copies to the committee, and this was before the days of scanners, he had to retype the entire 150 pages. The lesson, back up the back up, and always keep a hard copy of your most current drafts.

It is also critical to constantly communicate with your major professor to ensure that you are using the right protocol and strategy to navigate the briar patch. This is a challenge even when you are in residency, but it is particularly tough to manage when you leave the campus. Today's media avenues of social media, texting, Skype, and Twitter are most helpful, but the key is that a doctoral student must be persistent and diligent in keeping the lines of communication open with each member of their committee if they are to finish on time.

Too Stressed to Be Blessed

An aspect of doctoral studies that is rarely discussed is the physical, emotional, and psychological toll that it places upon both the student and their family members. Beyond the rigors of graduate course work is the high stakes game of being able to complete the program. The doctorate is an all-or-nothing proposition. It is critical that when considering doctoral programs, you research the PhD, graduation rates and estimated years for completion. While this number will fluctuate slightly each year, graduation rates below 50 percent bear scrutiny and should be a red flag to the prospective PhD student.

In Michael's case, he recognized that for his professional survival and well-being in the academy, the doctorate was essential for long term success. Although he had been hired with a master's degree and was an instructor on tenure track, he realized that the "handwriting was on the wall" as Lee College began talking about transitioning towards university status. His greatest fear at that point was his long-term retention. Laney noted, "I did not want to be in the situation of finding myself as a non-terminal degreed faculty member, over the age of fifty, with three kids in college and hearing them say, 'Thanks, but we need to hire a PhD, so goodbye." So, for Michael, as the head of household and sole bread winner, success was framed in terms of economic and financial security for his family of five. While some colleagues asked Leonora, "Why are you putting so much pressure on him to finish?" Her reply was "He's putting the pressure on himself, and we want him to succeed."

Michael recalls one incident when he arrived home after 3:00 a.m. after spending a long evening the Hodges Library in Knoxville doing research. He entered the house from the garage and was startled to find his nine-year-old daughter, Mikaela, sitting there in her pajamas. Shocked, he said, "Mikaela, what are you doing up at this hour, honey?" Her plaintive cry was "This is the only time that I can see you, Daddy. I missed you so much, and I love you." Ouch! On another occasion, when his seven-year-old son was being ushered out of the office area, labeled as "dissertation central" so that Michael could work on his research, his youngest son looked back with tears in his eyes and remarked, "When I grow up, I'm not getting a PhD because I want to spend time with my kids!" Wow, talk about a dagger through the heart. The cost to the family is real, and everyone pays the price for the pursuit of the doctorate by the family member. Laney likens the pursuit of the PhD to a marriage. "Engaging doctoral studies should be entered in only after sober, prayerful consideration and much counsel and wisdom. Be sure that you have counted the cost." In other words, don't strike out on this path just because you want some initials behind your name and you are enamored with the idea of people calling you, "Doctor So-and-so."

The level of stress one encounters in a doctoral program will, of course, be driven in large part by the personality of the student. As a "type A" personality, Michael was driven to succeed and do his best, so he pushed himself and was seeking to control as much as he possibly could; unfortunately, there are things in doctoral programs that you may have no control over. Michael's advisor and chair were pushing him to accelerate through the program because she needed to wrap up his program while she still was on the UTK payroll. She was pushing for a summer 1998 graduation (twenty-four months since the start of his program). The problem was that Michael, and some of his doctoral peers, like Reggie Murphy and Randall King at UTK, were doing pioneering online surveys in a time of the early development of the internet. In 1998 he was still at the leading edge of the technology curve, and Survey Monkey was still decades away.

Additionally, since his survey had to be placed within the hands of the religious community on their websites, no central database existed yet, so much of what he did required him to break new ground. Unfortunately, this resulted in small samples and poor response rates. Michael had chosen a quantitative dissertation because the research literature indicated that this methodology tended to be faster to assemble and formulate than qualitative narrative style dissertations. The Achilles heel of a quantitative dissertation rests upon the size of the sample, the response rate, and the quality of the data. When conducting online surveys, which are self-selected, the researcher needs much larger samples than what may be found in the typical focus group of a qualitative research project. His sample size was below threshold, less than 450; he would not be able to use this batch of data for his analysis.

As he trudged up the interstate that Sunday afternoon to break the news to his chair, he began to break down, sobbing and wracked with anguish. The stress of meeting the deadline, four semesters of course overloads, three thousand miles per month of driving, and the frustration of not having a working data set had finally taken its toll. He had dropped from 195 pounds to 165 pounds on his six-foot frame over the course of the summer. While some might say, "Wow, that's a great way to lose thirty unwanted pounds," it was so stressful that it brought no joy to him.

On that hot summer afternoon, as he pulled off onto the breakdown lane outside of Athens, TN, he wanted to quit and just return home and hang it up. Even suicidal thoughts entered his head of turning his late model Datsun pick-up truck into oncoming traffic. Instead, he cried out to the Lord for help. He was angry, frustrated, tired, and defeated, and he lashed out at God in his fury and his fear. Then he began to pray. After the prayer, he said, "It was as if a weight had come off my shoulders and a sense of peace flooded my soul." He met with his advisor, who had flown in from Florida to meet with him. She was understandably highly annoyed and upset that he had broken the agreement for a July graduation date. Like most doctoral candidates, Michael was completely self-absorbed in his own world and his own concerns. He had given very little thought to how he was impacting Dr. Zeigler or what she was spending in time, money, and effort to extend her assistance. It would be decades before he would discover that she probably had already departed sometime in 1997 but hung on to allow him to complete, such was the power of her commitment and her promises to her students. At the time, he was oblivious to any of her needs or concerns, and this was "all about him and his needs," but completing the dissertation did that to him.

Michael promised Dr. Zeigler that he would finish by December and defend no later than September and that he needed more time to rework the data set. While she did not appreciate the imposition, she stayed on with him, warning him that he had better deliver, as her relationship with UTK was ending. Encouraged and optimistic, he shared his prayer concerns with his church support group, and as previously mentioned, through divine intervention and the help of Kevin Chinn, a miracle happened, and the data began to flow in, more than enough to analyze and meet the rigorous requirements set by the statistician on the committee.

The takeaway on this piece is that, for Michael, his faith in God and the needs of providing for the economic well-being of his family made the difference between success and failure. When starting a doctoral program, one must be focused and driven to succeed; it must become a totally consuming obsession.

Avoiding the Dissertation Defense Drama

For Michael, the real challenge in his quest to finish by the summer of 1998 came after the course work was completed and in the run-up to the preparation to pass the comprehensive exams. The University of Tennessee requires grueling written comprehensive exams scheduled over a two-week period, focused on the foundational, theoretical, historical, and research areas of your discipline. If a student does not pass these written exams with the approved score, they must sit for an oral defense of their comprehensive exams. Michael interviewed ABD students as well as his mentors to help him prepare for "comps," and this paid off with a very successful score on the written examinations, which allowed him to go to proposal stage without a hitch.

Well before taking his comprehensive exams, he had been informed by his dissertation chair and mentor, Dr. Dhyana Ziegler that she would be going on sabbatical at another institution and that she would not be returning to UTK. She was committed to supporting him, but he would need to accelerate the process and complete within the next twelve months. She required that he submit the first three chapters as proposal instead of the typical twenty- to thirty-page proposal. While Michael's peers thought this requirement was onerous and suggested that he challenge it, since he did not know any better, he decided to do what his chair and he agreed to. Following his chair's guidance turned out to be a blessing in disguise. During the proposal phase of the dissertation, as Dr. Ziegler argued before the committee that since the candidate had already written 150 pages, the bibliography, and the first three chapters, no additional or significant changes would be accepted. Her advocacy was supported by the completed Chapter I, Introduction (pp. 1-31); Chapter II, Literature Review (pp.32-105); and Chapter III, Methodology (pp.106-137), which the candidate had placed in hands of the committee members. This left only Chapter IV, Results and Chapter V, Summary and Conclusions, to wrap up, allowing him to fast track his dissertation and complete it in record time.

Major lessons that were learned included the fact that not everyone wanted to see him succeed; some felt he was going through the program too quickly. Other faculty members wanted him to be their research assistant. Fortunately, he was able to decline these offers having secured the ACA Mellon Fellowship. This fellowship would require that, upon completion, he was to return and pay back seven semesters at his home institution. Michael recalled one occasion where he was waiting to receive graded comments back from a professor on a major term paper. While he had received an "A" for the course, he wanted to use the paper and the comments from the professor for inclusion in his growing bibliography and prospective dissertation chapters. When he finally could get an appointment, the professor almost, could not find the paper amidst the volume of clutter in his office. However, when he finally found the paper and pulled it out from beneath the stack, Michael reviewed it and noticed that there was not a single mark on the paper, no grade, no comment, not so much as or even a check mark. He decided to let the matter die and was thankful for having a "weighty paper that looked like an A."

Another committee member, a renowned researcher, would be a major stumbling block in approving changes and corrections to Michael's dissertation. He was the only committee member who refused to sign off during the dissertation defense. Michael had scheduled the defense during the Friday of the Labor Day weekend at 3:00 p.m., as he knew the campus would be deserted before a long holiday weekend. He had decided to make this strategic decision after observing a tenured faculty member during a public defense humiliate an African American student in front of the large, assembled gallery. Michael presumed that without an audience to perform for, he might be safe. While this assumption worked for the rest of the committee members, who try to work in a collegial fashion, it did not for this individual. The committee member refused to sign off on the dissertation until what he deemed "as major revisions and corrections were made." Michael agreed to work with him, recognizing that all changes had to be in by the Monday after Thanksgiving Break. Michael continued to send in weekly revisions, but the faculty member never responded. Finally, in sheer frustration and anger, Michael went to the faculty member's house the day after Thanksgiving and told him he would wait until he reviewed the changes and would make them on the spot.

The faculty member reluctantly agreed, took the changes back into his office, emerged three hours later, and approved the document as it was without making a single change or correction. Was it hazing, harassment, or simply spite? Michael will never know; maybe it was just "the cost of paying dues." Michael submitted his dissertation in time to graduate in the December 1998 Winter Commencement, completing the doctorate he started in June 1996. Dr. Zeigler flew in from Florida to congratulate him, and Vice Chancellor Dr. Bud Minkel performed the hooding ceremony. It has been suggested by some in the administration support section at UTK that this may be a record for completion within a time of two and a half years for a doctoral student in the College of Communications at the University of Tennessee. At this point, Laney neither cares nor knows for certain, but the most important fact was he was finished. After providing the customary copies to the members of the committee, Michael made sure that a copy was sent to Celestine Laney, to thank her for her support. Mom had made a huge sacrifice in purchasing his regalia, which cost more than nine hundred dollars at the time, as his graduation gift.

Michael loves to tell of his mother's response to the dissertation, entitled "Mediated Religion: Motivations for Religious Web Site Usage-An Exploratory Study of Christian Web Site Users." Celestine cheerfully noted that she loved his "book," "Oh son, when I can't sleep at night, I pick up your book, and before I know it, I'm out like a light and sleep so peacefully." Well, there you have it folks, dissertations rarely morph into best sellers!

Post-Graduation: Now the Real Work Begins

First Generation

On December 20, 1998, in the packed Thompson-Boling Arena, (now renamed the Pat Summit Arena in honor of the record winning UTK basketball legendary coach Pat Head Summit), Michael gathered on the hardwood floor with five thousand other undergraduate, masters, and doctoral students for the conferral of his degree. Doctoral students were presented their diplomas and their hoods after all the other students received their degrees. As the late Dr. C.W. "Bud" Minkel, his patron and benefactor, hooded Michael, his family and extended family looked on with pride and amazement. This was a historical event for both the Laney and the Sugg's family of Hampton, VA; the first doctorate in their collective family history was being conferred. Although Michael's ninety-three-year-old grandmother could not attend, as she was bedridden and living in Jacksonville, Florida, so proud of her grandson and so cognizant of the significance of this event, this woman, on a fixed income, sent him a graduation card with two hundred dollars in cash and a note praising him for being the "first in the line" for this achievement. Truly, it had been a long road from being a first-generation college graduate back in 1977 to the present, a twenty-one-year odyssey.

Unlike some of his freshly minted PhD peers on the floor, Michael was fortunate to be employed and had already returned to his teaching duties that fall at Lee University. Here he was, something of a rarity, an African American with a doctorate in communications. The National Science Foundation database tracks the number of doctorates conferred annually. That year, only 407 doctorates were conferred nationwide in communications, with 60 being conferred on African Americans (NSF Government Statistics, 2009). Upon the conferral of his degree, the Vice President for Academic Affairs and Chief Academic Officer Dr. Carolyn Dirksen recommended to President Conn to promote him from instructor to assistant professor. While securing the doctorate was a personal best for Michael, after the graduation party, it was just another day in the life of the institution. As an African American faculty member working in a small liberal arts university in the South, he was often challenged and, at times, insulted by parents and prospective students touring the campus on his academic credentials and pedigree.

How the PhD Opened Doors

Time has revealed that the guidance he received from his committee members in the crafting of his dissertation was invaluable, as it has produced several publications and opportunities to present his research around the world:

Laney, M. J. (1998) *Motivations for Religious Web Site Usage: An Exploratory Study of Christian Web Site Users*. Doctoral dissertation. The University of Tennessee, Knoxville. Motivations for Religious Web Site Usage: An Exploratory Study of Christian Web Site Users." *Journalism & Mass Communications Abstractions*. Volume 37, Spring 2000.

Laney, M.J. (2005) "Christian Web Usage: Motives and Desires" in *Religion in Cyberspace*. Editors: M. Hojsgaard & M. Warburg, Routledge Taylor & Francis Group Ltd. London. Laney, M.J. (2011) "From Drums to Cyberspace: Social media and beyond" in *The International Journal of Religion and Spirituality in Society*, Common Ground Publishing Company http://www.ijn.cgpublisher.com.

Laney, M.J. (2011) Associate Editor, *The International Journal of Religion and Spirituality in Society*, Common Ground Publishing Company. Volume 1, Issue 3.

Laney, M.J. (2012) Associate Editor, *The International Journal of Religion and Spirituality in Society*, Common Ground Publishing Company. Volume 1, Issue 4.

Laney, M.J. (2014) Associate Editor, *The International Journal of Critical Cultural Studies*, Common Ground Publishing Company. Volume 12, Issue 1.

Dr. Laney's research interests have grown but continue to build upon the foundation he received in his doctoral studies. He publishes and researches in the areas of

- Diversity in the Workforce
- Recruiting and Retaining a Diverse Workforce
- Christian Website Usage
- Minorities and Women in Media
- Minorities and Women in Religion
- Media Effects Studies and Research

Academic Administrator-Opening Doors for Others

Dr. Laney is now entering his nineteenth year of teaching and completing his second year as the dean of the College of Arts and Sciences at Our Lady of the Lake University (OLLU), a faith-based, Hispanic Serving Institution with 3,011 students enrolled (1,555 undergraduate, 1,372 graduate) over three campuses (San Antonio, Houston, and Rio Grande Valley), with a 15:1 student-faculty ratio, with 280 faculty. Dr. Laney supervises seven direct reports: Associate Dean for Accreditation, Assessment and Planning, Department Chairs, Coordinator of Operations and Research, Office Manager, and Administrative Assistant. He is also responsible for eighty-five full/part-time faculty and the delivery of instruction in twenty-two majors to 495 students.

Using the PhD As a Tool of Nurturing Christian Identity

Dr. Laney has chosen to align himself with organizations whose core commitments are in complete harmony with his own personal experience as a committed evangelical Christian academic in Christian higher education. Dr. Laney believes that student success in navigating the marketplace of ideas in our culture requires intentionality as it relates to their spiritual formation. He is an advocate for the primacy of the faculty in fostering the development and articulation of a biblical worldview as it relates to contemporary global issues and for creating access for students of color. He has invested almost twenty years of his life in service to this calling and continuously seeks maturity in his walk with Christ. He is drawn to institutions that allow him to further his own personal and spiritual growth in the areas of social justice and the development of the "beloved community." As a tenured professor, academic administrator, and an ordained minister with almost thirty years of ecumenical pastoral and teaching experience, (Baptist, Pentecostal, and Presbyterian), both domestically and internationally, he successfully bridges and advances the perspectives of the various constituencies that he serves.

Partnering with Presidents

Dr. Laney has spent his entire academic career at only two institutions, Our Lady of the Lake University in San Antonio, TX, and Lee University in Cleveland, TN. He was recruited to both OLLU and Lee University, breaking the color barrier as the first African American as a dean at OLLU (2012) and as the first African American faculty member at Lee University (1995).

As a military broadcaster and telecommunications manager in the communications-electronics area, he retired from the United States Army in 1995 as a young major with twenty years of federal service. At Lee University, he established the telecommunication program for electronic media in less than eighteen months with an enrollment of 138 students. Within ten years, he was promoted to the rank of professor. Dr. Laney aspires to serve in capacities of increased responsibility in higher education. His strengths lie in the areas of servant leadership, service, and vision casting. He accepted the call to servant leadership while serving our country in the armed forces. With a solid record of accomplishment in being a partner to those he served under and alongside, he has been able to successfully transfer these skills into the area of higher education administration, resulting in improved training and mentoring, particularly amongst faculty of color, improving their level of retention within the organization.

In partnership with the three presidents he served, which would have been impossible without the doctorate, he has been instrumental in helping his institutions raise large sums of money, expand the university's footprint and visibility in the marketplace, as well as in the African American community and, particularly, in the local churches of color. In his present role of dean at a Hispanic Serving Institution, his research study skills have allowed him to develop additional expertise and sensitivity in working with large numbers of Latino/a students and their families through establishing a dual credit program in a predominately Latino high school. Shortly after earning the PhD, due to the shortage of faculty of color at Lee University, students frequently turned to him to help sponsor events and mentor the growing number of African American students on campus he began to attract, as his image was marketed heavily in institutional promotional materials. Dr. Laney has worked to facilitate numerous opportunities to attract high caliber part-time faculty, women into leadership positions and STEM arenas, staff and students of color to the campuses he serves. His record of achievement demonstrates that he is an effective and successful bridge between the president and the various academic divisions because he is flexible and adept at adapting to several different leadership styles.

Promoting Positive Relationships

A review of Dr. Laney's record demonstrates that he is a mature first-generation, educational,bleader who is committed to faith-based institutions of higher learning. He has developed a proven track record of excellence in teaching, research, and outstanding service. As a bridge-builder, he is effective in bringing together diverse constituencies. He has learned that to survive in higher education, one must be flexible and can adapt to a dynamic and rapidly changing environment. He is a committed supporter and advocates for shared governance and affirmative action/equal opportunity. In his various leadership roles, Dr. Laney has successfully overseen an eclectic mixture of disciplines, which is typical in liberal arts, as well as having experience with forming partnerships with key stakeholders both on and off campus. During his tenure as dean, he has worked closely with a wide range of disciplines, such as art, biology, chemistry, communication, drama, English, history, humanities, kinesiology, mathematics, Mexican American studies, music, physics, physical science, philosophy, political science, public relations, religious studies, Spanish, telecommunication, and theatre. His doctoral education exposed him to the importance and the benefits of embracing a strong interdisciplinary and collaborative approach to higher education. Therefore, he has been successful in building harmonious relationships, which engendered true camaraderie and professional collegiality across disciplines and perspectives.

Building a Learning Community

Dr. Laney has also developed expertise in creating diverse programs, which has been a major by-product of his doctorate. He has become adept at delivering and marketing higher education opportunities on multiple platforms, in various modes, both traditional as well as emerging demographics. At OLLU, the undergraduate population is over 60 percent Latino/a, with a rich representation of veterans, international, non-traditional students, and a surging online population. Building a strong academic community requires positive and effective communication skills, and trust, to move fluidly between the silos that hide us and the walls and labels that separate us: "Staff," "Student," "Faculty," "Administration," and "Alumni." In his interactions with faculty, Dr. Laney's leadership style has been described as participatory and nurturing in tone and approach, while effectively working to draw faculty members out of their silos and into the wider university community. Michael perceives his role as that of being a team player and chief advisor and advocate on all academic matters. In 2004 he was nominated, along with sixteen other fellows from across the nation, to participate in the Council of Christian Colleges and Universities' Leadership Development Initiative for Emerging Leaders program in Sumas, Washington. Dr. Laney encourages excellence and student success in the classroom from his faculty and outstanding customer service from the staff. Additionally, he possesses strong, creative problem-solving skills. The strengths and gifts he brings to any administrative team are described in Gallup Strength finders as strategic, learner, maximizer, achiever, and input.

Advocating the Academic Enterprise

In his various capacities as professor, chair, and dean, Dr. Laney has served as both a vigorous and rational advocate for the liberal arts, scholarship, funding for research, student support services, and library and technology infrastructure and for advancing the cause of Christian higher education. He continues to be a passionate, responsible advocate for the faculty, staff, students, and administrators he serves in his role as a servant leader. Faculty and staff members with whom he has served in his previous positions as department chair and dean describe him this way: "Dr. Laney is the most proactive, even handed, and hardest working dean I've served with in seventeen years of teaching. He does a great job performing a very challenging task and is effective doing it in a servant-like manner and is an excellent academic and administrator."

"Dr. Laney is an exceptionally good leader for the Communication department. He leads with courage, fairness, and discipline. It is wonderful to have such a boss. Maybe I'm biased, but I think that we've got the best chair of all the departments."

"Michael is an excellent CAS Dean. He is a strong advocate for our college and truly cares about his faculty. It is a pleasure to work for him and to work hard. Excellence is expected and he gives back excellence."

"Dean Laney is doing a great job leading CAS. He appears to be aggressively pursuing excellence and advancement for all of the academic disciplines represented. Dr. Laney, you have done so well here at Our Lady of the Lake University in such a short period. Your joy, compassion, and dedication to each one of us are appreciated and we are inspired by your devotion to us as individuals. Thanks again for doing the research on the payroll mix-up. At our department meeting, I could help explain the problem to others who experienced the same result. You made it so easy to communicate on all levels. Believe me, this is our best time. I'm so privileged to be a part of this growth. Please stay here at OLLU forever, or at least until I must quit teaching, which should be about twenty more years (I'll be 102 and a half. Dr. Dyer said I could take off the last semester before I died at 103 years of age.) I love her. I love you both. Along with President Slater, I am finally enjoying true leadership. Thank you."

Cultivating Institutional Effectiveness

Dr. Laney relishes his role as a mentor to the faculty, staff, and the students at OLLU and to every student who has ever stepped into his classroom since 1995. He has also been recognized for his achievements in this area by students, peers, and administration and was awarded the Excellence in Teaching Award in 1999, the highest recognition given at Lee University. Many universities in Africa are seeking partnerships with Christian universities in the USA and, particularly, with African American PhDs and professors. It was in this setting Dr. Laney had the opportunity to expand his expertise in curriculum and program development.

During a one-year sabbatical, he served as a visiting professor in the Communication Department at Daystar University, Nairobi, Kenya, during the period of summer 2006 through summer 2007. Michael and Leonora sold "Faith House"—their dream home, to make this experience possible for their family and relocate to Kenya. Daystar University has the distinction of establishing the first communication program on the continent of Africa as well as having the premier Christian liberal arts program in Kenya. The vice chancellor of Daystar directed Dr. Laney to revamp the MA in corporate communications as well as develop their first doctoral studies program at Daystar. Under Professor Laney's leadership, the faith-based, Afro-centric communication doctorate program was developed and launched in August 2010; the program has been exported to twenty-two African nations. Daystar University informed Dr. Laney that it was the first of its kind. As the first African American missionary many Kenyans had ever met, who was serving in East Africa, he was able to draw attention to the vast range of resources that African American PhDs have at their disposal to aid and assist their brothers and sisters in East Africa and the rest of the educational institutions residing on the African continent; the opportunity for these emerging partnerships can expand, as the number of African American PhDs grow and expand their horizons to include performing service in Africa.

Building a Legacy

Dr. Laney believes that the Lord used the PhD to open to door to a host of blessings, recognitions, and honors, but it also involved giving back to his community in the form of servant leadership. Some of his recognitions include UMOJA Award-Outstanding Community Service Leadership Award, Inaugural Recipient—2012; 100 Black Men of Bradley County Inc. President's Award—2011; Cleveland Media Association-Excellence in Communication Award—2005; King's Men's Production-Minority Teacher of the Year—2005; NAACP (National Association for the Advancement of Colored People) Bradley County Life Time Achievement Award—2005; CCCU Leadership Development Institute Fellow—2004; Alpha Kappa Alpha Sorority, Community Service Leader Award—2004; National Register's Who's Who in Executives & Professionals—2004, 2005; Who's Who Among America's Teachers—2000, 2002, 2004, 2005, 2006; Africans Who is Who in USA-2000; 100 Black Men of Bradley County, Inc. Mentor of the Year—2000; Lee University Excellence in Teaching Award—1999; Mellon-ACA Doctoral Fellowship—1998; Kappa Tau Alpha (Mass Communications Honor Society)—1998.

During this next phase of his career, Dr. Laney is looking to use his expertise, networks, and gifts to build a legacy of excellence in faith-based higher education as he seeks to mentor the next generation of African American scholars and students.

Provoking One Another to Good Works

In the spring of 2006, while serving comfortably as a department chair, Michael attended the Council for Christian Colleges and Universities (CCCU) International Forum in Dallas, TX. He was presenting his research on the lack of diversity in hiring of faculty and administrators of color in Christian colleges and universities, "A Seat at the Table: Guess Who's Coming to Dinner?" As of June 2014, no CCCU member institution has placed a person of color at the helm of their institution as president; even though a few successful African American provosts have held the number two position at CCCU member institutions (Dr. Herma B. Williams, Fresno Pacific University; Dr. Joe Jackson, Point Park University; and Dr. Bob Suggs, Ashland University), to date, none of Dr. Laney's mentors have been tapped for the presidency of a CCCU institution. They have either retired or have moved on to other more profitable opportunities.

A former dean at a CCCU member institution challenged Michael and told him that he was "sitting back and resting, had become comfortable, and needed to step it up so that he could open the doors for others." This dean went on to become a provost but has not broken through the CCCU's presidential glass ceiling yet. Michael was initially furious at this man, who barely knew him, to make this assertion after having sat in Michael's presentation in diversity in hiring. However, in hindsight, his challenge made sense. If the CCCU was to have a person of color as a president, then now was the time to be preparing prospects for leadership. Little did Michael realize how distant and far out of reach this dream remains.

During his sabbatical year at Daystar University, Nairobi, Kenya, (2006–2007), Vice-Chancellor Godfrey Nguru, a fellow alumnus of the University of Tennessee-Knoxville, strongly encouraged him to seek the presidency upon his return to the USA. "Professor Laney, you should be seeking a presidency; you will make an excellent president and now is the time to begin." A similar comment was made by a tenured communication faculty member from Calvin College, who was a visiting professor at Daystar University. Buoyed by this support but still a department chair, Michael applied for provosts, vice president for academic affairs, and presidential positions with barely any acknowledgement from prospects. When pressed, the response was "The position requires at least five years of experience in academic leadership at the level of dean or higher." One candid president in 2007 told him, "I would love to hire you as my executive vice president or provost. I came out of the vocational world, but I could never sell your candidacy to my faculty if you had not been at least a dean." There it was, no amount of corporate, government, or military experience was going to allow him to fast track the process; he would need to "punch the ticket" just like everyone else and hope and pray to not age out of the process in the pursuit of a presidency as his mentors had before him.

The academy, for all its trappings of adaptability, advancement, and progress, is a very traditional, class-conscious, pedigree-oriented (Ivy Leagues and private versus public), and rank-sensitive institution. Highly traditional and very suspicious of those who have not come up through the traditional rank and file, the system tends to promote and reward those who look like them and have a similar pedigree. While Dr. Laney has seen an influx of minorities entering the ranks of the faculty, increasingly, faculty of color coming into higher education enter as a second career. They tend to transition from non-traditional sources, such as business, law, government, or the military. While these individuals, in many cases, had extremely successful careers and demonstrated remarkable leadership abilities, this does not matter. The academy, it appears, starts the clock as of one's initial entrance into higher education. Most importantly, time toward promotion does not count until after completion of the doctorate and your demonstration as a published scholar. Thus, for many faculty of color, decades of non-academic leadership experience are simply discounted. Additionally, these non-traditional leaders are commencing a second career and are more mature. Entering the educational workforce between the ages of forty to fifty usually works against some of these applicants as well. Since the typical path to the university presidency tends to be a traditional one, one must ascend through the ranks of the professoriate and contribute service as chair, dean, vice-president/provost, and president.

Frequently, this will entail moving and relocation to various colleges and universities to "punch the ticket" because of lower glass ceilings at many institutions. For example, in Dr. Laney's case, he hit the glass ceiling at the department chair level. The dean's position was filled, and the institution was extremely stable with administrators holding their positions for ten to twenty years or longer. The only path to promotion was outside of his host institution. The risks of following such a traditional path means that one may need to commit as much as twenty to thirty years to the process. This, of course, assumes that the faculty member of color has successfully navigated the minefields of tenure and promotion, which are littered with the casualties of the system, especially faculty of color. This is especially apparent when observing the audience composition and demographics of academic conferences. When surveying the landscape, faculty of color, while clearly underrepresented, are still in the picture. However, when the conference attendees are department chairs, the absence of diversity becomes more apparent, and when the attendees are deans, the number of faculty of color can be counted on two hands. However, at the provost and vice-presidential level, the number of faculty of color who are in these positions can be counted on a single hand, much like the professional drafts for the NBA or NFL. Ultimately, many prospects from these non-traditional paths, who are highly qualified, age out before being eligible for consideration by most university search committees, whose membership came up through the ranks of the academy and their first job out of graduate school was in higher education as staff, adjunct, or faculty member.

Competition and High Risk

In the current economy, the number of qualified people competing for deans, vice president for academic affairs (VPAA), or provost continues to surge and makes for a very tight labor market. Often executive search firms are employed in these national searches and can pull as many as fifty to one hundred applicants for a single position. Dr. Laney recalls that the dean searches that he participated in before landing in position at OLLU had similar numbers, and the VPAA and provost searches at select institutions may have doubled this number of applicants. Along with high competition, for faculty of color, comes high risk for failure in the position. Dr. Laney has observed in his role of chairing search institutional and infrastructure issues (accreditation issues, low salaries, turnover, fiscal challenges), committees, that when it is revealed or the candidate discovers that the position is high risk, due to white males particularly drop out of the pool, because they believe that they will have better options either at their current location (they have used this interview as a bargaining chip) or for a lateral promotion at a more select school.

Dr. Laney recounts how he was working to recruit a highly talented white male vice president for Enrollment Management; however, when the candidate became aware of the instability in the office of the president, he withdrew his consideration and returned to his current institution and parlayed it into a promotion at his current location. Often, minority members may feel compelled to accept the offer of a risky position at a troubled institution because they may feel as if they have fewer options to fall back upon. Dr. Laney admits, "I laugh when I hear my white colleagues telling me that I'm so qualified that I'd have plenty of offers to choose from! "While I am qualified, no one is beating down the door to offer me or any other African Americans that I know jobs." Of course, if the African American candidate is successful in the risky administrative position, he or she may be able to leverage it and move into a higher position. However, they also run the risk of being "typecast" as "a fixer" or "troubleshooter." Once this occurs, one may find that they are limited to working in high risk and highly stressful positions, which can take their toll mentally, emotionally, and physically upon the African American scholar.

Beyond the Horizon

Dr. Laney remains an "optimistic realist" about his promotion opportunities and potential; however, he concedes that the color barrier for presidents in faith based, and particularly, CCCU institutions will most likely be broken by the current undergraduate students who are enrolled in over two hundred federal TRIO educational programs like the McNair Scholars Program. *The Ronald McNair Post-Baccalaureate Achievement Program* was named after the late astronaut Dr. Ronald McNair of the ill-fated January 1986 US Challenger space mission. The program, founded in 1986, is designed to attract and recruit students of color and promise into graduate and doctoral programs while they are traditional undergraduate students. If these students successfully navigate their doctoral programs and land faculty positions before they are thirty, some of them could be on the traditional trajectory to the presidency. Given the fact that this program has been around for twenty-eight years, alumni from this program may now be entering those key positions that will soon groom them for the presidency.

In the meantime, Dr. Laney works to mentor students and faculty of color and promise in his various leadership roles in the academy and in the community, and he trusts the Lord for the outcome. He places his hope in two promises in scripture, Psalm 75: 6–7 KJV, "for promotion comes neither from the east, nor from the west, nor from the south. God is the judge: he putteth down one, and setteh up another." Also, Jeremiah 29:11 NIV: "'For I know the plans I have for you,' declares the LORD, 'plans to prosper you and not to harm you, plans to give you hope and a future.'" "It's all good," says Dr. Laney. "I have been so blessed, I could have never imagined that I would be able to serve in this role, and if the Lord never blessed me with another promotion, my life would have been complete, rewarding, and a success. The rest of my days and my future are completely in the Good Lord's hands, and if nothing else, my life story has demonstrated that God certainly has a sense of humor, so there is no telling how this story turns out—stay tuned."

• • •

CHAPTER 3

Dr. LaJoyce Chatwell Lawton

Principal Consultant, Lawton International
Pastor/Professor, The Multitude Experience

BIOGRAPHY

Lawton International

Dr. LaJoyce Lawton is the principal of *Lawton International*, a continuing education consultancy based in Cypress, Texas. She is a sought-after speaker. Dr. Lawton has spoken at conferences both nationally and internationally on global and educational issues. Most notably, she has spoken at conferences in Argentina, Austria, Jamaica, Bermuda, Swaziland, Lesotho, and other countries. Since 1975, Lawton has served as consultant to corporate, military, and student personnel with overseas assignments. She provided Business English training to Japanese executives in Tokyo and Yokohama.

She has made numerous media appearances. She has appeared on WGN's *Minority Business Report*. She was a co-host on *Creating the Future* and host/producer of Oklahoma *World View* on Cox Cable. She has been interviewed in the *Exhibitor*, *Tradeshow Week*, *Entrepreneur*, *Indianapolis CEO*, and *Black Enterprise*. Lawton founded *Oklahoma Women in World Trade* and was instrumental in the establishment of *Bermuda Women in World Trade*, both *Organization of Women in International Trade* (OWIT) affiliates. She is a member of the San Antonio Ladies-Talented Tenth (SALTT).

CREDENTIALS:

- EdD, Adult and Higher Education, *University of Oklahoma*
- MA, Curriculum and Instruction, *Michigan State University*
- BS, Home Economics, *Lincoln University*

"If we have the courage and tenacity of our fore bearers,
who stood firmly like a rock against the lash of slavery,
we shall find a way to do for our day what they did for theirs."
~ Mary McCloud Bethune

***Disclaimer:** The stories in this chapter reflect the author's recollection of events. Some names, locations, and identifying characteristics have been changed to protect the privacy of those depicted. Dialogue has been re-created from the author's memory.

The Multitude Experience

It's not unusual to find the Reverend Dr. LaJoyce Lawton participating in liturgy during worship services, praying, visiting, teaching, preaching, administering sacraments, or completing ministry projects in various locations. Rev. Lawton preached the baccalaureate worship service at Piney Woods School (MS), was the commencement speaker at Boley School (OK), and planned/facilitated a citywide Juneteenth worship service in San Antonio, TX. While serving as executive administrative assistant to Bishop (then Pastor) Sarah Davis, she actively worked in the successful campaign toward Episcopal service.

Education, especially faith-based education, is her passion. Since earning a Doctor of Education degree from the University of Oklahoma in adult and higher education, Dr. Lawton has continued making contributions within various educational arenas. This pastor/professor specializes in "sweet beginnings."

- Founding faculty, Texas A&M University – San Antonio.
- Founder/past president, Oklahoma Women in World Trade and instrumental in the founding of Bermuda Women in World Trade.
- Instituted San Antonio campus of the Interdenominational Theological Center Certificate in Theology program; established The Multitude Experience Certificate in Ministry program.
- Consultant to the founder of I Am Destined Specialty Academy and I Am Church in Tema, Ghana.

Team member, development of Training and Development certificate program for University of Oklahoma College of Continuing Education.

A part of the team that provided teacher education training in Southern Africa led by Bishop Vashti McKenzie, Dr. Lawton shared lesson-planning strategies with teachers at faith-based schools in Swaziland and Lesotho. She supervised an Oblate School of Theology intern and currently trains clergy and lay ministry leaders. LaPrensa Foundation, Inc. has named Rev. Lawton "Outstanding Woman in Action" (Religion Award - 2008). Dr. Lawton received a ministry grant from Inspire Women to create teaching materials for training clergy in Ghana. As a Trade Adjustment Assistance for Farmers consultant, she worked with Gulf Coast shrimpers to assist them in completing business plans which enabled them to improve their current endeavor or launch a new venture.

Ordained in 2004, Rev. Lawton has served churches in Kerrville and San Antonio. This Methodist minister speaks at Christian conferences/retreats and is a lifelong learner who continuously completes seminary courses and theological workshops.

LaJoyce is married to Billy Lawton, Program Leader (AGNR), Cooperative Extension Program, Prairie View A&M University (retired). Their daughter, Kimberly, and grandson, Ke'Mar, live in Mansfield, TX.

Part One: A Strong Determination to Succeed

The women in my family are the role models who have inspired me. I'm researching them now. The path to leadership for women descending the Prier/Richardson family tree has been paved with perseverance. One of the reasons the women in our family have moved from a boarding school experience to sitting on boards, from illiteracy to terminal degree is the persevering spirit that runs through our veins.

The Women Who Have Inspired Me

Nancy Prier

My grandmother told me that Nancy was from Virginia. I continue researching Prier/Richardson women but haven't found evidence of her birth, to date. The 1870 census lists her as Nancy Foreman and there are seven children are listed on this census with her. By the 1880 census, there were two houses included in the Prier … Foreman census report. House 171 lists Jacob Foreman, WM, 61 yo, farmer, single; and Nancy Prier, BF, 44 yo, widow, laborer. House 172 lists William, 18 yo, BM, laborer; June, 15 yo, BF, laborer; Myme, 13 yo, BF, laborer; Laura, 11 yo, BF, laborer; Caroline, 9 yo, BF; Hampton, 5 yo, BM; Kit, 1 yo, BM. There's a 15 October 1879 birth record that includes the following information: 10 Mill Street, Charleston, SC, Father: John J. Prier, waiter; Mother: Nancy Prier, maiden name Nancy Williams.

Laura Richardson

Laura made the South Carolina … Georgia … Florida migration that had been made centuries before. Fort Mose in St. Augustine, Florida, was the first free black community in what is now the United States. Africans running from slavery in British Carolina fled south into Spanish Florida. Laura, known for her rice cooking, worked as a farm laborer/cook, servant/cook, or maid/cook while serving four employers throughout her lifetime: a farmer, a physician, a chain drug store owner, and an international art collector.

My mother shared lots of information about my great grandmother. I was two years old when Laura died. Though she was illiterate, I learned that she did her grocery shopping by identifying logos on products, i.e., the picture on a red baking powder can. She had four children. The boys died young in life. One daughter was sent to the country to be raised by relatives, because she looked whit. She sent my grandmother to boarding school, "disowned" her when she got pregnant, and, later, made a home for her and her children. She developed ways to cope throughout life. Several years ago, I discovered two photographs of her that my mother had put in a frame behind a photo of my grandmother. What an incredible blessing! After many years of begging, my uncle gave me correspondences, that was written to her between 1923 and 1937. There are postcards postmarked Havana, CUBA, and letters postmarked from states up and down the Atlantic coast. I am currently cataloging the Letters to Laura Collection.

Floria Richardson Holley

I have wonderful, fond memories of my grandmother. We spent many summers with her in St Augustine, Florida, and she spent lots of time with us in St. Louis, Missouri. She was originally from Georgia and had relatives in New York. She had run away from boarding school in Aiken, South Carolina, and given birth to my mother by the time she was seventeen. Two years later she was a married woman with two daughters, and later, two sons followed. Her husband was a merchant Marine. I am told he was older than she was. He died when my mom was twelve. By the age of twenty-nine, Granny had four children to raise and no high school diploma. She did a lot of domestic work for the Lynch family in New York. When my mom was a teenager, she went with her mother during summers to help. Ultimately, she became the chef at Flagler Hospital in St Augustine, Florida, where she worked until retirement. She sent all four of her children to Florida A&M University. She completed her GED after my mom was an adult. My grandmother played with the hand that had been dealt her.

Lois Holley Chatwell

My mother was sick all her life, and I believe it was because she wasn't true to herself. I don't know who her father was, but I'm researching the women in my family now. I don't believe my mother married her true love, but I watched her work very hard at marriage and with her family. Her marriage lasted thirty-nine years until her death at the age of sixty-two. She had three children, one of whom recently "found himself." My mother wanted to be a dietitian. Armed with a degree in home economics, she needed a year's internship and to complete the national exam required to earn the registered dietitian (RD) designation. In those days, the closet place she could meet that requirement was in Chicago. She didn't live during the era of commuter marriages. A married woman with a daughter just didn't do that (even though St. Louis and Chicago aren't that far apart). I learned that my parents went to these locations to party. She started her career as assistant director for a daycare center, worked as a dietetic technician, and, ultimately, taught home economics in St. Louis public schools for many years. I admired her tenacity and the way she lived her life so much that I chose to pursue home economics as an undergraduate major.

Mom sacrificed her hopes, desires, and aspirations for her children. What happens to a dream deferred? It's these models of perseverance that intersected to deposit me in this place where I can exhibit community leadership and exert small influences on the lives God places in my space.

Part Two: College Educational Experiences

I grew up in a home where there was never any question as to whether we (my siblings and I) were going to college. It was a fact that we were going. Ever since I was twelve years old and had a pen pal from Tanzania (at that time Tanganyika), I've had a desire to see the world. I informed my dad that I was going to Africa when I was twelve, and he laughed in my face. Never laugh in my face. With my limited knowledge of life, I felt the way to see the world was to join the military or to become a flight attendant. Each time I pursued one of those professions, my father told me, "You're not doing that. You don't have to go to college to do that." My mom and her sister graduated from Florida A&M University. Both of their brothers attended FAMU but later graduated from other colleges. My dad's people were high school graduates or less; some dropped out of high school. Money was always tight in our household. I was always told we were poor, and I hated hearing that.

After hearing about FAMU all my life from my mom and my aunt, I wanted to go there. My parents said no because of out-of-state fees. My mom grew up in St. Augustine, Florida, but she moved to St. Louis, Missouri, to marry my father. They wanted me to attend Harris Teacher's College. I felt that going to Harris would be just like going to high school. I would ride the bus back and forth and live at home, plus I had no desire to teach.

I had seen my mom and my aunt work as teachers and earn absolutely no money. I quickly told my parents that I would marry my high school sweetheart, whom I thought I dearly loved. Then one day, they asked if I wanted to go to Lincoln University in Jefferson City, Missouri. My dad had attended school there for one semester, and ironically, while I was in the sixth grade, I had taken a class trip to the campus. I eagerly went to Lincoln, and my parents were quite surprised my sweetheart had also registered to attend Lincoln. They were equally surprised when we broke off the relationship toward the end of my freshman year.

Statistically, I'm one of those people who should never have finished undergraduate school. I entered the university with a low-grade point average, and I quit school twice. I finally decided to buckle down and do the work. I remember my major professor telling me that I was an underachiever. She had asked me what would motivate me to work toward my potential. I finally understood many years later and began doing the work. The fact was, I wasn't stupid, merely unmotivated. During my undergrad studies, I had been married and divorced; this helped me make up my mind to make my own way in life.

I retained a loving relationship with my favorite undergraduate professor, Mrs. Beatrice Moore Smith, until her death. She came to know my husband. There was a time, one morning, when she called to request a recommendation letter because she was being considered for the rank of professor. I admired her so much that I wanted her and my mother to meet. Unfortunately, they never did meet; however, both my mother and Mrs. Beatrice Moore Smith were my mentors. They were both very smart and had overcome many adversities.

When I arrived at Lincoln University, I wanted to major in library science, because I loved to read. Unfortunately, there were no library science courses there. I was so anxious to leave home that I agreed to go to Lincoln without checking what majors were available. After wandering from table to table at registration and reviewing requirements for different majors, I considered having an undeclared major for the first semester. I then decided to major in home economics. My rationale was that my mom was a home economist, and I greatly admired her and applauded her accomplishments. My grandmother was a hospital chef. I had come from a long line of good cooks. My decision was made, and I graduated with a degree in home economics.

When I moved to Miami, Florida, unlike many of my classmates, I didn't have any job offers before I finished the undergrad program. I made the decision to move to Florida because I had spent most of my summers with my mom's people and loved it there. I had many pleasant memories my times with relatives and friends throughout the state. I began to work as a nutrition educator for a community health center. When that federally funded center suffered budget cuts, I saw the handwriting on the wall and began to search for new career opportunities. The man I was dating at the time was a teacher who suggested that I become a teacher. His reasoning was, you get out at 3 p.m. and have summers off. I remembered my mom saying one of the things she enjoyed about teaching was that she was off the same time her children were off. I personally never had a desire to teach, but this had become my destiny. Later, my being a teacher afforded me the chance to achieve a lifelong goal—to see the world. After teaching home economics in Miami, Florida, for three years, I was more than qualified to apply for a Department of Defense Overseas Dependent Schools teaching position. I also had a few graduate education courses which made me more marketable.

When I began to pursue Florida certification, a Department of Education employee recommended that I take graduate courses, therefore killing two birds with one stone, i.e., becoming certified and working on a master's degree. A colleague, Evelyn Woods, was instrumental in getting Rocky Mountain College to offer graduate courses in education at the high school where we taught. From this action, I had fallen into pursuing graduate degrees in education! The year I was accepted by DODDS, three thousand people had applied, but only three hundred were accepted. My thought as I reflected on the past, "Ha! Ha!" an underachiever was in the top 10 percent.

I returned to the States after teaching for DODDS in Japan for four years. I had completed a master's degree, plus thirty (Michigan State University Graduate Education Overseas Program and had a desire to pursue a doctorate. With these qualifications, I could teach at a university and have a training and development consultancy.

Part Three: Experiences Entering Doctoral Study

At some point while living in Oklahoma City, I applied for a position at Oklahoma State University. After the panel had interviewed me, they asked me to work on my doctorate. There had been a PhD in home economics and an EdD educator on the panel. The doctorate would have been in home economics education. I went home and excitedly told my husband about the opportunity. His response was that my working on a doctorate rather than earning an income would be a financial disaster for our household. Not wanting to cause dissention in the home, I found a job.

Ten years later, I was very active in my local chapter of the American Society for Training and Development (ASTD). I had a training and development consultancy and was determined to pursue as much professional development as possible. It was confirmed that adult education is my forte. I served as president of my local ASTD chapter. As president of the chapter, I was instrumental in establishing a training and development certificate program. Initially, this certificate program was sponsored by our ASTD chapter and Metro Community College. Garland McWatters had brought the idea to the chapter. The certificate program was so well received by the community that the University of Oklahoma College of Continuing Education asked to make it a part of their educational offerings. That program is now conducted in three states. Dr. Gary Green, who was an ASTD chapter committee chair and professor of education at the University of Oklahoma, later became my committee chair.

As Gary and I worked together on ASTD projects, I believe he observed some of my capabilities. One day he asked if I were interested in working on my doctorate. He also mentioned that some minority fellowship funds were available. Certainly, I don't want to cause any dissention in my home, but I knew that I would pursue this opportunity no matter what my husband's response. When I returned home and told my husband about this opportunity, he told me to do it if that was what I wanted.

I began the application process. Gary walked me through everything step by step, i.e., taking the GRE, completing paperwork, being interviewed, customizing my program, selecting my committee (I didn't know anyone on the faculty at OU except him). Gary was my biggest supporter. He selected my committee based on colleagues he got along with. Since I provided international business protocol training and development as part of my consultancy, Gary did agree that I could have two business professionals on my committee: one specialized in international business and the other in human resources management. I was off to the races to pursue a doctorate in adult and higher education with an emphasis in training and development.

Part Four: Experiences in Doctorate Study

I always say the process of completing a terminal degree in academia is about five men (sometimes a few women) deciding whether they will let you enter "their club." It's whether you will enter the old boys' club resulting in being addressed as doctor. Will they deign to allow you entrance into the "doctor's club"?

In my case, two Native American men were the "minority" representation. You must have an advocate; otherwise, it is even more difficult to move through the process. Not only is your advocate in your corner, but he/she persuades the remaining committee members to accept your premises and work.

I moved through class work in three years. Since I had my own consulting practice, I could attend classes day, night, summers, intersession, regular term, anytime. I took advantage of all the different times classes were offered. I even taught classes as a graduate assistant. These classes were listed in the schedule under my chair's name or listed under both of our names. I could even teach some undergrad courses I had developed during intersession under my own name.

I do have vivid memories of one course. Once I began attending classes, I realized I had no interest in the content at all. Instead of checking to see if I could have this course dropped from my program of study and add another course, I suffered through it. I found most of the requirements pointless and, therefore, did my own thing. Of course, that didn't go over well with my professor. I earned the only "C" in my doctoral program. The experience was so negative that I did not feel the professor (a member of my committee) was an advocate for me and my education. I asked that she be removed from my committee. My chair handled the paperwork for her removal. I later learned that she had once stated she would no longer serve on any EdD candidate committees because their research emphasis was different than that of PhD candidates. I was grateful to learn of her mindset but certainly wish I had known about her thought processes before I enrolled in her course.

In retrospect, I wish I had done an ethnographic research project. By the time I learned what ethnography was, I was already knee-deep in my work with my committee chair. Perhaps I'll get to do some ethnographic research now. I'm currently cataloging correspondence my great grandmother received between 1923 and 1937. "To God be the glory."

I decided to take an oral general exam in lieu of written generals. I felt it would be a dress rehearsal for defending the dissertation. This process included writing a mini proposal for your dissertation and submitting it to your committee members for review. Then everyone comes together at an appointed time to discuss your proposal. This process is similar to defense, and I felt it would me give an idea of what to expect during the defense. As soon as I walked into the room, committee members began slamming me into the wall. I was asked questions that I could not answer or answered poorly. Obviously, I had no idea how to prepare for this process. Once again, I had not worked with my committee chair to prepare for this segment of the process. When I was asked to leave the room so that my committee could discuss answers, I walked out feeling that I had failed my general exam. My only thought was how I could tell my husband that I had failed. We were about to move to Indianapolis (for his job). I knew I could write my dissertation anywhere and communicate with my committee electronically. I did not want to move to Indianapolis with a failed general exam hanging over my head. I didn't want to fly back to Oklahoma to defend again, if taking the exam again was even allowed. When called back into the room, I was told that I had passed and given numerous recommendations as to how to proceed with writing my dissertation. Oh my God!

Rotating Committee Members

When your process evolves into a three state, ten-year endeavor, there will be members who rotate off your committee for various reasons. Here's a snapshot of my "rotating" experiences.

Dr. Valdrie Walker was a sorority sister whom I loved having on my committee. It was a joy to talk with her about my proposal. She gave me invaluable insights about moving through the doctoral process in general. It would have been an incredible blessing to have had Dr. Walker on my committee throughout the entire process. She truly represented the kind of support doctoral students need. She (and her son) moved back to Virginia and returned to university administrative duties—her first love. She later became an administrator at Edward Waters College in Florida.

Dr. Lawrence McKibbin is a South African. Imagine that! His sister moved to the States to attend Oklahoma University undergraduate school, and we all spent time talking about the prospects of providing training and development in South Africa. He left to acquire a dean's position at a small college in Kansas. He made me aware of university international student programs, which, in the past, I hadn't known about.

Dr. Ramon Alonso retired while I was in process. We had many wonderful conversations about global education and international business protocol.

Dr. Connie Dillon and I did not come to a meeting of the minds. I requested that she be removed from my committee because I did not believe she was an advocate for me during the process.

Dr. Grayson Noley (Member of the Cherokee Nation) joined my committee when I was almost finished with the process.

Doctors Gary Green, Robert Fox, Jerry Bread (Member of the Kiowa Nation), and Michael Buckley remained constant and provided continuity on my committee throughout the process.

Part Five: Dissertation Experiences During Doctoral Work

Each time I moved (due to spouse's career), I put writing my dissertation on the back burner. Granted, my husband did wait to begin making moves until I had reached the writing stage. He had been asked before but declined, because I was either taking classes or hadn't completed generals. Once these processes were finished, he couldn't hold the company off any longer, so the moving began. In each new location, I busied myself establishing the household and seeking opportunities for generating income from my consulting practice.

Of the four years we lived in Indianapolis, I submitted a proposal in the fall of each year for the first three years. Each time, my chair rejected my proposal stating he didn't believe my committee would accept it. Each time, disappointed, I threw the proposal on the back burner and continued attempting to grow my consulting practice. At least I could generate some income to maintain myself. In retrospect, this would have been the time to ask my chair for clarification and for help in writing something the committee would indeed accept. I also could have asked colleagues in Indianapolis to review my proposal and give me their input. Instead, I handled everything alone and in my own way. Certainly, that was not the best way to handle my challenges. One of my husband's coworkers told him, "Chances are she won't finish—the longer you stay away from the process, the more likely you are not to finish." Never say that!

While living in San Antonio, Texas, I finally had my proposal approved. I also landed a very taxing job with a huge learning curve. I spent every weekend studying and preparing for the next week. Mentally, I was not in a frame of mind to write. All my mental faculties went toward studying for my job. Then a few situations began to converge.

My time was running out. I had only one year left to complete my degree. My chair was retiring at the end of the year. I knew no one else on my committee had the interest in my future that my chair had. No one would advocate for me like he did.

Meanwhile, on this demanding job, I had been denied a vacation request. This vacation request had significance. This was a timeframe that I had to accompany my husband on a big, national corporate business trip with customers. It was an annual time to entertain important customers and their spouses. One year before, when I put in for my annual leave, I had requested several small vacations with an explanation that all other dates could be refused, but the time requested to accompany my husband was very important. A few days before it was time to leave with my husband, I received my response to leave request. All vacation had been approved except the dates needed to accompany my husband. Long story short, after talking with everyone up and down the chain of command about taking the necessary days off, I resigned.

Resigning freed me to write. I could now concentrate on my writing. I had all day to write, and I could concentrate on my writing. I wasn't confined to merely writing evenings, holidays, and weekends. I had one school year to write. The first thing I had to do was look at all the suspense dates and plan my submissions accordingly. With those dates posted on my bathroom mirror, I began writing. My husband handled all finances (household and dissertation related), which gave me freedom to write, write, write every day.

When I stepped into the room for my defense, I immediately began putting overheads (yes, overheads!) on the projector. By the time I had gotten to the third overhead, committee members had begun telling me of small changes I needed to make to get my work published. Once committee members begin telling you they will be disappointed if you aren't published, then you know you have passed! The process was complete. Praise the Lord! They began working on the signature sheet.

Lesson to be Learned

- It's a very political (and often a racist, sexist) process.
- You must learn to play the game.
- Setbacks can move you forward.
- Timing is everything.
- There are unexpected joys.

Part Six: Post-Graduation: Reflection on Being an Educated and African American Female

As I was moving through my doctoral program, I knew that I had no interest in working toward tenure "rainmaker" research or the publish/perish scene. I enjoy teaching at the university or college level and writing about what interest me, i.e., my ancestry research. Working at a small college/university are both enjoyable to me.

I also enjoy adult and continuing education very much and have been blessed to work in those venues. Since I've always marched to a different beat, I discovered that I do my absolute best work when I chart my own course and create my own path. Having a terminal degree gives me the "credibility" needed to establish my own educational organizations and be a serious contender in the field of continuing education. Being an educated woman means I can enter conversations with university presidents about collaborating on programs. Being an educated woman allows me to be taken seriously by men.

Having that credibility allowed me to establish a continuing education consultancy. The consultancy has two divisions (for-profit and non-profit). I enjoy both aspects.

Lawton International is for profit, and *The Multitude Experience* is non-profit. Work samples are included below:

Lawton International

Lawton International initiative was to serve as a Business Planning Consultant for Trade Adjustment Assistance for Farmers and Fisherman. (TAA). This was a three-year federal program where we worked with Gulf Coast shrimpers on improving their operations or transitioning from said operation into another career. We consulted with them and helped them to write business plans.

The Multitude Experience

We launched *The Multitude Experience* (TME) to serve those with a passion for specialized ministry. TME offers:

- A customized blended learning format.
- An opportunity to earn IACET CEUs.
- Here's our rationale:

A Certificate in Ministry

Ministry today is challenging, complex, and specialized, so a commitment to upgrade skills is necessary. Work at the certificate level is often voluntary, so this pursuit highlights personal commitment to excellence and professionalism.

Earning a certificate in ministry demonstrates A willingness to pursue the skill sets needed for effective ministry performance as well as a commitment to staying current regarding ministry issues.

- An ability to apply course work curriculum to ministry experiences.
- A working knowledge of faith-based topics.
- A capacity for handling advanced ministry responsibilities.

Pursuing A Certificate in Ministry with The Multitude Experience

Multitude Experience administrators have planted their own ministry and/or serve as ministry leaders at their respective churches. Administrators can help certificate participants prepare to successfully complete seminary or upper division university work.

- Multitude Experience administrators have
- Adult and Higher Education experience.
- Seminary experience.
- Pastoral experience.

As a sole practitioner, it's imperative that I have a support network. Jesus, our greatest teacher, had His team. John Maxwell reminds us that "talent is never enough" and "teamwork multiples your talent." Those listed below are an advisory board of sorts, helping me to navigate the growing pain continuum. We want to establish official advisory boards for each division to facilitate our work. We have begun working on succession planning.

As I prayed about establishing The Multitude Experience, I met with Dr. John Kinney, Dean of Samuel DeWitt Proctor School of Theology. He counseled with me and offered recommendations. He shared with me that once I had achieved a certain level of success, there would probably be one of two outcomes: (1) faith-based HBCUs would seek to collaborate with us; (2) a majority faith-based institutions would seek to incorporate our curriculum and establish an African American division. I respect Dr. Kinney's accomplishments and value his opinion. I'm grateful that he was willing to share his time and thoughts.

Dr. Gwendolyn Johnson hired me for my first higher education teaching position. She has served as assistant dean and dean at major universities. She also has HBCU experience. She counseled with me about the mistakes I made as a new professor and celebrated with me once I achieved glowing student reviews. She was always ready to advise me, serve as a reference, and fellowship with me. She, too, has invaluable input for our growth.

Dr. J. Brendonly Cunningham was a mentor and prayer warrior. I watched her successfully matriculate the challenges of one of the major denominations. She kept me grounded, letting me know when I was wrong or right. She advocated for me and helped me avoid some pitfalls. She was there for me since before the time of ordination and walked me through my denominational transition process.

Wearing Two Hats - Ministry and Education

Since completing my doctorate, I have followed a unique progression. I began the decade as one of two the founding faculty for the new campus of a state university. We served non-traditional upper division and graduate students. They were second career or working toward improving their career status. These success stories include student teaching overseas, teaching overseas, becoming department heads, and being officers in professional development organizations. Their community contributions are varied and extensive.

During the next chapter of my life, I was pastor of a small congregation. I was responsible for all spiritual and administrative aspects of the Body of Christ. We experienced a wealth of outcomes, i.e., viable youth ministry, training on collaborating with a large congregation, a strategic plan, computerized membership, and finances. Identifying officers and ministry heads to continue the work, meeting financial obligations ahead of schedule, and experienced numerous professional development opportunities. It was an incredible experience and confirmation that being a senior pastor is not my forte.

After having worked in a certificate program for a nationally known seminary, I established a theological institute. My previous certificate experience was wonderful, and it allowed me to envision much more work that could be done. The harvest is plentiful, but the workers are few. Hence, The Multitude Experience (a multifaceted ministry) was born. Our target population is one that is underserved. We work with lay and clergy who will not attend seminary but realize there must be preparation for God's work. Their ministries have a direct effect on children, family, and community. We seek participants who want to increase territories, expand knowledge bases, and sharpen skill sets. We provide training in a format where busy professionals can participate while still meeting their current work, family, and community demands. We produce ministers and ministry leaders that are better equipped for Kingdom Building.

Four cohorts graduated, and the outcomes were incredible. I'll share a few of God's manifestations I observed among participants who completed certificate programs I have administered. One woman went to the annual conference of her denomination and came back ordained and assigned to pastor a church. A man accepted his call to ministry, and he and his wife (an ordained minister) planted a church. A man received a youth pastor position, along with other increased responsibilities, at his current church; he's now being considered for a pastor's position. Several participants were licensed or ordained by their respective denominations. Lay participants expanded or started ministries. One licensed minister has an online devotional. One of our graduates, now ordained, is pursuing a women's respite. A blessed camaraderie developed such that when I needed participation in a citywide Juneteenth Worship Celebration, all I had to do was ask. God continues to move in miraculous ways. However, as it is written, "No eye has seen, no ear has heard, no mind has conceived what God has prepared for those who love Him." (1 Corinthians 2:9 NIV.)

My view of working with adult learners is very eclectic. This comes from having taught at the university level as well as having facilitated faith-based and continuing education programs. Primarily, I know that all participants can learn any material. The key is to use a variety of methods in each course so that no one will be left out. Each participant has an opportunity to be successful, and success breeds success. Our curriculum has included field-based assignments, group work, projects, panels, guest lectures, field trips, presentations, book reviews, portfolios, case studies; the methods continue... Adult students have much to offer and to share their life experiences throughout the course in many ways. Classes are performance based—students "do" what we study via Ministry Projects and field assignments.

I am a strong proponent of lifelong learning. I got my library card as soon as it was allowed at the age of six and have been reading ever since. For many years, I enjoyed reading novels, but that soon changed to reading for information gathering. I constantly complete courses, both for credit and non-credit. I've been blessed to travel to over thirty countries, which remains an education. These trips represent ministry, work/service, completing graduate courses, and vacations. I feel that professional development is an important component of lifelong learning. I'm active in professional organizations related to my ministry and work. I encourage participants to do the same. I begin exposing them by making sure we attend conferences and meetings during our time together.

God has allowed numerous success stories among former students. My university students have viable teaching or training and well-developed careers. Among them are department chairs and individuals who are active in professional organizations. One who did her student teaching in Italy, and another who is teaching in Germany. Former students have served as mentor teachers to subsequent pre-service and student teachers. My ministry students are working successfully as pastors, youth pastors, and ministry leaders.

As I reflect on all that God has deposited in me, I'm amazed. However, as it is written, "No eye has seen, no ear has heard, no mind has conceived what God has prepared for those who love Him." (1 Corinthians 2:9 NIV)

Educator's Litany
© 2012 LaJoyce Chatwell Lawton

This is an excerpt from a moving speech Dr. LaJoyce gave during the celebration honoring the Exceptional Scholars (now the Talented Tenth of San Antonio) in 2012. She and 19 African American Women were honored by Carver

Library for their accomplishments and receiving their PhDs or EdDs in various fields of study. In 2011, 16 African American Men were honored for their accomplishments with PhDs in various fields of study. These scholars' dissertations are catalogued into the San Antonio Public Library System to be used by the public as reference material.

ALL: We must teach, teach, teach.

ONE: Let us teach our males that sagging pants was the way the slave master deterred us from running.

MANY: Teach sister teach.

ONE: Let us teach our young women that when boys say "If you love me-you will" that boy's actions, "ain't about nothing."

MANY: Teach sister teach.

ONE: As we teach our young people parenting skills let us model that hitting is not the only way to discipline.

MANY: Teach sister teach.

ONE: Let us teach our young people when to use who, whom, and past participle because "massa" uses language to disqualify us.

MANY: Teach sister teach.

ONE: Let us teach our young people that body piercing, grills, and tattoos are not keys to climbing the corporate ladder.

MANY: Teach sister teach.

ONE: Let us teach our young people to use Mr., Mrs., Miss and other appropriate titles rather than disintegrating into a chasm of informality that the majority culture has.

MANY: Teach sister teach.

ONE: Let us tech our young women that walking across campus Half-naked is not a path toward internships?

MANY: Teach sister teach.

ONE: Let us teach our young people that not working while on duty as a student worker does not translate to recommendations for graduate school or corporate positions.

MANY: Teach sister teach.

ONE: Let us teach our university students why texting during class or while attending campus seminars is not acceptable.

MANY: Teach sister teach.

ALL: We must teach, teach, teach!

This is an excerpt from a moving speech Dr. LaJoyce gave during the celebration honoring the Exceptional Scholars (now the Talented Tenth of San Antonio) in 2012. She and 19 African American Women were honored by Carver Library for their accomplishments and receiving their Ph.Ds or Ed.D.s in various fields of study. In 2011, 16 African American Men were honored for their accomplishments with Ph.Ds. in various fields of study. These scholars' dissertations are catalogued into the San Antonio Public Library System to be used by the public as reference material.

• • •

CHAPTER 4

Dr. Sharon Small

CEO/Early Head Start Director, Parent Child Incorporated (PCI)

BIOGRAPHY

Dr. Sharon Small is the chief executive officer of *Parent/Child Incorporated* (PCI), a family-oriented agency focusing on early childhood education and development from birth to five through the *Early Head Start Program*, *Day Care Homes*, and the *Child and Adult Care Food Program* (CACFP). These programs collectively serve over four thousand children and families daily. She is a former principal and math teacher.

She is an active member with *National Association of Female Executives*; *National Education Association*; *Phi Delta Kappa, Inc.* Dr. Small has won numerous awards such as *Who's Who Among American Teachers*; *Doctoral Recognition Award - Texas Alliance of Phi Delta Kappa, Inc.*; *Educator's Hall of Fame*; *Who's Who Among America's Teachers 1996–2000*; and won an award for *Teacher of the Year*. She is a member of the *San Antonio Ladies-Talented Tenth* (SALTT).

CREDENTIALS:

- PhD in Leadership Studies, *Our Lady of the Lake University*
- MA in Special Education and Teaching, *Our Lady of the Lake University*
- BA in Education, *St. Mary's University*

"Set your goals. Make the commitments and stick with them until they become a reality."
~ *Sandra Bates, Entrepreneur*

***Disclaimer:** The stories in this chapter reflect the author's recollection of events. Some names, locations, and identifying characteristics have been changed to protect the privacy of those depicted. Dialogue has been re-created from the author's memory.

My Journey to the Doctorate

Personal Background

Dr. Small entered the field of education in the Edgewood Independent School District in 1981. In 1986 she was encouraged by Mrs. Mary Burns Michael to continue the zeal for teaching in the Northside Independent School District. While being employed in Northside ISD, Dr. Small became vice principal of Oak Hills Terrace Elementary and, in 2003, principal of Shirley J. Howsman Elementary.

Dr. Small received her undergraduate degree from St. Mary's University in San Antonio, Texas, a master's in special education from Our Lady of the Lake University in San Antonio, Texas, as well as a Masters of Education in mid management administration. In 2003 she completed doctoral studies in the Philosophy of Leadership Studies at Our Lady of the Lake University. Her dissertation: "The Relationships of Transformational/Transactional Leadership Behavior of Elementary School Principals with Teacher Outcomes: Extra Effort, Effectiveness and Satisfaction." The PhD was awarded August 6, 2003.

Dr. Small was baptized at an early age from West Laurel Baptist Church in San Antonio, Texas, where the late Reverend Richard P. Owens was the pastor. While a member of West Laurel Heights, she participated in the choir and the usher board. Uniting with Grace First Baptist Church in 1985, Dr. Small has participated in the Sanctuary Choir, has been announcement clerk, and participates in Sunday School. Dr. Sharon Murphy Small is a native of

San Antonio and the sixth of seven children born to Mrs. Calasca Murphy and Mr. Porter Murphy Sr. (both deceased). On June 22, 1985, Dr. Small united in holy matrimony to Mr. Ernest (Ernie) Small.

Moved By Faith

Born breech may be somewhat of a negative concept to many pregnant women. However, because of how I was born, being a breech baby, I believe it was a message to who and what I have and will become in this life. As stated, I was born breech. X-rays were taken during a time of my mother's pregnancy that perhaps should not have been. This was in the 1950s, so technology then is not anything of what it is today. Because of the X-rays, I entered the world with extremely dry skin. I must have looked strange because my mother prayed for me more than she had for any of my other siblings…*so I hear*. Mom stated that she "gave me back to God" and asked him to make me special and make me stand out from the others. I am the sixth of seven children, and all siblings born prior to me and, of course, my mother attested to two things: (1) how I looked and (2) Mom's prayer for me. I still have dry skin today but thank God for the makers of lotion and Eucerin! Growing up and even today, I feel God's favor. Placing the right people in my path was a blessing, beginning with my older sister Paula. Because of Paula, I had a good grasp on learning and reading, because whatever she would learn at school, she would come home and teach me. I began school ahead of many.

In high school, I had a band director who saw something in me that I did not see. I can recall being in band practice and playing clarinet; we were rehearsing for the annual concert contest. There was a lead part that the first chair first clarinetist had to play. One day, during practice, she was absent, so as second chair, first clarinetist, when the solo part came around, I played the part without being told to do so. The director, Anthony Castellanos, stopped directing and stopped the entire band. He made everyone stand and give me a round of applause. He said, "Murf… (my maiden name is Murphy) "Murf...I knew you had it in you." I was shy in those days, and still am to some extent, but I had been taught responsibility at an early age and believed in following through. Mr. Castellanos may have never known what an impact he made on me that day, but his belief in me has meant more than he would ever know.

His faith in me gave me courage for days and years to come.

Very rare growing up was to see all members of a family go to college or have some type of trade. I witnessed my older siblings attending college or a trade school. My brother, Porter, attended St. Mary's University. He graduated and entered the army as a second lieutenant. His major was mathematics. I saw his work ethic and silently told myself I wanted to be like him. Ultimately, I attended St. Mary's University and received a Bachelor of Arts in education. Last, I was blessed with a husband, Ernie Small, who is a Christian. With his encouragement, I could receive two master's degrees and the PhD. So, I can literally say my mother's belief in God, her giving me back to Him and asking Him to give me favor, my sisters, brothers, and my teachers, my husband and my father, who was a thinker and I believe was brilliant…all these factors have made me the person I am today. But I truly believe.

Life Lesson Learned

"I'm Better Than This, but Not Without God."
There is more to come.

College Educational Experiences

I received my undergraduate degree from St. Mary's University in San Antonio, Texas. There were second thoughts about becoming an educator, mainly because all my sisters were nurses. So, I shared with my mother my doubts. She allowed me to transfer to Incarnate Word College, but I soon learned nursing was not for me. It wasn't the courses that stomped me but the clinical… giving injections to oranges and visiting/assisting in the nursing homes. I just didn't like seeing people hurt.

Another discussion with my mother ensued about returning to education at St. Mary's University. She acknowledged knowing nursing was not for me but wanted me to experience nursing for myself; thus, the decision would be mine and not hers. God blessed me with a one-of-a-kind mother. I returned to St. Mary's University and still graduated within the four-year timeframe. Next, I received a master's in special education from Our Lady of the Lake University in San Antonio, Texas. The reason for pursuing this degree was to assure I was providing my special needs children in my classroom what they needed. Each year, as a classroom teacher, I would receive what seemed like the majority of the special needs children in that grade level. I knew how to work with all children, as should all teachers, but my greatest concern was if I was giving these children what they needed to be productive in life. So, I chose to go to learn about the children I was teaching through formal education.

I could have remained a classroom teacher and math specialist forever, but I was encouraged by my principal to utilize my skills to help more than just the children I touched daily by becoming an administrator. I had registered to begin classes at Our Lady of the Lake University in the summer of 1996 when something unexpected took place—my mother passed away. She was not ill. She was simply sitting in her favorite chair reading her Bible and passed away. I had spoken to her three times earlier that same day. Mom was such a positive force in my life, and I loved her so much that I was going to cancel my classes and ultimately not pursue a Masters of Education in mid management administration. My sister, the same sister who taught me how to read, Paula, told me mom had recently shared with her that she was pleased I was going to school to become a principal. So, I received the Master of Education in mid management. I became the vice principal of Oak Hills Terrace Elementary in Northside ISD soon after.

In 2000 I began my educational dream…a doctorate. I had always wanted a PhD because I felt it was the ultimate sign of a true scholar. The challenging part of it all was where would I go having a full-time job as an elementary vice principal and then a principal, because my work ethic was, and is, one of quality. I completed my doctoral studies in the Philosophy of Leadership Studies at Our Lady of the Lake University. My dissertation: "The Relationships of Transformational/ Transactional Leadership Behavior of Elementary School Principals with Teacher Outcomes: Extra Effort, Effectiveness and Satisfaction." The PhD was awarded August 6, 2003, on my husband's birthday and two days before my mother's birthday. My biggest regret was that my mother was not physically there to see me receive my doctorate degree.

Life Lesson Learned

> "Start by doing what's necessary; then do what's possible;
> and suddenly you are doing the impossible."
> ~ *St. Francis of Assisi*

Experiences Entering Doctoral Study

As mentioned before, I pursued a doctorate in leadership studies at Our Lady of the Lake University in San Antonio, Texas. Entering doctoral studies was positive, mainly because the university of choice was local and could accommodate my schedule on the weekends. Also, I was quite familiar with Our Lady of the Lake University, having two other degrees from there.

I first needed to know how getting a doctorate in leadership studies would help me in my current field as an educator and administrator. It was a perfect fit! My experiences were majority positive, but there were some negative.

First life lesson: ask questions prior to beginning a doctorate program. You must know how this all fits in with all that you are expected to do. Second life lesson: be sure those around you know that you have embarked upon a study that will take much time and they should expect changes in lifestyle with you as well as be understanding when you must say no, you are asking for defeat or a loss of friendship.

Experiences During Doctoral Work

I'm sure you have heard the quote "It takes a village." This ancient African proverb teaches eternal truth. No man, woman, or family is an island. I think of my experiences during doctoral work as a village journey. There is a need for so many people and so many things. As I stated earlier, it is important that those who surround you understand the journey you have embarked. I surrounded myself with people in my corner, thus making my dissertation journey a positive one. I can't say I didn't have obstacles at times, but my faith allowed me to overcome those obstacles and made them part of the journey. My village included people who cared—people who pitched in to help when things got rough. I was encouraged by my husband, Ernie Small, to consider the leadership program since it was something that he knew I wanted to do. Since the home going of my mother, Alaska Murphy, the ultimate encourager, I really needed someone to say, "Sharon—do it. I'm behind you." That's exactly what took place for three years. My husband stood by me, cooked for me, shopped for me, and attended many functions alone—just to make life a little easier for me while I was in this program. And he did it all without complaining or making me feel guilty.

My family was a part of that village—my dad, my brothers and all my sisters, my nieces and my nephews, and my brothers-in-law and my sister-in-law, all who had faith in me. My brother Gary was an extremely instrumental part of my village—getting the surveys out. I couldn't have done it without him.

Dr. Mark Green was the chair of my dissertation committee and a major player in my village. Dr. Green showed what "servant leadership" was all about.

Dr. Malcolm Ree was the statistical whiz of my village. With such a soft demeanor, he enforced *dependent and independent variables*, *multiple regression analysis*, and *ANOVAs* in my head until I got it.

Dr. Jackie Alexander has been an important individual in my village three times! The PhD was the third degree received under her watch.

Another important part of my village was the late Dr. Phil Linerode, who made it possible for me to do research in Northside ISD.

Life Lesson Learned

Remember the dissertation topic chosen may not be your topic of choice. But keep in mind you will have time after you receive your doctorate to do research on any topic you choose.

Post-Graduation

My mother often said to me, "Sharon, good, better, best, never let it rest until your good is better and your better is best." My mother was speaking from her experiences, descended from parents in which her dad was a Baptist minister and expected the best out of her and her siblings. As a woman of color who has just completed eight years as the CEO of a non-profit organization and twenty-five-plus years in the public-school setting, I feel I have accomplished something I have always wanted. Throughout my education and life,

I have believed "Knowledge is power!" and that if I continue to learn my discipline well and became a proficient teacher, mentor, and leader, I would be successful. Not just successful for myself, but for others who may need my assistance and direction. I am a beneficiary of God's grace.

I am now the chief executive officer of Parent/Child Incorporated (PCI), a family-oriented agency focusing on early childhood development and education through the Head Start and Early Head Start Program, Project Success, Day Care Homes, and the Child and Adult Care Food Program (CACFP). These programs collectively serve over four thousand children and families daily. I am confident that helping others less fortunate than I, being a servant leader, is what I am called to do. I realize I have attained much through the gift of knowledge.

I give credit for all accomplishments, past, present, and future, to my Heavenly Father; a Christian household, in which I was reared by a God-fearing and praying mother; a supportive and loving Christian husband; and a strong and encouraging Christian family.

Life Lesson Learned

- Favorite Scriptures - Isaiah 40: 28-31 and Philippians 4:13
- Dr. Small's forthcoming book is titled *I'm Better than This, but Not Without God.*

• • •

CHAPTER 5

Dr. Shantana L. Robinson

Business Consultant/Expert and Scholar

BIOGRAPHY

Dr. Shantana L. Robinson is an accomplished business consultant/expert. She has twenty years of experience in business in different industries. She is a United Way ambassador and has held numerous offices in her sorority Sigma Gamma Rho, Inc. on a local level, including president, vice, treasurer, and secretary as well as offices on the regional level.

Currently "Dr. Bridge Builder" is actively building and running the largest business owners Facebook training group in San Antonio, Texas, ROOTS. She also was the capacity building program coordinator for Bexar County, where she helps businesses, particularly minority-owned businesses, reach their full potential. Through her AABE (African American Business Enterprise) Initiative, Bexar County has seen a 36 percent increase in Black-owned firms registering with the county supplier portal over the past year.

She has an extensive list of accomplishments, to name a few: Who's Who in Black San Antonio; Member of National Association of Female Executives (NAFE); Charter Member BWIB – (Black Women in Business); Member of Walker's Legacy; Member of the Alamo City Black Chamber of Commerce; Former Black Contractors Association (BCA) Steering committee member; Certified Higher Education Professional (CHEP); Instructor of the Quarter; Instructor of the Year nominee; numerous radio and TV appearances, including co-hosting "Sista's In Business"; first African American female instructor at Sanford Brown School of Business and Merchandising; and first African American female professor at ITT Tech – Northwest in their School of Business and Leadership.

She attended Texas State University, then called Southwest Texas State University (SWT) home, where she received her bachelor's in fashion merchandising with a dual degree in business. She received her Master of Business Science and Management degree, with honors, from Colorado Technical University. She completed her doctorate in business administration from Northcentral University. She has presented at the Academy of Business Research Conference as well as worked on two research teams that have presented at the ABR Conference. She is a four-time winner of the award for Best Research in Marketing at the ABR Conference.

CREDENTIALS:

- Doctorate of Business Administration (DBA), *Northcentral University*
- Master of Science in Business Management (MSBM), *Colorado Technical University*
- Bachelor of Science (BSFCS) in Family and Consumer Science, *Southwest Texas State University*

"Be like a tree, bend don't break."

~ *Joanne Raptis*

***Disclaimer:** The stories in this chapter reflect the author's recollection of events. Some names, locations, and identifying characteristics have been changed to protect the privacy of those depicted. Dialogue has been re-created from the author's memory.

Diary of a Determined Black Woman

I was born in a small town in Texas in the seventies, where football was king and still is. My mom was a track star and one of eight born to a mother who was a housekeeper and father who was a truck driver. My grandfather served in the Korean War, and my grandmother was an amazing cook; when she was not cleaning homes, she worked at the county jail as the lead cook as well as at numerous local mom-and-pop restaurants, never to be seen nor heard, racism was and still exists. Many times, my mother accompanied her; as soon as she was of age, she was employed at some of the restaurants. I was born her junior year of high school; when you have a teenage love affair between athletes, out pops a baby.

I had a village from an early age, and my mom moved out of my grandparents' house and down the road. Mom's neighbor's house turned into my favorite place. It was a large farm owned by a woman that was mystical and hauntingly unique; till this day I cannot tell you about her beginnings, her parents, where she came from, or the exact year that she was born. She looked perhaps and Native American or Native American by itself and practiced what I would later call "root work." She rarely went to the grocery store, as she completely lived off of her farm and the land that it set on. It was at her property I developed an appreciation for animals and Mother Nature as a whole. She never worked a day in her life, never married or had kids of her own, but she always took care of her farm and her babies, as she called us. I remember her telling me at an early age I was extremely smart and unique, my path would not be traveled by many. She also told me my soul was old and that I had been here before and that, in the previous life, there were decisions I needed to rectify in this current life. As well as people that I needed to help and save a long way.

On one eventful night my mom went out with her sisters, she met and fell in love with an army man. They married in the summer of '83 and, shortly thereafter, moved to the big city. I rode shotgun in my little pink rocking chair. The man that my mom married came from a large extended family, and with his military background, education and order were important to him. Believe it or not, standard education did not come easy for me in the beginning. I did well in kindergarten and first grade, but around the time I got to second grade, I was struggling with reading. After my mom met with my teacher, my parents enrolled me in an afterschool reading program, and they also enrolled me in a version of the speech club for elementary students. With guidance from my teacher and parents, as well as extra reading assignments, my reading improved greatly. I also developed a love for reading fiction, realizing that there were many places that I can escape to, far-off lands and distant places that I had never been to or heard of before.

To make sure I was well-rounded, my parents made sure that any opportunity for growth presented to me I took advantage of it. From ballet to swimming lessons, they had me signed up. In some cases, the employees would look at me strange, knowing that my fellow students and I came from a certain area of town or, in their eyes, associated certain socioeconomic background or stereotypes on us. Those opportunities laid the foundation for what I became. When there was a trip or even a museum day, I went. By the time I was in junior high, I was on the honor roll, reading avidly, and had started my own version of a library. During my first year of junior high school, I was accepted into a magnet multilingual program where I fell in love with Spanish. I had also developed a passion for the arts and continue my love for nature as a whole. In the multilingual program, I started learning Spanish and felt good that I did not continue to perpetuate the stereotype of a traditional student being an athlete.

I also volunteered in the library to continue my passion for interesting places. I developed a strong bond with the librarian Ms. Kearney, and she would encourage me to read even more and also suggested different books to read as well. Ms. Hill, my sixth grade English teacher, invited me to join a club she ran called the "Charm Club" to practice my speaking as well as etiquette and show young ladies how to be a lady in society. Outside of my third-grade teacher Mrs. Polk, I had not had an African American teacher until Ms. Hill. My reading was getting stronger by the minute, as well as my speaking. I was introduced to the student council, and as eighth grade approached, I was also inducted into the National Junior Honor Society. My parents and I were also deciding where I should go to high school.

My stepfather graduated from the school that was directly across the street from my current middle school; that school is predominantly African American and had a fabulous band and football team, but scholastically, they really were not high on the list. My current middle school, Jeff Davis, was primarily African American and so were a lot of the instructors. I was exposed to the Black Greek life, strong women (outside of my mom and grandmother), as well as overall cultural awareness. That being said, most students at Jeff automatically went across the street to Sam to continue their "Black Experience." I wanted this, too, but I had heard horror stories about the school and their test scores and just overall scholastics. Outside of football and the band, what did Sam Houston produce on the academic side of the house? My other option, Brackenridge, was on my list because I was in the multilingual program as I mentioned earlier. If you were smart enough through junior high with your chosen language in the program, you can continue that program through high school.

In the spring of 1992, while sitting in my eighth-grade honors science class, gunshots rang out from across the street at Sam Houston high school. The early 90s was the height of the gang epidemic. When we heard the shots, we all hit the floor, and the school was on lockdown; this was not the first time. That moment solidified my decision to continue the multilingual program and attend Brackenridge High School in the fall. My years at Brackenridge High School were full of challenges, fun, and filled with great events. I continued in the multilingual program, studying Spanish. I also developed a love of doing hair and enrolled in the cosmetology program. Since I was AP, I had already taken majority of my classes. I also joined the student council and help form the Black Student Alliance. I struggled with tests my ninth and tenth grade year; this was nothing new for me; even though my grades were decent, I needed them to be higher than what they were. I knew the information, but for some strange reason, my tests were not reflecting that.

Then, in my sophomore year, my English teacher asked me to take a test revolving around numbers and formal and informal sentences. Me thinking it was a standard test, I took it; a couple of days later, she called me into her office after removing me from my current class to tell me, according to the test she gave me, I was dyslexic. I had never heard the word before, didn't think I had any type of illness or learning disability; my teacher then informed me that she wanted to have a meeting with my parents to go in further detail about exactly what dyslexia was and what it meant for my future education. At the meeting, a game plan was created to make sure that I was able to understand test taking with this disability and to get a clear understanding of what laid before me. Highlighters, tape recorders, and bookmarks became my best friend; still right today, I have to read some things more than once to make sure I get it.

As I approached my junior year, time was quickly winding down me. Now that I was at Brackenridge, where majority of us were AP, many of the students had parents who graduated from college or already knew where they wanted to go. Whether it was because their parents went there or because it was a top school. The discussion came up about where I wanted to attend school. I really had not put much thought into attending college; I was quite happy doing hair and nails and was looking forward to starting my own business. I really did not think I could do another four years of education. Especially since I was recently diagnosed as dyslexic. During my junior year, my counselor informed me he signed me up for a program for minority students to find out more about PWIs (predominately institutions). The program would send minorities to campuses for Friday and Saturday, where they get the college-life experience.

One of the campuses we went to was Southwest Texas State University. Even though attending college was not top on my radar, I still wanted the experience. As soon as we got to Southwest, I fell in love with the campus. The class sizes were great, and the instructors knew what they were doing, and the student life was nice as well. There were other institutions that we checked out—St. Mary's, Texas A&M—College Station (which I really did not like, by the way; they were not warm or inviting to minority students) as well as other schools. Still, with all of the visits, Southwest Texas State University was still number one on my list. I spoke with professors about the school and my vision for myself as an adult and was informed if I wanted a good foundation, it would make sense to go to college and possibly look at a degree in business. I was going to be a first-generation college student, not just for my nuclear family but for my family line as a whole; our roots go back to the 1800s, but it wasn't until I came along in 1996 that our DNA officially was enrolled on a college campus.

My dilemma as I went into my senior year was now that I knew I wanted to go college, I didn't know if I want to go to PWI or HBCU. Both had their pros as well as cons. At an HBCU, I would feel right at home; at a PWI, I would have to venture out and try new things and get outside of my comfort zone. It was that challenge that led me to my final decision for my undergrad degree. I closed out my high school years with a 93.4 GPA, seventy-ninth in my class of fourteen hundred, with honors, with college credit, with a multilingual background, and state board certified with my cosmetology license.

College Experience

After much debate between where I was going to attend college, I started at Southwest Texas State in the fall of 1996. Believe it or not, during high school, I was actually undecided if I want to go to college as I was in the VICA program and on my way to get my cosmetology license. I just wanted to do hair and nails and maybe open up my own salon, as I mentioned earlier. I realized my junior year, with guidance from Ms. Ponce (my cosmetology instructor), I needed a solid foundation for my hair salon, which was similar to the conversation I had with the professors at Southwest when I visited my junior year. Arriving to Women's Residence Towers with my parents in a U-Haul, I was scared, excited, and tired all at the same time. My roommate and I had already talked via the phone. We had decided who was bringing what and how we would lay out our room. I knew going into a predominantly institution the odds of me having a roommate were slim, and I actually did not mind; my main concern was whether or not she was messy or snored.

On move-in day, we finally met her face to face,, and her father (who was a contractor) had already laid down carpet in our room. We had suitemates we had not met until that day. I had never experienced direct racism until that day, when our suitemates, who were both , decided that they wanted to change rooms. They had met my roommate earlier and were completely fine. But all of a sudden, right after I introduce myself, they wanted to move across the hall; however, it worked out for the best, as they swapped with twins from Brownsville, and they turned out to be great and helped me with my Spanish. That move-in day told me a lot about what to expect on this journey of college at a PWI.

My freshman year was rough, first time away from home, trying to get adjusted to being on my own; it was a lot. I also was working full time; funny, even though my family was not wealthy, according to FAFSA, my parents made too much money for me to get any kind of financial aid. The scholarships I received went books and other needs, but nothing toward tuition. Luckily, I had worked since my sophomore year, and by the time I was eighteen, I was already a key carrier at a retail store, so working was nothing new to me. Because of my love of fashion and beauty, I declared merchandising management and business as my major. I got involved in BSA, NAACP, as well as dorm life; with all of this, I barely finished my freshman year with a 2.0 GPA. Time management, at that time in my life, was not a strong suit. Furthermore, this was the year that I had a history professor that had a fascination with the N-word.

It became clear that minority students were treated differently than other students in his class. Many minority students, including myself, failed (my first and only F) his class. I still remember being sick and not being able to come to campus and not even being able to eat. I left him a message on his phone (no email yet). And when I went to his office to request the makeup for the class I missed, I was told that I should have come in anyway; he wanted to see that I was actually severely ill. I ended up taking the class with another professor and getting a "B." A grievance was filed on the other instructor, and issues were found with him, and he was later sued and terminated from the university. That first year laid it all out for me; I got exposed to all the good, the bad, and ugly that freshman year.

During the summer of '97, I came back to San Antonio and enrolled at St. Philip's College and took two classes, both basics, so that I could get them out the way. Something else I was happy about was all my years of Spanish paid off in the multilingual program, and SWT was able to waive and give me credit for all of those years. Over the summer, I got better with time management, learned how to say no, and not to stretch myself so thin. It also was a time I saw myself officially closing out my teen years. I came back in the fall to SWT ready to conquer. I had met businesswomen over the summer who all had degrees as well as solid connections. I made sure to build those bridges; I even joined a sorority, Sigma Gamma Rho, Inc.; they were known on campus to be bookworms and educators. I love that about them, since those are both things I am passionate about. The school paid for members of the sorority to go to leadership and professional development conferences; after we submitted for grants, we were able to go. At these conferences, I learned new skills, develop tools, as well as made connections and friendships, some of which are still in play twenty-two years later.

While I attended college, I continued to work, even did some hair, as well as sold Mary Kay for extra income. I have always been a fabulous dresser, and soon, people in my business classes were asking me to help them with their job interview questions, set up mock interviews and meetings, and also picking out outfits for them to make sure that they look professional. My years of undergrad went by superfast, and coming up on the closing of my junior year, we were required to do an internship, and I did mine at a retailer called Harold's. Learning the inner workings as well as a corporate culture of the world of retail was fascinating.

When graduation season came around, I had numerous offers. Many people were running the banks and large companies. I, on the other hand, went to Target Executive Team Leader Program; I had heard numerous great things about it and also knew quite a few people who went through it and had nothing but great things to say about the program. The training they received was not only good just for Target but also just for any career or leadership move in general. I applied and was accepted into their program; it required me to be stationed in Austin, Texas, and up under their sister store, Mervyns. I graduated from SWT on a Saturday and officially started the EIT program on the following Monday.

Doctoral Debate

I took a four-year break to settle into adulthood and my management role at Mervyn's. I never stopped reading or gaining CEUs. I was sent to all professional development events the company deemed important. I was also researching master's programs; many stated that having a master's degree would take me to the next level. I had concluded, from research and experience, I would be better going at my own pace and not on the ground (campus) in a classroom. After much research on different master's programs, I settled on CTU—Colorado Technical University, in 2005. They were a fully accredited university, and it only took two years for their master's in business administration; also I did not have to take the GRE, and as we know from my previous discussion, me and tests are not friends. The class sizes were small and independent; we did have some group work but not a lot, and I also appreciated the fact that majority of the studies were surrounded around real-world experience. The classes actually felt like they were a long project that got drawn out. In some ways, I do believe that my master's program prepared me for my doctorate program.

The master's program went by super quick, and before I knew it, I graduated with honors. While I was going through the program, I had assisted others with their resumes, cover letters, as well as their overall image. I started a small business to bring in extra money to help with the program and any needs that I had from it. After completing the program, I told myself I would not be going back to college and that I was done. However, over a seven-year time span, I saw so much research being done on minority business owners and the need to get them exposure, but no one was really talking about where they intersect. To be more specific, no one was discussing minority female businessowners and their factors to success and how it relates to their community as a whole. During this time, I was adjunct instructing on two college campuses in their school of business. Even though I was the instructor at the school, I still was learning myself, from my students, as well as learning outside of the classroom on my own with my own research. I finally decided if I was going to do that, why not go ahead and put it a doctorate degree? One of the schools I was an adjunct at had a Certified Higher Education Professional Program, where they literally had us take classes for CEUs. That was great, but once again, it was on the higher education side. I wanted my research to be more based around businesses, particularly minority businesses.

After a seven-year break and much research, I decided to go to Northcentral University and pursue my doctorate. Their doctoral program is fully accredited and has an awesome business program. Their program was also voted one of the best online business programs in America. I entered NCU in 2014, and my decision to go back for my doctorate was not easy, especially since I took a nice seven-year break, and on top of that, as many know, college can be expensive, even with financial aid. One of the big things I ran into was the concept of profit versus non-profit with colleges and universities. When in actuality, unless you get a fellowship or full scholarship, you will be paying a college either way; it's just there are institutions that are a little bit more expensive than others.

Doctoral Studies

My doctorate studies started off quickly once I was involved in the program. I officially started my first class on January 2014. The portal they have for students was very easy to use, and I also liked the fact that it was one class every eight or twelve weeks completely done online. I never had to go to the campus or do a residency; being that I was working full time, I did not want to have to take time out to do a residency. There were boot camp options available, held every semester, where you could come to the campus and do a one-week boot camp or cohort study with other students. My first few classes were based around me getting used to the campus and this overall doctorate journey. Those classes were considered introductory courses; they got me familiar with the layout of the dissertation process's many different theories as well as the process in the long run of what a chair was responsible for, an academic reader, and the different chapters in the book.

I had never been on a journey where writing would be this important. I knew that course research would be an integral part of the journey; I just did not have an idea that I would be writing, in some cases, ten- to thirty-page papers weekly. However, my chair guided me through the process and was very wise when she stated to make sure I researched material that would tie into my dissertation in the long run. The first couple of months started out fine. I went through the classes, got A's, turned in work on time, and yes, there were some long nights and very early mornings. Once those base courses were done and I was officially introduced into the person would be my chair, the process got a little scary.

My new chair was wonderful in that she had great knowledge about her field but with that great knowledge came many people pulling her in numerous different ways, including her working at six different schools as well as lecturing internationally. It soon became impossible to reach her; I even had a moment where I went a total of three months without a word from her. I had tried email and even a phone call—someone picked up and told me that it was a hotel and she had checked out over a month ago to move on to her next lecturing journey. Even the school could not track her down, and finally, after four months, a notice was sent out to me as well as some of her other students that she had been terminated. While waiting for them to decide what they were going to do, luckily, I had continued to work and turn in material, which was graded by another professor.

My second chair came in, and she was great; she gave me a whole bunch of solid feedback and had a very unique way of micromanaging her students. She gave us a welcome packet with her expectations as well as what she was bringing to the table, and I can appreciate that, because I am one that likes to know what I am getting into and what is expected of me. We could also schedule meetings with her on a weekly basis if we chose to. And she was very thorough with any information she gave her students; her turnaround time was also very quick as well. She was the first person to tell me that the main point of my dissertation was that I should research something I was passionate about and find the gap; the gap would literally be my topic and what I was going to research for my dissertation. So "Fill in the gap" became a motto for me, and I also hired an outside coach and did two sessions with her as well.

One of the main things the coach stated on our first call after reading over some of my work was that she wanted me to make sure that I worked on my alignment. This was because my thoughts were there, but they were just not aligned properly. I had never read so many articles for one particular thing in my lifetime; by the time I got two years into the program, I was no longer in just the base courses, such as statistics or English and business management. I was now starting to actually take some theoretical classes as well, and these were leading up to my comprehension exams. I heard horror stories about these exams, and with my particular institution, you had to get an eighty on all three questions at a minimum in order to pass.

The three questions that made up my comp exam were not short but very detailed questions; there was a minimum of thirty pages for each of the questions. So, in essence, my comp exam was a ninety-page paper that had a six-week deadline to complete and submit. I broke the questions down, took my time, and thoroughly researched my answers. I had to become very familiar with philosophers and great thinkers like Drucker and many more. I had a reference list of around sixty different articles that I was utilizing to bring my thoughts altogether. I submitted my comp exam on the dead day, and I had a fourteen-day wait before my results were to be sent back. I got an alert the comps exam had been received and had been graded. I went into the portal they had to look at your final grades as well as the comments that were received from your committee. Students do not get any assistance with rewrites of any kind with their comp exam. When you submitted, that was the final copy for submission turns. I passed two of the three questions, and because of that, I had to retake that portion only, and I was given an additional six weeks to complete. And once I took it over and really put more thought into it and focus just on the one question, I was able to finish it up in under a week submitted and get it regraded and pass that part as well.

I was officially notified by the institution that I was now considered a doctorate candidate, so began my process of gathering my research on something that I had been so passionate about for so long. That passion was about African American female businessowners and the community they reside in and the success that intertwines them both.

It took me two years of extensive research and reading close to one hundred articles as well as purchasing around twelve different books related to my research topic for me to develop a great understanding of what it means to be an African American female businessowner and what role that plays into her community. I did extensive rewrites of my chapters; chapter two—the literature review—being the longest, took the most time. Being that I am a girl that has some country roots it was hard for me to make sure that my grammar was scholarly. I also have a habit of speaking from my own point of view (first person) that was something that I had to work on as well.

During this process, I also lost my second chair; she left the institution for a full-time job as a professor at a prestigious university. So, I was handed a third chair as I headed into the final part of my dissertation. This chair was actually a male, and he gave me great feedback, had set office hours that you could book online, and was determined to make sure that I finished the program by the summer of 2019. During this time, I had done numerous rewrites of the first three chapters, with chapter two giving me the greatest heartburn. One of the biggest things I had to understand was whether or not I wanted to do a qualitative or quantitative study, and for the longest, I was unsure until I really dived into my research. My chair explained I needed to make sure my dissertation reflected what I wanted to do and what I was passionate about; he also told me to make sure that my dissertation was narrowed down and focus. That was how I concluded to have the study done in Bexar County. I also got very familiar with data saturation once I got the final approval on chapters one through three; I was ready for my IRB approval.

Unlike most doctorate students, my IRB application process went smooth. I completed my application process utilizing the steps that the school had online. I submitted it, and it was approved in less than forty-eight hours. There were a lot of things I had to turn in, but I had already started to get my mind wrapped around what I wanted to do for the study as far as location and how I wanted my flyers to look, so a lot of that came with ease when the time came. With the IRB approval, I hit the ground running and immediately pushed out my flyers looking for African American female businessowners and also partner with the sites I was going to do my interviews at. The interviews started up the following week, and before I knew it, I had reached saturation; I had over twenty business owners who wanted to be part of the study. Some of the business owners who applied did not meet the qualification standards, and so, my total for the study ended up being exactly twenty. The information I received from these businessowners laid the framework for my dissertation as well as the framework for the relaunch of my business.

Chapters four and five came with ease, being that they were a reflection of my interviews with the subjects and the conclusion of my findings. I was able to finish both of those chapters in under two weeks and get them approved. By Christmas of 2018, all five chapters of my dissertation were approved; it was the greatest Christmas gift that I could give myself.

Tassel Is Worth the Hassle

My oral defense was scheduled for February 21, 2019. I had a whole month to prep and get myself together and ready. This included my speaker notes as well as my slide presentation. I am a visual learner, so putting together a slide presentation was not complicated or hard for me at all. However, making sure it met the specifications of what was needed for a good oral defense was my main concern. Luckily, the university had many different templates and tools to give students an idea of what they could possibly utilize for a good oral defense. It was also nice that my final chapters were so well put together that I could bring that information directly into my oral defense. On February 21, I went into one of the digital libraries in San Antonio, Texas, and presented my finding. I had invited my whole entire Facebook friends list as well as friends and family to witness me defend my dissertation. The oral defense went well;

my chair as well as co-chair were pleased with my oral defense. They asked numerous questions about my study and what I planned to do with it in the long run as well as what I planned to do once this was all over. I proceeded to tell them I would continue to help small businesses in my home state and continue to run my business. They did not even put me on hold and told me "Congratulations, Dr. Robinson!" My heart skipped a beat, as I have finally achieved one of the greatest achievements in my lifetime.

Post-Graduation Reflection

The journey to get my dissertation had many bumps, including having three different chairs, three different academic readers, months where I did not hear from people, and feeling like I was in the dark. There also numerous late nights and early mornings; Sunday mornings at 5 a.m. to about 9 a.m. became my favorite time to work on my dissertation. I fell in love with the library again because we are so tech driven, I had not been in one in ages since I could find everything online. If I could change anything about the process, I would definitely say I would be more active in the student portals to reach out to students who had been through the program before; that can save you a lot of heartache. I found that out after I finished some courses the end of the program, and once I decided to do that, a lot of things became a lot smoother. I talked to people who had been on the path already. This process has exposed me to a whole different gamut of individuals, and I even utilized the tutoring and proofreading service numerous times.

I joined Research Gate, and it exposed me to some of the greatest minds in the world; it is a beautiful thing to share that space with those individuals. I was asked to be part of a research team and got to do my first presentation, even though I had not finished my doctorate at the time. That exposure of doing my first presentation at an academic conference was moving, and it taught me a lot. I developed long-lasting relationships with people from the cohort online, and it was a beautiful thing meeting all of them in July at our graduation in Arizona. It was also beautiful to see so many minorities faces who were part of the graduation for 2019 as a well. I would also say, make sure, before you begin your doctorate journey, to check with the school or institution regarding chairs and how long they have been in place and also read their bios to see what else it is that they are involved in. I would hate for someone to have to go through three different chairs like I did; that process is not fun, and it is very time consuming and draining.

I have found out, since I am done, that I have a lot more free time on my hands, and my brain seems to be a little bit clearer. Mainly because I do not have thoughts running around my head. The research team I am a part of has won three awards, and we are getting ready to compete again in October. I can truly say this process has also shown me who my true friends are as well as how strong my family can be and rally around me and beside me. And, in my acknowledgments, I made sure to thank them for everything that they did for me; you truly have to have a village in order to finish this process. As I close out this chapter of my journey and start a new one, I will continue to be an advocate for minority businesses as I run my own, and I will also continue to teach students the important values of entrepreneurship on a college campus as well.

I will also continue to do research tied into my actual doctorate itself; my chair, who now considers himself my peer, has informed me that we will be getting together to do a version of my study in other cities. Disparity studies are needed in our communities so that we can find out exactly what is going on and find ways to rectify the issues at hand. That is why studies like mine are so important. All of the different articles and books have exposed me to a world that I had no idea about seven years ago. The research is ever-changing and ever-growing. When I started my dissertation, there were a few articles about small businesses owned by minorities but nothing as significant as it is now; that is why it is so important that, as you go through the process, to keep your articles in your research fresh. Most instructors would tell you three to five years for all of your references, and I highly agree. You also may want to look into having your own workspace strictly for the process as you go through it, and organization and time management will become your best friend, so be prepared. I wish you the best on your journey, and just like one of my favorite quotes that guided me through this journey, remember to "Always be like a tree, bend but never break!"

• • •

CHAPTER 6

Dr. Lawrence Scott

Professor and Researcher, Texas A&M University-San Antonio

BIOGRAPHY

Dr. Lawrence Scott currently is an assistant professor at Texas A&M University-San Antonio. He is also the executive director of the Community for Life Foundation, a scholarship fund that has given over half a million dollars to eligible students nationwide. Prior to teaching in higher education, Dr. Scott served over sixteen years in the K-12 sector as a secondary teacher, coach, guidance counselor, district-level curriculum specialist, and administrator in San Antonio ISD. Dr. Scott began S.E.N.D. Consulting, which he has given trainings for many universities, school districts, churches, and organizations such as Teach for America, SA Youth, Catholic Charities, and the Federal Bureau of Investigation (FBI).

He has won numerous awards: Golden Key International Honor Society Educational Leadership Award—University of the Incarnate Word, Teach for America Leadership Inspiration Award, Phi Delta Kappa Educator's Hall of Fame, San Antonio ISD Foundation Innovative Educator of the Year, Presidential Award Recipient—St. Mary's University. Most recently he was selected by the San Antonio Business Journal's 40 Under 40 for 2018. Also, he won the San Antonio Business Journal's 2018 Man of the Year Award. He is a member of the Talented Tenth Scholars of San Antonio (TTSA).

CREDENTIALS:

- PhD in Organizational Leadership, *University of the Incarnate Word*
- MA in Educational Psychology/Counseling, *University of Texas at San Antonio*
- BA in Political Science/History, *St. Mary's University*

"Believe in Life!"

~ *W. E. B. Du Boise*

***Disclaimer:** The stories in this chapter reflect the author's recollection of events. Some names, locations, and identifying characteristics have been changed to protect the privacy of those depicted. Dialogue has been re-created from the author's memory.

My Journey Through the Ivory Tower

We Are Created to Serve

I grew up on the east side of San Antonio, Texas, where I learned very early that life is not worth living unless you are serving others. Through the many challenges I experienced early, I learned that my life could serve as a model for others. If I can make it, anyone can. My parents divorced when I was about eight. I was moved back and forth from Charlotte, North Carolina, to San Antonio, Texas, every year until my high school years. This back and forth movement prevented me from establishing and maintaining serious friendships. I did have several friends in San Antonio and Charlotte, but our contact was intermittent due to the distance.

My mother went through many hardships as she navigated the life of a single mother of two African American boys. Seeing her struggle with two jobs and going to school while rearing my brother and I was inspiring, although it was difficult as well. I knew that I would one day get married and didn't want my wife working as hard as my mother had just to survive. My mother would always tell me she would make the sacrifices now so that my brother and I would have the opportunity to live better lives. I am so thankful she is now able to see her grandchildren grow up with opportunities we had only envisioned in our dreams, such as international traveling, educational escapades to the museums, career inquiries, and college tours.

My father wrestled with a drug addiction that nearly ended his life on several occasions. Seeing him go through years battling this addiction helped me realize that we all suffer from addictions, and only something greater than ourselves can liberate us from the addiction. In our case, it was our belief and personal relationship with Jesus Christ. My dad later joined a local church and became a bass player. Most people can talk about spiritual power, but I could see it firsthand as the change unfolded in my father's life. I was vaguely able to get some of his musical talent, but he gave me a stronger trait that I am extremely thankful for, that of persistence.

My older brother, who was six years older than I, is the epitome of a hardworking, giving man. He would give you the shirt off his back if you asked. He also shared some of the similar struggles of an African American man caught in the malaise of growing up in an impoverished area. He kept me when our mother worked all day to provide for us. I believe his keeping me after school and on weekends did not allow him to pursue many of the educational opportunities offered at his school; so much of his learning occurred on the streets and through the struggle. When you are in survival mode, the standardized test (SAT and ACT) preparatory classes were the nebulous concepts reserved for the "White Kids" or the "Rich Black Folks."

My brother helped me get my first job. I started working at fourteen, but my first official job was with my brother as a dishwasher and busboy at a local restaurant. I worked long hours and, sometimes, during the week. I worked because the students at school were relentless when they joked about my shoes with holes, and they were not name brand, such as "Jordan's" or anything from "Nike." It was an exasperating time, but I knew if I wanted to keep up with the latest style, I couldn't be a dishwasher for the rest of my life!

We didn't have many professional male role models in our neighborhood in San Antonio, Texas, or Charlotte, North Carolina. In fact, when I moved to Charlotte, our neighborhood was full of young African American drug dealers endeavoring to make a name. On a side note, I was not surprised when my neighborhood in Charlotte was featured on the television program *Gangland*, which showed some of the worst gang-infested neighborhoods in America. Some of my closet friends from the neighborhood were involved in criminal activity, and some did not make it to see their twenty-first birthday. However, I did meet several successful Black men when I attended high school in North Carolina. My coaches, teachers, and even principal were all strong (Bible-carrying and were mission-minded) Black men who demanded excellence from their students. I was particularly drawn to my English teacher and basketball coach Mr. Darryl Bego. I met him when I joined the basketball team during my freshman year. I didn't have a ride back home, and I wanted to play on the team. He offered to take me home, even though this was a twenty-minute detour from the usual route. When we were on the way home, he would simply just talk to me about God, family, and education. He didn't realize it but being someone I could look up to and see that this measure of success was possible was all the help I needed to catapult me to a desired lifelong outcome. Unbelievably, he had a wife and two children of his own. He was still able to make an indelible impact on my life and the lives of many others.

I could participate in sports, the student council, a mock trial team, and even was a DJ at the school-sponsored radio station. I was also student council's school president while, in the same year, excelled as a superb defender on the basketball court. I was on Who's Who of High Schools of America, and I had won the Presidential Award, which was bestowed by the founder of the school, Pastor Dr. Robin Gool. Now, there was nothing I felt I could not do. Placing me in leadership at an early age was the beginning of a series of events that would solidify my academic and professional success.

I, however, felt uneasiness or a hole in my soul, like what I would hear from other people when they had everything but felt empty inside. While on the cusp of finishing a momentous high school career, with admission letters from various prestigious colleges, I knew that my life was headed success (which was not clearly defined at the time). It was through several experiences while in college that I realized success in my life had to be redefined. Success would later be defined not by what I could amass (accolades and the trappings of life) but by what I was willing to sacrifice. My life would not be my own. I was created to serve!

When in Rome, Let It Change You

When deciding which college, I wanted to attend, I considered being away from my family in San Antonio. I had spent my high school years in Charlotte, North Carolina, and wanted to be closer to my family that I had missed so much. I also wanted to become an attorney, and the local, private university was reputable for producing great attorneys with regional notoriety. I had worked assiduously in my pre-law and political science classes. I became a member of the student government and, eventually, worked my way up to the first African American vice president of the university's student government.

During my junior year, my whole life changed. I was dating a young lady named Trisha who would always teach me that success in life is defined by helping others. When Trish and I broke up, I was distraught, but I didn't just lose a girlfriend, I lost my muse! She would challenge me to think beyond the finite success of this world. She didn't know it, but she inadvertently introduced me back to the tenets of my faith that my teacher Mr. Bego and my mother had taught me. Furthermore, the young lady I dated before her was also a Christian, and her dad was a minister in their church. Relationship with both women was not sexual, even though I was heavily attracted to them. They both taught me the true meaning of sacrifice.

I had a good friend in college named Jason Smola, who was a natural-born leader. Although I had positional power and influence, he influenced people to get involved in service opportunities. He ran a classroom supply distribution initiative, along with a tutoring and mentoring program, all while taking a full pre-med class load, including labs. When I broke up with Trisha, I was so lost that I immersed myself in service work. Every initiative Jason created or was involved in, I wanted to be there. I remember having a conversation with a good friend of mine who asked me whether to run for student government president, which was a goal of mine for quite some time and would be a great culmination for my last year in college. Ultimately, I decided, instead of running for this prestigious position, I would spend some time finding my true mission.

A friend of mine named Bryan Leroux was going on a study abroad program located in London, England, and asked me if I wanted to go, because there was only one spot left. When I went to the coordinator's office to inquire about the program, he let me know that the spot had been taken. I didn't fret because I knew I was on a mission to crystalize my purpose in life following this huge paradigmatic shift of success being defined by positions and accolades to now believing success being defined by service to others and doing God's Will. I received a call from the coordinator of the program who told me that a spot had opened. This would be the call that changed my life forever.

While in London during the study abroad program, I could see and experience things I have only heard about or seen in movies. Here I was, from a working-class family in San Antonio in San Antonio to seeing the Louvre Museum in Paris or attending the Oktoberfest in Germany. My first life-changing experience occurred when I took a trip to Rome, Italy. When I first arrived in Rome, I was tricked by a taxi driver who swore he could not speak English. He charged me $165 dollars for a ten-minute drive. I tried to argue my case, but the communication barrier was evident, and in the event of police intervention, it was my word against his word. Then he proceeded to take my wallet out of my hands and took the money directly out of my wallet. Please be mindful that I only had $185 for a five-day trip, and I was alone. After visiting a host of museums and eating a meal, I ran out of money. This was the worst thing I had ever experienced in my life—to be without food, money, family, friends, and still having three more days to go before I could take the scheduled Channel ride back to London. I did not do adequate research on what to do in emergency situations; therefore, I did not know about the US Embassy. My first and only thought was, *how will I survive?*

I began a rationing system immediately. I used four Rice Krispie treats I had carried along for snacks in my bag as meals. I slept with the rest of the homeless people in the streets or on park benches and inside stairways in buildings. I finally found comfort at the local train station because there were police around. It got to the point where I had no more pride. I would do anything to meet Maslow's basic needs hierarchy. I began going to restaurants and beg for leftover bread that I would carry with me. I went into McDonald's restroom to fill my water bottle, to wet my palate after walking about three miles between each site. Since I didn't understand the phone system, I couldn't call my parents collect. No one spoke English, and those who did refused to take time to try or translate who had the answer to my question. This action is like the way many Americans treat people from other countries.

I had a burst of hope when I remembered that my mom had sent me a fifty-dollar money order from Western Union. Even though I found a Western Union office at the train station, I was unable to cash it because I was told that Europe didn't have a transferable money order system. At this point, I was beginning to lose my faith. I reached the edge of despair when I had waited for twelve hours for the first train to Paris so I could catch the Channel to get home. When I boarded the train, I was so excited. I couldn't believe I was finally going home. I was then tapped on the shoulder and told, through broken English and with numerous hand gestures, that I could not use my Euro-pass; this pass was to allow me to travel anywhere in Europe on this train. The conductor told me that the train was for sleepovers only and that I would have to pay thirty-dollar USD (US dollars) to get on; after pleading, begging, and vehemently arguing with three of his colleagues, I got off.

I was in despair. I did not know what to do. I did not have any money, food, or any way to get in touch with anyone. I was feeling extremely weak because I hadn't eaten in two days or showered in four. I realized that I had one last hope. I remember my mother and my grandmother telling me that God can deliver you out of any situation if only I believed and released my faith. I pondered the absurdity of this idea, seeing that I was simply limited to my finite understanding of miracles, and I had only entertained thoughts of how I did not have any means of getting home. At that moment, as I was walking toward the phones to call my dad, I miraculously saw two young ladies from St. Mary's University study abroad program. They had come to the train station to see when their train from Naples would leave. They saw me sitting on a bench at the station crying profusely. They gave me enough money to get food and catch the overnight train to London. I now truly believe in miracles!

The fun and exciting part of this learning process occurred immediately after my arrival in London. I experienced an overwhelming feeling of excitement knowing that anything is possible, especially when you have faith. It meant a great deal to me to see the sage words of my mother and grandmother materialize in my life. I learned that all things are possible to those who believe outside of their normal understandings, surroundings, cultural upbringing, or paradigms.

I believe I played a subsidiary role in my own learning process. For example, the airline I initially was scheduled to take went bankrupt the weekend before I flew to Rome. Deep inside, I knew that it was a part of my indescribable destiny to go to Rome that day. After I was notified at the airport about the airline bankruptcy, I still insisted I fly out to meet my destiny.

People told me beforehand to "Beware of Rome." Others insisted that I not go to Rome alone, but I simply ignored common sense gestures to pursue what undeniably became my fate. My professor admonished us to do extensive research prior to our departures, but I knew I wanted to be independent of admonishment. After the experience and the two young ladies who saved me and told me that they, too, believed in miracles, I realized that miracles truly exist. They are inexplicable or immeasurable, even with an empirical analysis.

My most distressing learning experience occurred when I found out I placed a great deal of my self-worth on the acceptance of others. I have learned this in a time span of five years. It has taken another two years to figure out how to rid myself of this cancerous disposition. This learning process was problematic in several ways. First, I had to come to the realization that I either don't know myself enough or know myself too well to like myself. Secondly, I had to do a self-inventory to find whether my actions were because of genuine servitude or simply an effort to please others. Lastly, I had to assess whether my "I can't say no" problem was a result of being a people pleaser. It was difficult to face the idea that some people will not like me no matter what I do. I always thought, as a teacher and an aspiring politician, I must be liked by all people, all the time. Some people will not like me for doing what is right, while some will not like me for doing what is wrong. I had to understand that "Everyone will not like me all of the time!"

Other people have helped me see that this "people pleasing" attitude is curable by understanding who I am, my past, and my purpose in life. My ex-girlfriend illustrated ways in which I inadvertently sought attention from others. While I have allowed some people to perpetuate this demeanor by giving me positive reinforcement or punishment for things I did or did not do, I have learned that my insatiable desire to please others stems from feelings of inferiority and fallibility. This epiphany is troubling in many ways, because the career fields I have chosen are conducive to serving people or making people happy.

These experiences have given me insight on my meta-cognition; as a learner, I understand I need to listen more and talk less. For years, I have always felt that I have been chosen to do great things. After my Rome incident, I was assured that my purpose in life was to help others, even if they don't speak my language, live in my country, share my experiences, or live in poverty.

The Day I Met Michael Jordan

Throughout my life, I have met many well-known people. I was blessed enough to know at a young age that there was something different about my life, because these exchanges did not enchant me. I always wondered whether these people were happy pursuing their purpose in life. This uncanny inquisition even occurred when I met Michael Jordan, arguably the most well- known basketball player to ever grace the game. When I was in the eighth grade, I went to a family gathering with a good friend, James, from school. His sister had married into the Jordan family. I vividly remember arriving at Michael Jordan's parents in Wilmington, North Carolina; I was in a sense of awe.

Naturally, the youth congregated together and went upstairs to play video games and play pool. After about two hours, the doorbell rang; you could tell that something momentous had occurred because there were clamorous shouts of joy coming from downstairs. As we descended downstairs, I saw a tall, dark man sitting down and conversing with relatives around him. I went up to him and said, "Hey, you're Michael Jordan." He laughed and facetiously responded, "Yes, I am, and you need to take off that Spurs gear in my momma's house!" At that time, I was a huge Spurs fan, particularly David Robinson, Avery Johnson, and Sean Elliot. I was particularly drawn to the way the Spurs worked as a unit, had a great reputation on and off the court, and was led by a Christian leader, "The Admiral" David Robinson. Michael Jordan was not at all the cocky persona I saw on TV. He was genuinely concerned about the people he interacted with. He was very laidback and had a great sense of humor. Here I was, the only person there that was not a part of his family, and he spoke with me for about ten minutes, gave me autographed shirts, and let me see his championship ring, which had MJ engraved on the side.

This experience let me see that our heroes are no different than we are. They long for the constant to intermittent connection with those they are close to, as making new connections and experiences. They must recharge batteries as well, so they can have enough energy to give back to the millions of adoring fans. And, lastly, they sacrifice their own privacy and, in some cases, their security to activate their fullest potential as a person on a mission. Even though I do not possess millions of dollars, or even have millions of fans, I have the unparalleled privilege of making a difference in the lives of young people. I get an opportunity daily to help someone realize their purpose and provide a road map for them to pursue their dreams and ultimately become a hero for someone else. Every day I look at my daughter Gabriella and my son Christian and think of how God used me and my wife to break intergenerational curses.

Meeting Michael Jordan did illustrate to me that it doesn't take a great deal to be a hero, a mentor, or a leader. It just takes someone who is willing to set aside time to make the connection with another human being pursuing their God-given purpose and using their God-given talent. On the day I met Michael Jordan, I was an eighth-grade boy, who later became a public-school educator and college professor.

The Beginning of the Doctoral Process

When I first started the PhD program, I was immediately made aware of the sparse number of African Americans and the few of African American men in my program. With a class of thirty-two, there was only one other African American male and one African American female. I was the only African American in most of my classes. This disparity was the impetus I needed to begin research in African American male academic attainment. There were also anecdotal occurrences that solidified the need to pursue a doctoral degree. I have been in the educational sector as a teacher and as a coach and I was now working as a guidance counselor for over eleven years. I had become tired of seeing our African American kids under perform, even though they received the same instruction as their White and Hispanic counterparts. I knew that there were non-cognitive factors, such as cultural ethos, socio-economic, equal access to early childhood education, that could play a factor in the educational attainment of African American men.

I had great professors and advisors who guided me through the process to make sure that my research was representative of my mission. One professor would always talk to me about the need to make a difference by gathering candid stories of successful African American men that were difficult to get by my counterparts. Other experiences illustrated that there was a need to discuss African American scholarship and my research could be a catalyst to perception change. I can vividly recall a time when one of the professors asked me whether I was coming to pick up the trash out of her classroom, if I was a janitor. She exclaimed, "You can start in my room; there is a lot of trash in there." To her dismay and embarrassment, I told her I was taking her class as a doctoral student.

I knew that my role as a graduate student went far beyond the confines of studying or writing research but becoming an example of male intellectualism to counterbalance the ubiquitous anti-intellectualism that has plagued our community for generations. I knew that my time was limited, that something must be done, and I was up for the challenge to change the educational outcome in my family lineage for generations to come.

Time Management

When I was growing up, time was not a concept that mattered. Each day, my friends and I would find new ways to cause mischief, converse with girls, and waste our time. When I became more involved with my church, I developed an authentic relationship with God. I started developing a sense of purpose. My prayer changed from "God, I want" to "God, help me serve."

I vividly recall a teacher in middle school giving me a spiritual book and a few Christian tapes. There was also a basketball coach and English teacher in high school who taught me about time management and balancing the many roles a successful man would have to assume. As timed progressed, I began to understand the brevity and finality of life. I realized that you only have one chance to make an indelible imprint on the world and that the world would be a better place because you were born. I further realized that your children's children and their grandchildren would be able to feel the impact you created by walking through your purpose.

Through my role as a husband, father, and active participant in the community through church and other civil organizations, I experienced a great deal of time management issues. Time is the one commodity everyone will eventually run out of. I learned we are all equal. We are all given the same amount of time, but it is how we use this time that matters. An African American male pursuing a PhD was evidently in high demand with regards to heading up community initiatives, speaking at programs and forums, and, essentially, making an effectual difference. I had to learn the secret of balancing my time and being circumspect about the commitments I made outside of my home. It was as if I was juxtaposed between spending time with my wife and kids or helping a few young men through a mentoring program or handling a situation of a mother facing challenges with her teenaged son, whom I was mentoring.

I have learned that there are seasons for everything. There are times it seems that your community involvement and mission overshadow your family life or that you are not doing enough for the community or your family. Sometimes it will seem that these two important seasons are converging, but with the right level of balance and surrounding yourself with the right kind of social network and friends that can keep you grounded, this balancing act becomes easier as you become more skillful in how you allocate your time.

Money Is a Factor

As a doctoral student, I faced some financial hardships as well. I grew up in a lower working- class community in which higher education was considered only for the rich folks. It wasn't until the beginning of my senior year did, I get serious about college admissions and scholarship exploration. By that time, most serious students were clear about which college they were going to attend and were expending their time and resources on scholarship applications. I knew I wanted to be a lawyer and knew about a local private university that also had a law school, so this is where I applied. I didn't consider how much it would cost me annually, my estimated family contribution, scholarships, and the fact that I would have to work while attending school. In my junior year, I had to work three jobs and take twenty-one hours just to graduate from college within a five-year duration. Albeit, I did change my major to education, which necessitated an extra year of schooling. In retrospect, I would have heavily considered going to a community college for my prerequisites and subsequent transfer to a four-year university. Therefore, it's critical to have a good guidance counselor, informed parents who are actively involved, along with a team of mentors who are in college and some who have graduated.

The Dissertation Process

While in my doctoral program, I mastered the art of presenting research, analyzing, and discussing the assigned readings. I made all A's and one B (in statistics, consequently), proving that the coursework was easy for me. I struggled heavily during the dissertation process because there are no reminders, no exams to study for, or timelines to follow. Everything is predicated on your ability to do your own research and motivate yourself when you become tired or completely saturated with all the research. The first thing I readily noticed was that I loved the subject I was studying. I gained a sense of purpose beyond obtaining a doctorate degree, which became my mission. Every time I would see a negative portrayal of a Black man, I was reminded that my research would help to eradicate the negative depictions and caricatures.

After about two years of dissertation writing and attending summer sessions, I began to get tired of the inundation of information. No more could I go to the movies or watch television without the thought of how this was impacting the African American male experience.

When I discussed issues in class, gave lectures, or wrote commentaries, I would always filter everything through the lens of the African American male's plight or success. It became my passion, which then became my mission and, ultimately, my duty. Now that I have gone through the process, I fully understand that writing a dissertation gives one the skills to do in-depth research and to provide a blueprint to engage one person, or a few people, and then a community to affect change. I have reached my goal, and I am living my dreams. I have become a positive difference maker who will continue to create other positive difference makers and change lives through education. I have become "The Miracle" for someone else.

• • •

CHAPTER 7

Dr. Linn R. Waiters

Principal and Founder, Waiters Educational Vision, LLC

BIOGRAPHY

Dr. Linn Waiters is CEO/founder of *Waiters Educational Vision*, a non-profit organization focused on improving educational, economical, and skills-based opportunities on the Eastside of San Antonio, Texas. She has an extensive background in K-12 public education, working with at schools in *Ohio*, *Texas*, *Washington*, and the *Department of Defense/Education*. She has an incredible success story of earning four college degrees, including a doctorate, despite being a victim of domestic violence in her former marriage and coming from an impoverished background. Yet, she still became a success and an example for her children and family.

Most notably she has won numerous public speaking awards, taught internationally in countries such as *Germany* and *Turkey*, was a keynote speaker for Black History events, and has presented at conferences around the country. She is a member of the *San Antonio Ladies-Talented Tenth* (SALTT).

CREDENTIALS:

- PhD in Entrepreneurship, *University of the Incarnate Word*
- MEd in Education, *Wright State University*
- MA in Management, *Webster University*
- BSOE in Education, *Texas State University*

> "Education empowers you; it places you able to verbally challenge people who are giving you a whole lot of nonsense."
>
> ~ *Camille Cosby*,
>
> Television Producer, Author, Philanthropist

***Disclaimer:** The stories in this chapter reflect the author's recollection of events. Some names, locations, and identifying characteristics have been changed to protect the privacy of those depicted. Dialogue has been re-created from the author's memory.

My Journey to the Getting A Doctorate

Personal Background

I was born on Monday, May 13, in the Wheatley Courts, a low-income housing project in San Antonio, Texas. Both of my parents were nineteen years old when I was born, and they were divorced by the time I was eighteen months old. Between the two of them, by the time I was seventeen years old, I had ten sisters, one brother, and one stepbrother.

For the first nine years of my life, two sets of grandparents raised me. From Sunday evenings until late Friday afternoons or early Saturday mornings, I lived with my mother's mother, Mama Linnie, and her stepfather, Charlie, whom I called Pops. When I left Mama Linnie and Pop's house, I went to my father's parents' house, and their names were Ellen and Dillard, who lived at 206 Del Rio Street. Their house was on the Westside of a low-income housing project called the East Terrace. As a teenager, I can remember walking to my grandmother Ellen's house early on Saturday mornings, and from a distance, I could see her sheets hanging on the clothesline, gently swaying in the wind. To this day, I have never seen sheets as white as hers or that smelled as good. By the time I was six years old, my mother had a downstairs apartment in The East Terrace at 306 Goldsmith Walk.

Shortly after starting the fourth grade, Mama Linnie and Pops bought a house in a predominantly white neighborhood. My cousin Penny Boy, Luiet Eugene Coleman Jr., and I transferred from Booker T. Washington

Elementary, an all-Black elementary school, to Elizabeth Tynan Elementary, a newly integrated White school. He was the third Black male, and I was the third Black female in the school. I don't remember having any problems adjusting to this new environment or being called derogatory names by the students. I remember it was at Tynan Elementary that my love for books and reading began.

Mrs. Klein, my fourth-grade teacher, on Friday afternoons, would tell us to put our heads down on our desks for the last twenty minutes to thirty minutes of class while she read the next chapter of the book she had selected for us. This had not been done at my old school. Listening to Mrs. Klein as she read to the class was the highlight of my week. To this day, I still love the books like, *The Black Stallion*.

At the age of ten, my sisters, Rita and Wendy, and I went to live with my mother in the East Terrace. At ten years, old, I was old enough to wake up my sisters and get them and myself ready for school each morning, and for us to walk a little more than a mile to school and back each day. Today, this is almost unheard of, but I never thought of it being unfair or hard. I was the oldest child, and that was my job, and my responsibility, and I had no problems doing it.

When I was about eleven and a half, my mother married my stepfather, Walter, a sergeant in the US Army. About eighteen months later, we moved to a house they had rented on Dawson Street. I now had a baby sister named Sandra, and we needed more room. Until then, my sisters and I had always shared the same room and the same bed. Now, I had not only my own bed but my own room.

After completing the sixth grade, I went to Ralph Waldo Emerson Junior High. I was an above-average student who usually made at least one "C." My grades were usually two As, three Bs, and one C. So, I was only on the Honor Roll my first semester with three As and three Bs. I was also the tallest girl in the school for three years. In fact, there was only one student taller than me, and he was on the basketball team. Just before turning thirteen years old, my mother allowed me to take "company" on Sunday afternoons during Christmas vacation. His name was Roosevelt. The relationship didn't last long because, one Sunday, in February, he accepted a piece of lemon crème pie that my mother offered him. I thought he should have refused, so when he finished the pie, I told him to never come back. I guess the pie meant more to me than he did.

It was shortly after this that my mother began saying that the most important thing, I could do in my life was to graduate from high school without getting pregnant. That was to be my goal. Making decent grades were desired but making excellent grades and attending college was never discussed or stressed. My mother's oldest sister, Louie Mae, was the only person who ever talked to me about attending college and what it could do for me.

In the tenth and eleventh grades, I attended George W. Brackenridge High School. As a sophomore, I joined the pep squad, called the Purple Jackets, and participated in all the football game halftime shows, Fiesta parades, and other school or community activities. With my boyfriend, who was an officer in the ROTC, I attended every major function the school had, and my grades suffered. Therefore, in my junior year, the only things my mother allowed me to do were go to school, to church, and to attend only one major school activity in the fall and one in the spring.

My extracurricular activities, as a sophomore, resulted in my earning two failing grades in academic classes at the end of the semester. According to Texas education rules at that time, that meant I would have to attend summer school if I wanted to graduate on time with my class. There was no way I could tell my mother. She was shorter than me and weighed only one hundred pounds, but she had already emphatically said on more than one occasion that our job was to go to school and learn. It was not a fun activity. She would in no way pay or assist us in paying to attend summer school. This would bring shame to our family. Going to summer school said that a student wasn't smart enough to learn during the regular school year and needed extra time. She knew that that was not the case for me.

During the summer, before my senior year, I could talk my mother into letting me attend school in Los Angeles and live with her father, Ollie, and her stepmother, Miss Lilly, who I called "MaDear." While on an earlier trip that summer, I had talked with some of my cousins and knew that if I wanted to graduate on time, I needed to complete my senior year in LA. The California school system allowed students to take seven academic classes each semester, which allowed me to make up the classes I had failed in the tenth grade. So, my senior year of high school was at John C. Fremont High School in Los Angeles. I graduated on June 19 on time, with a B-minus average.

College Experience

Attending college was a different experience. During my first and only semester until after my children were born, I acted just like I had in the tenth grade. The lessons about studying and making good grades still had not been learned.

After graduating from high school, I moved back to San Antonio and attended San Antonio Community College. With my newfound freedom and popularity, I skipped more classes than I attended, and my grade point average was nothing to be proud of. My family refused to waste any more of their money for me to attend the second semester and told me to get a job. Any future educational expenditure would be on me. I did as my mother suggested. I got a job and worked as a cashier for the H.E.B. grocery chain for about six months, after which I was hired by the State of Texas as a teacher's aide in the newly established Teacher's Aide Program. I worked until the end of the school year in May and got married two weeks later. Two weeks after that, my husband and I moved to Seattle, Washington, where his family lived.

I had been married about five years, had worked for the Boeing Airplane Company, and was working for REI (Recreational Equipment, Inc.) when I began thinking about attending college again and what it could do for my children and me. The Civil Rights and Affirmative Action movements were providing work and educational advantages that had never been available to minorities or women. Privately, I had always dreamed of being an attorney. But then I remembered people's reactions the few times I had told anyone about my dream. They either laughed or thought I was joking. The Dean of Women at Brackenridge High School had told me, "Linn, you know there is no such thing as a Negro female attorney. Why don't you just keep studying to be a good clerical employee or maybe a schoolteacher?" This was just before I met Barbara Jordan. If it had happened after, I would have had a good response to her statement.

My husband was not a proponent of women's education. He thought it was a waste of time and money. So, without telling him, I registered for classes at Seattle Central Community College. I had been taking academic classes (one here and one there) for over a year when he found out. He came to the college and, without my knowledge, withdrew me from the school. Then, he came upstairs to my classroom, called me out of the room, and when I came out, he took me by the arm and led me from the building. He threw all my textbooks in the trash as we quickly exited the building. I didn't scream or holler because husbands could do this type of thing in the 1970s.

When we got home, he told me that he wasn't upset about my going to college. He was upset because I was taking academic classes. If I wanted to take tailoring, cake decorating, or any type of coursework that focused on improving domestic concerns, he did not care. He would gladly pay for them and even watch the kids if the class was an evening class. So, I took tailoring classes, cake decorating classes, and any other classes I could to keep my mind active.

The marriage lasted until 1980. Our divorce was final exactly four months' short of fourteen years. Now, I am a single parent with two teenage daughters, good clerical and work skills, but very few college credits. The US was in an economic recession and most of the jobs I wanted, I had the skills required for the job but not the education.

After being divorced two years, my ex-husband and I agreed to joint custody of our children, and in September of 1982, I moved back home to San Antonio, Texas. Things had not gone well for me in Seattle after the divorce, and I needed the encouragement and stability that my family could provide. In 1983 I enrolled in St. Phillips College. In 1987 I graduated from Southwest Texas State University (now Texas State University) with a Bachelor of Science degree in occupational education and certified as a secondary business and English teacher. In October 1989, I graduated from Webster University with a master's degree in management. Ten years later, in December 1999, I graduated from Wright State University with a second master's degree in higher education administration. It was not until I began attending Wright State University that I had an African American professor (male or female).

Taking classes taught by an African American professor was the highlight of my educational experience. It was exciting to see them work and interact with the students. None of my teachers had been African American since the first, second, and third grades at Booker T. Washington Elementary. These professors, though not direct mentors, inspired me to further my education and "cover all the bases" (first base—high school diploma; second base—bachelor's degree; third base—master's degree; home base—doctorate degree).

My academic career has always been non-traditional. I have always had to work full time and take classes when I could. Most of the time, I attended school during the day and worked either swing-shift or graveyard shift. When

I began attending Southwest Texas State University (now Texas State University), I had to drive 120 miles roundtrip five days a week to attend classes. My grades lowered during my junior year because I missed three classes due to a female medical issue that I had to have emergency surgery for. The college would not even accept a doctor's note. This dropped my grades and grade point average a whole letter, but I still graduated on time.

Doctoral Studies

In 2002 I was accepted into the Educational Leadership Doctorial Program at Our Lady of the Lake University. Classes for the program were taught on Saturdays and Sundays, and I thoroughly enjoyed my studies there. But, in the spring of 2003, one of the professors I was looking forward to learning from left the program. This was a critical factor for me, so I applied to the University of the Incarnate Word just in time to be accepted into their International Education and Entrepreneurship Doctorial Program. This was a very good move for me. For the first time, in a college outside of Ohio, I would have a Black professor.

Dr. Francis Bokari, in my eyes, was the most effective, creative, knowledgeable, and mentoring professor I ever had. He had been born and raised in Western Africa and completed his advanced studies somewhere in Midwestern America. We talked about my educational concerns and direction, class assignments, and the importance of cultural acceptance and diversity. He gave me instruction, direction, and communicated with me on an educational and personal level that White professors had seemed reluctant, unable, or just refused to do.

One of the most important lessons Dr. Bokari taught me was about if the meaning of a simple word was the same for everyone. In class, he asked the question, "What is the definition of home?" Most of the American students in the class giggled and responded with positive affirmations about Mom, Dad, Thanksgiving, Christmas, and apple pie. Then he asked some of the non-American students from other countries and experiences to respond. Very few of their responses were like ours.

In a number of instances, their responses were shocking. Many of their definitions of home focused on anywhere they were not beaten, molested, ridiculed, had enough food to eat, or where they were warm and dry. His asking this question helped me to realize that my reality, in most cases, is not the same reality for a large portion of society. I had to become more aware of my responses to questions that assumed the same reality for everyone.

As basic studies go, I had no problems. I planned and tried not to procrastinate when it came to completing assignments. I studied and was prepared for class. As an African American non-traditional student, and usually the oldest student in the class, I had learned there would be no second chances for me. I had to get it right the first time. If I disagreed with a professor, I would discuss my point with that professor, but if they continued to disagree with me, I did it the way they wanted. However, there were times when I won the discussion and could do things my way. Knowing who has the power and accepting that fact is critical in life. I knew that once I had my degree, my professors and I would be equal—to a certain degree.

While teaching in Germany, as part of my externship credit for living and working in a foreign country, a requirement for international education, I had to write a paper about my experience. My academic advisor and I had a somewhat heated disagreement via email concerning some of the statements I had made about not having any problems adapting to living and working in a foreign country.

My final explanation to him after returning to the United States for Christmas vacation was (a) He was a Caucasian man and I was an African American woman; (b) He was a member of the dominant society, and I was a minority; (c) He had been raised from a position of authority, and I had been raised and trained from childhood to be cognizant of my surroundings and to be able to adapt if or when necessary; (d) As a member of the dominant society and an American, without realizing it, he acted as if he were better than others. As a minority, I did not exhibit this behavior and was willing to learn; (e) He was not raised from childhood to adapt to Arab, Asian, Mexican, and various other nationalities and cultures to include (German, Jewish, and Scandinavian etc.), but as an African American born in the late 1940s, I was. Therefore, since I was born, raised, and educated in adapting to whatever I was in, he in no way could tell me what I did not experience. To my surprise, he agreed with me, and we became good acquaintances. This was my only negative, though somewhat exciting, experience during my doctoral studies.

Dissertation Experiences

This was a long but exciting time for me. My writing skills are above average, so I thought I would complete the entire dissertation process in no more than six months. It took me almost a year and a half to do the literature review. Doing the research was easy. Figuring out how to put it together and how to write it was a different thing altogether.

After reading several books and articles on writing a literature review, one Saturday morning, while sitting in a laundromat and reviewing my notes, the lightbulb came on. All I had to do was to organize the literature review into topical segments, then write each segment as a long, detailed authoritative essay. This revelation made the whole process flow like water on clean glass.

The most important element of the dissertation process is the committee and, most importantly, the committee chairperson. My chairperson and committee were the best people possible for me. They could get into my head and help me focus and figure out what it was I was trying to say. They listened to my suggestions, and when they disagreed with me, told me why and suggested how I could do things in a better and more scholarly fashion.

When it comes to writing, everyone has their own style or routine, but making the corrections suggested by the chairperson and the committee should be done in a timely fashion unless you think what has been suggested changes the focus and or the intent of the research. Arguing with the chairperson and committee about mundane issues will only prolong the process, and doctoral degree credits are not cheap. Just get it done. After the dissertation has been defended successfully and your title is conferred, you can go back and do whatever you want. You are now a doctor. This is what I did.

Post-Graduation

Post-secondary education did not begin for me until I was in my mid-thirties. I wanted to be an example for my daughters, grandchildren, great-grandchildren, and other family members. I wanted them to see and know that a dream can be achieved when you take a chance and believe in yourself, work hard, don't listen to people who talk in the negative, and believe that God has a positive plan for your life.

My doctorate degree will not do for me what it could have done if I had achieved it earlier in my life, but I have no regrets. I have covered all the bases. If someone rejects me for an employment position, it won't be for inadequate education. It will probably be because of my age, but so what? Now maybe I will organize and create a charter school that will fill a much-needed void, and/or write a book. Never think there is nothing left for you to do. There is always something else to do. God will always give you another dream and another goal if you are willing to "Cover All the Bases."

• • •

CHAPTER 8

Dr. Nicklas Cormier

Administrator and Educator (Retired)

BIOGRAPHY

Dr. Nicklas Cormier is a retired US Army master warrant officer. He is also a retired public- school administrator, and a retired college professor. Dr. Cormier has vast experience in the public education and higher education. He currently serves on the Board of Directors of *Catholic Charities*, the Foundation Board of Directors of the *School of Excellence*, and the Board of Directors of the *Knights of Peter Claver* Texas State Conference. Dr. Cormier is a member of the *Knights of Peter Claver, Inc.* He is a *fourth degree Knight* and has served as Faithful navigator of *William A. Killian Assembly* 21, Grand Knight of *Holy Redeemer Council.*

He has served as third vice president and first vice president of the *Texas State Conference* and is currently serving as president of the *Knights of Peter Claver*, Inc. He is a member of the *Talented Tenth Scholars of San Antonio* (TTSA).

CREDENTIALS:

- PhD in Education, *University of Texas at Austin*
- MS in Business Administration, *Boston University*
- MA in Education, *Texas State University*
- BA in Economics, *Park University*

"The test of character is the amount of strain it can bear."
~ *Charles Houston*

***Disclaimer:** The stories in this chapter reflect the author's recollection of events. Some names, locations, and identifying characteristics have been changed to protect the privacy of those depicted. Dialogue has been re-created from the author's memory.

The Path to Obtain a Doctorate Degree at a Research 1 University

My Background

I was born in New Iberia, Louisiana, a small town in south Louisiana, to a father who had no formal schooling and a mother who only went to the fourth grade. These humble beginnings would not suggest I would become the first master warrant officer in the United States Army Signal Corps, or to earn four college degrees: a bachelor's degree from Park University, a master's degree from Boston University, another master's degree from Texas State University, and a doctoral degree from The University of Texas. However, to understand how this happened, one would have to understand my parents.

My father had no formal education but was a hard worker and knew how to handle the money he earned. When he died, he owned more property than all his educated children put together. My mother only had a fourth-grade education, but she was very concerned about the education of her children. She enrolled all seven of her children at St. Edwards Catholic School. While St. Edwards only went to the eighth grade, this education gave me the foundation I needed to be successful in school.

My first day at St. Edwards was something. My mother took me to school on that first day, and I was introduced to my teacher and given a seat. Mother talked with the teacher for a while than she told me to be good and walked out of the door. I immediately jumped up and ran after my mother. She had a talk with me and took me back into the classroom. I did not like school very much after that experience, and this dislike showed in my early days. I had to repeat the first grade, but I think there were two reasons for my not being promoted to the second grade. I was born in November; therefore, I was five years old when I started school. Secondly, I did not do very much in the classroom that first year. When I finally got promoted to the second-grade things got better. My teacher, Sister Helen, was terrific, and I learned a lot.

When I was held back again in the third grade, I began to question my academic ability. It was in that second year in the third grade that the light came on. I learned to read, and school became easier. After seven years at St. Edwards, my older brother, Harvey, and sisters, Barbara and Lillie, went to public high school, and I went to the public middle school.

Public school was different from St. Edwards, but I was surprised when several of the teachers came to my room to see me on that first day of school. I asked why and was told I had scored at a ninth-grade level on the Iowa Achievement Test. The teachers wanted to see this little sixth-grade teacher's favorite student. Miss Davis would ask me to work math problems on the board and explain the process to the students. I was ahead of all the students in the sixth grade in all subjects. The sixth grade was no problem, but seventh grade was a big hurdle.

I played hooky, or skipped school, and my father was working out of town. I did stay in school all day on Friday because it was test day in all subjects. I don't know how I did it, but I passed every test. Something happened that stopped me from skipping school completely. I would skip school to caddy at the golf course. But one day, a group of older boys, who had quit school or had graduated, called the police on us for skipping school. When the police came, we ran into the woods. The older boys then ran after us and caught us and turned us over to the police. We were then taken to jail and locked up.

We only stayed locked up for a short period of time, when one gentleman from my community saw me in jail. Mr. Polk immediately went to my home and informed my mother. We were taken back to school, and we stayed all day. The skipping school group was met by the principal, and he got his belt out and gave each of us a good whipping. When I got home, my mother was waiting. She talked to me about skipping school. During this time, my father was in town working, but my mother told me that she was not going to tell my father because he would kill me for going to jail and skipping school. That was the end of my skipping school. I completed seventh grade and was promoted to the eighth grade, which was located at the high school. The eighth grade was fun for me, but the teacher would put me out of class so that she could teach. I had to work with the custodian most of the year. I made it to the ninth grade. I was finally in Jones Henderson High School.

The ninth grade went well. I was on the football team, and to my surprise, I was named starter on the high school team for the first game of the season. I didn't realize that I was considered a good football player. This was a huge accomplishment, because we played in one of the largest districts in the state. The first semester was good, but in January, at the very start of the semester, my mother died. I was devastated. I remember going out in the fields and cried. I promised that day, to my mother, that I would make something out of myself. The remainder of the ninth-grade year was very difficult. I made C's, D's, and a few F's. My grades were terrible, but in the tenth grade, I was star on the football field and a running back. I had very good support from the teachers at Jones Henderson High School. They were all African American teachers consisting of men as well as women. They were the best and the brightest in the African American community. The teachers were smart, but because of segregation, and the limitation placed on these brilliant individuals, they were not able to obtain employment in corporate America, so they became teachers.

Teachers like Mr. Brooks, Mr. Hadnot, Mrs. Moore, Mr. Porter, Coach James, and Coach Brossard helped me through my struggles in high school. I did not do very well academically that first semester in the tenth grade, but the second semester, the light came on. I began to make the honor roll and made A's and B's in the eleventh grade. At the end of my eleventh-grade year, I was selected to go to Bayou Boys State by the high school. Bayou Boys State was held at Southern University for what the school considered future leaders in the state.

My senior year in high school was excellent; I was selected the most outstanding football player of the year and made the honor roll each period. I was offered a scholarship to play football at Dillard University, but I refused to go to Dillard because they could not compete with Southern University and Grambling in the state of Louisiana. I was offered a partial scholarship to Southern University, but the coach told me that my fees would be covered at the school, but I would have to work for at least two years because he could not give everyone a full scholarship. All the colleges in Louisiana were segregated, and African Americans were not to play against s in colleges throughout the south.

I was accepted at Southern University but didn't go. That Friday before I was to leave for school, I lost all the money I had saved from working on road construction that summer. My father was working in Nebraska. I called him, but he said that he could not help me. I believe that he felt that high school was enough education. I then decided I would join the army.

The army was a very good place for me to start adulthood. I decided I wanted a college education and started going to college as I soon as completed my training. At my first duty station, I enrolled at North Texas State University in the evening program. I finished the semester and was sent to Korea. While in Korea, I was working on the evening shift and did not think I could go to college. I would educate myself. I went to the library and got books on math, science, and logic. I read and studied the first year in Korea. The second year, I was promoted to sergeant in two years, so I asked my sergeant major if I could go to college in the evening. He said I could, and he added, after I finished class, I was to come to work. This was my opportunity to complete my education.

I moved quickly up the ranks, and I was selected for warrant officer after only six years in the army. I was the youngest warrant officer in the entire Signal Corps. I was assigned to Vietnam as a young warrant officer. I enrolled in college in Vietnam. After my tour of duty in Vietnam, I applied for the Degree Completion Program. I was accepted and told to pick any college in the United States, and the army would pay all my fees, and I received all my salary and allowances for two full years.

My selection was Park University, a small, private school in Parkville, Missouri; because eighty percent of their graduates went on to get graduate degrees. I had some great experiences. While at Park. I played on the college basketball team and lettered in golf. After graduating from Park *Summa Con Laude* with a 3.89 GPA, I was provided the opportunity to go to Boston University. I was excited about being submitted to the Boston University Graduate Business Program. I knew Dr. Martin Luther King and Barbara Jordan both attended Boston University. I just knew that I had to be successful at Boston University.

Business Boston University of Management had a rigorous program. I would say those professors would even flunk their friends. Several of the Ivy

League School graduates did not make it through the first semester in Boston University's School of Management. This elevated my level of concern in every class. I had a very good experience at Boston University, and I knew that I could go toe to toe academically with anyone at any graduate school in the country. I got a Master of Business Administration from Boston University.

Military Assignments

My army career was going extremely well, and I was promoted to the highest warrant officer grade of chief warrant officer four. I was also selected to be the first master warrant officer in the Signal Corps. During my career as a warrant officer, I was selected for some outstanding assignments at the highest levels.

Assignment that consisted of going to:

- Saigon, Vietnam
- MAC V. Headquarters, Berlin, Germany
- Panama
- Korea, 8th Army Headquarters
- Fort Hood, Texas 3rd Corps Headquarters

Fort Sam Houston, Texas, in San Antonio, these were all considered outstanding destinations. It was while I was assigned to Fort Sam Houston, Texas, serving as the director of the Counter Signal Intelligence Division that I was selected for master warrant officer.

Before I could be promoted to master warrant officer, I had to go to Fort Rucker and attend the Master Warrant Officer Course. The course lasted for six months ,and after completion of the course, which was like a high-level graduate program that prepared warrant officers to serve at the highest levels of command in the United States Army, I was promoted to master warrant officer, becoming the first master warrant officer in the United States Army Signal Corps. I had finally reached the very top of my career field. I retired after thirty years and embarked on my new career as a teacher and coach.

I have taught and coached for six years in the San Antonio Independent School District. While I was teaching, I also obtained a master's degree in education and an administrative certification. Teaching and coaching at a middle school were rewarding. I taught sixth, seventh, and eighth grade students in a special education self-contained classroom for emotionally disturbed students.

At first, this was the most difficult job that I had ever held, but during my second year, I was given a class of eleven sixth-grade students. I only had sixth graders. This was great. I could achieve excellent results from the students. I kept these students for three years until they completed the eighth grade and then the moved to high school. I got a tremendous amount of satisfaction from this job. I also experienced success as a coach. During this timeframe, I coached football, basketball, and track.

As a first-year coach, I was amazed at how things were done in middle school, football being the first sport of the year, and we got off to a great start. We won every game until the first six weeks' grades came out. We lost our quarterback, who was our best defensive lineman, and several other starters who did not pass all their subjects. We lost half of the fifty-six players we started with. After the six weeks' grades incident, we did not win another game for the rest of the football season. I asked the coaches about this and was told that it was okay, because now we could have only one team per grade level. I then set up a system to check grades every week and insisted that all schoolwork must be completed before any student could practice. I also checked on how the students were behaving in class and made sure that if I received an unfavorable report on any athlete, that individual had some extra work to do before practice. The environment changed in the athletic department. In the six years that I coached, we won four football championships and six track championships. I was the head track coach, but I had a great track coach helping me, named James Griffin. Coaching and teaching were amazing in the San Antonio Independent School Independent District, but I wanted to have more of an impact on the school system. I then moved onto the field of administration in the Austin Independent School District.

While in the Austin Independent School District, I could have an impact on the entire school. I wrote a school-wide behavior management plan for Burnet Middle School. I enjoyed working in this middle school. I had a great principal, Linda Van Horne, who trusted me to help improve the school, and the very best assistant principal I have had the opportunity to work with; Jo Dawn Robinson helped me become a better administrator. Working as an assistant principal was very rewarding, but I wanted to do more in the public-school system, so I decided to apply to the University of Texas at Austin for their doctoral degree program in education.

The University of Texas had an assessment center that selected applicants to attend before admission. All the three-hundred-plus applicants were screened, and only thirty were selected to attend the assessment center, and only fifteen would be admitted to the doctoral program. I was one of the thirty selected to attend the assessment center.

I had to teach a class in San Antonio, Texas. Doctor Nolan Estes oversaw the assessment center, and he recommended I come in a little later to start the assessment process. This being the first day of my class, I had to meet with my students and get the class started and head back to Austin to attend the University of Texas and start the assessment process. When I got into Austin, my car stopped. I was already late, but I got out of the car, walked around the car, and said a prayer. I got as far as the State Capital building, and the car stopped again. Being close to the university, I got out of my car and started to walk, but I thought I would try to start one more time. The car started again, and I made it to the building where the assessment was being held. By this time, I was late; the twenty-nine applicants had already completed the morning session. It was now time for lunch. I found D. Estes, and he said, "You need to complete a test, then you can join the other applicants." I completed the test and went into the lunch area to join the others.

When I arrived into where the other twenty-nine applicants were, I noticed that all of the men had their best suits on, and the ladies were wearing their best dresses. They were really dressed up for the occasion. I, on the other hand, I was wearing a polo shirt and a pair of Levi's. I felt completely out of place. After lunch, the afternoon session started. We were put into groups and given a scenario that included the problem that the group had to come up with a solution. Each person was given an opportunity to participate. The process was observed by a group of professors who were seated around the room and the participants were evaluated. After the scenario was completed, each applicant had to go, one by one, to be interviewed by a professor from the Education Department.

I had an interview with a professor who had been at the university for a very long time. We sat together in a room where he asked me questions for about an hour. After each question, he evaluated me. After this one-on-one session, we were given another a scenario with another problem, and we were evaluated again. The process lasted all day. After everything was completed, I then had to complete the portion I had missed. I completed everything. I had done the best that I could, but I felt I would never be accepted by the University of Texas at Austin.

I got the letter from the University of Texas at Austin, but I was afraid to open it. I just knew it was filled with bad news. I opened the letter slowly. It read, "Congratulations, you've been admitted to the University of Texas at Austin's Executive Leadership Doctoral Program." I was accepted into the program. The coursework during the first year was overwhelming. Two of the fifteen students dropped out during the first semester. The experience was so intense, one wanted to commit suicide. The workload was too much for one person, but the professors hadn't told us what to expect. You had to figure everything out for yourself; with this new information, a group of us got together and divided up the work.

While attending undergraduate school, a student can work on their own. Doing the master's program, you may be able to complete the program with very little group work, but in the University of Texas at Austin's doctoral program, it is impossible to go it alone. You should work together to have a chance to complete all the course work and have opportunity to advance to candidacy.

At the University of Texas at Austin, to start writing your dissertation proposal, you must advance candidacy. To advance to candidacy after all coursework is completed, a specialization paper must be written and graded by three professors. You must get a passing grade from two of the three professors for your specialization paper, and you must pass your comprehensive examination, and I advanced to candidacy. After advancing to candidacy, you must select a dissertation committee.

Selection of Dissertation Committee

Selection of a dissertation committee is one of the most important tasks a doctoral student must complete. You must have each of those five professors sign and approve your dissertation, or you cannot become a doctor. All five signatures are required. My committee of four professors from University of Texas at Austin (UT): Dr. Martha Avondo, Dr. Donald Phelps, Dr. Oscar Meeks, and Dr. Charles Clark. The final professor was Dr. Jean Madsen from Texas A&M University. I don't think everyone at UT was happy with me, placing a professor from A&M on my committee, but she was an expert on diversity, and my primary focus was diversity. Dr. Madsen served as the co-chair of the committee. As I was about to complete my dissertation, the chair of my committee, Dr. Phelps, passed away. I did not know what to do. Dr. Nolan Estes said he would be the chair of the committee to help me complete the process.

He told me, "I had been there long enough already." Upon hearing these words, I was so happy. My committee was set, and I was preparing to move on to the proposal.

Dissertation Proposal

This was the time that the dissertation proposal had to be written. The dissertation proposal is the first three written chapters of your dissertation. The topic selected for my specialization paper was related to my dissertation, so I had a good start for my proposal. This would serve as part of my literature review, or chapter two of my dissertation proposal. To improve my dissertation, I took a dissertation proposal writing class from Dr. Avondo, and she was amazing. She helped me with those three chapters. I completed my proposal, met with my committee, was approved, and began my research.

Now that the proposal was completed, I had to start my research and begin to write the first two chapters. I decided to write a dissertation focusing on diversity in public school leadership. The title was "The Perceptions of Principals of Color, and European American Principals of African American Superintendents." I did a qualitative study, using three African American superintendents and fifteen principals. I used five principals from each school district. The research was completed, and I wrote the last two chapters. After the dissertation was finished, I had to schedule my defense. After scheduling was completed, the five professors showed up. They kept me defending for over an hour, and they finally asked me to leave the room and wait for their decision. I became worried as I waited for what seemed to be forever, but finally, Dr. Nolan Estes came out and said, "Congratulations, Doctor," as he gave me a super handshake. It was over. I had finally earned the right to be called Doctor.

Reflecting back, I can remember sitting in the class at the University of Texas and thinking African Americans were not allowed to play football at this school when I finished high school. That thought gave me determination to graduate from the program, and with the support of my wife, Patricia; my sisters, Barbara, Irma (Priss), and Lillie; my brothers, Phillip, Tyrone, and Harvey; and my three sons, Bret, Nick III, and Omar, I was awarded a doctoral degree from the University of Texas at Austin. During that year, I retired from the public-school system and started teaching for Park University at Lackland Air Force Base.

Life is full of ups and downs, but I credit one book that I read a long time ago by Norman Vincent Peale, *The Power of Positive Thinking*, for the achievements in my life.

• • •

CHAPTER 9

Dr. Chanel Young

Clinical Psychologist, United States Army and Private Practice

BIOGRAPHY

Dr. Chanel Young is a clinical psychologist in the *United States Army* based at *Fort Hood Army Post*. She has been a clinical psychologist for eighteen years. Previously, she worked at *Brooke Army Medical Center* (BAMC) in San Antonio, Texas. She has an extensive psychology background through working with multiple clinical disorders to include mental retardation, depression, anxiety, and post-traumatic stress. During her years of extensive training, she worked with local youth as a juvenile corrections officer and public affairs coordinator for the *Department of Military Affairs.*

She is planning to expand her clinical practice the fields of trauma and health psychology. Her plan is to build her clinical psychology practices to provide consultation to the military. She will integrate Psycho-Educational Seminars and the practice of health psychology and women's issues in clinical psychology.

CREDENTIALS:

- PsyD in Clinical Psychology, *Argosy University-Virginia*
- BA in Psychology, *Norfolk State University*

"He who asks questions cannot avoid the answers."
~ *African Proverb*

"I will not let you fail."
~ *Marva Collins,*
Founder, Collins Westside Preparatory School

***Disclaimer:** The stories in this chapter reflect the author's recollection of events. Some names, locations, and identifying characteristics have been changed to protect the privacy of those depicted. Dialogue has been re-created from the author's memory.

My Journey to the Ivory Tower

Hard Work and Determination

As the youngest of four children, and the "baby-girl" of the family, I considered myself a "Southern Bell" with a zesty twist! I was born in Suffolk, Virginia. I grew up enjoying pep-rallies, peanut festivals, small-town parades, family reunion celebrations, playing spades and Bobbie-jacks, and, most importantly, blue crabs from the Chesapeake Bay. Suffolk, Virginia, is identified as the largest land mass in the entire state. However, many passers-by are unaware of Suffolk's simple treasures. Hence, the name on the various roadway signs: "SURPRISING SUFFOLK." In all its subtly, it is most commonly known as the home of one of the famous peanut factories called "Planter's Peanuts." If it's not obvious, I am very proud of my southern heritage, as well as my diverse culture. In 2004 I learned that my family has strong ties to the Algonquian Indians on the Trail of Tears and a large portion of my ancestral roots are entrenched in Manteo, North Carolina, where my great grandparents resided.

Given my heritage of both African American and American Indian roots, I am proud to share the story of my path to academia. Others within the larger western culture may see me and label me as just another minority. This raises an important question: Which came up with the term "minority" anyway? The term alone (minority) closely resembles a reverse psychology of brainwashing technique neatly tucked away and embedded into societal norms. If one redefines or recreates social norms based on this ideology, it seems pretentious, to say the least. In a world where most ethnic groups outnumber those who identify themselves as Caucasian or of Anglo-Saxon descent both nationally and internationally, how can the majority be defined as the minority, and vice versa, as it relates to cultural representations within the subset of Western society? Nevertheless, we learn to accept societal labels and stereotypes and adjust fire accordingly.

Since I was in grade school, I chose not to view myself as just a "minority" in the traditional sense of the word. This was not an attempt to deny the rich aspects of my African American roots. Considering my southern accent, humble beginnings, and caramel skin tone. I couldn't escape my roots if I tried. However, my view of myself as something greater than a subpar label was my defense against becoming subjected to prejudgments, stereotypes, and "isms" that are routinely indoctrinated within the larger culture identified as the western worldview. However, I planned to view myself as a person with a plethora of diverse ethnic traits and cultural characteristics that have helped me evolve into the unique individual I am today.

Coming from parents who worked in the human services field, I could precisely construct those cultural experiences into a profession of interest. My father was an entrepreneur who specialized in the art of cosmetology. My mother worked in the field of mental health as a case-manager for the homeless and the mentally ill. From a young age, I was molded into an individual destined to be in the "helping profession." My journey along the road of psychology began with an interest in working with various dually diagnosed individuals in home-based, residential outpatient and military mental health settings for fifteen years. During these years of extensive training, I worked with local youth as a juvenile corrections officer and public affairs coordinator for the Department of Military Affairs. While immersing myself in the mental health arena, I could gain a more expansive understanding of psychology through working with multiple clinical disorders to include mental retardation, depression, anxiety, and post-traumatic stress.

Having a variety of vocational experiences and clinical training, I later obtained a doctoral degree in clinical psychology from Argosy University in Arlington, Virginia. Prior to earning doctoral degree, I obtained a bachelor's degree in psychology from Norfolk State University in 1995. I also obtained an associate degree in mental health, which I earned from the Community College of the Air Force, and currently maintain a certification as a substance abuse counselor in the state of Virginia. In addition, I completed two master's degrees in community clinical psychology. To date, I am currently enlisted as a United States Army officer and have had the opportunity to serve as an equal opportunity advisor and behavioral health officer to military members in that capacity.

Moving to Texas

In 2010, I moved to San Antonio, Texas to establish myself as an army psychologist through an intensive pre-doctoral internship and post-doctoral residency. Currently, I provide individual, family, couples, and group therapy to military members at Brooke Army Medical Center in San Antonio, Texas. During the past two years, I have worked toward completing the United States Army's internship and post-doctoral residency program at Brooke Army Medical Center in San Antonio, Texas. My professional passion is heavily rooted in trauma work with the military population. Through this work, my love for clinical practice challenges me to continue to expand my knowledge and expose myself to new ventures in the fields of trauma and health psychology. My future goals include military consultations, the integration of Psycho-Educational Seminars, and the practice of health psychology as it relates to salient women's issues.

This interest stemmed from both professional and interpersonal experiences during my doctoral studies. These experiences challenged me to grow not only professionally but personally, as an older student who happened to be female. I was an older student when I decided to return to graduate school. I quickly realized that it would be a process of adjustment as I transitioned from clinical practice back into the world of academia. I recall having to adjust to using software in online classes and taking a little longer to process information during class lectures. I was a little embarrassed initially, as I found myself frequently comparing my performance to my much younger peers who seemed to be some sort of "JET-EYE MAGICIANS" at pulling "all-nighters'" and integrating technology into their presentations and assigned projects. Later, I learned that this was not totally about aptitude and declining intelligence quotients (on my part), but this had everything to do with differences in learning style. Once I realized that my learning style primarily incorporated visual, auditory, and sensory cues involving my hands (Typing, writing notes, or using index cards), I was much more comfortable in my own skin and simply adjusted in how I prepared for required academic tasks (test, presentations, group projects, or clinical assessments.)

More specifically, I struggled with being one of the few African Americans in my cohort in an academic setting where African American students were typically less aspiring than the general student population. Through these experiences, I could reflect on what it meant to be a person of color and a professional in a field that often emphasized Western philosophies and views that were much different from my own, for example, many (not all) Western-based theoretical orientation or modalities within psychology practice view clients from a perspective rooted in psychopathology. In other words, the client's presentations of symptoms are identified based on a label or specific diagnostic criteria independent of many important factors that vary from client to client. For example, culture and their rate of assimilation to Western societal norms, religious views/affiliations, age, situational stressors, social-economic status, and educational level are all factors that may vary and impact the presentation of symptoms that clients experience and present. Coming from years of community-based clinical practice, I prefer to integrate psychological principles criteria that treat clients from a holistic or bio-psychosocial perspective, inclusive of all the variables. Becoming experts in clinical diagnosis and assessment is paramount if the field of psychology. However, we must understand the necessity and importance of a comprehensive approach. This is, quintessentially, what allows intervention to be implemented from a strengths-based perspective rather than a framework rooted solely in maladaptive functioning and diagnostic labels.

After attending an Historically Black College (HBC), I quickly found myself in a "culture shock" upon entering my graduate program, and I knew that I would have to slowly adapt to be successful. Unfortunately, I had previously been conditioned to function in a collectivist environment. This is primarily the environment in which the underlying philosophy is that "it takes a village to raise a child," academically or otherwise. In the collectivist environment group, participation is warranted and is encouraged. It is what fuels the ego and sustains the subsequent development of self-esteem. It breeds a supportive and encapsulating foundation for autonomy and a sense of competence within clinical practice. To the contrary, the new academic environment was one in which the message "every man for himself" echoed throughout the classroom and campus. Group work or collaborative efforts were often viewed as a threat to the autonomy of the self. In cases in which collaboration was implemented on the part of the student, the environment became extremely competitive and punitive at times. Statements such as "At this stage in your professional development, you should know this" or "At this stage in your professional development, you should be ready for independent practice with little feedback from superiors."

It is this thought process that resembles an oxymoron. How is it possible for the student to be ready for independent practice if they are clearly in a structured program in which the overreaching goal is to subject them to clinical training required to obtain the necessary skills and abilities identified in that specific field of practice? It wasn't until I found myself in a situation in which my integrity was questioned that I began to realize that vast differences and distinctions across both academic settings. It started with a situation in which I was accused of cheating and was faced with potential disciplinary action from the dean of the program. At this moment, I found myself not only fighting to remain in my program but also to prove myself and maintain a sense of personal integrity. It was clear that the view of the majority culture had a significant impact on the perception of the truth. Nevertheless, I completed the program in a timely manner and went on to complete another challenge to reach my goal...the dissertation!

The dissertation is another feat that comes along with the doctoral experience; however, prior to attending Argosy University, I had limited exposure to what a dissertation would require academically (writing style, research requirements, preparation time, etc.). During previous academic experiences, I had not been required to write a thesis. My program was designed in such a way that the student could take comprehensive exams in lieu of writing a thesis. However, the thesis remained optional. Therefore, I had great angst regarding how the entire picture would come together. I knew that this would require a great deal of time, effort and began to immerse myself in the research.

What I found most the most challenging was that I had to multitask while on a full-time intensive pre-doctoral internship. Consequently, I spent countless hours researching my topic of interest to develop a cohesively written body of work. This feat followed me just like a dark cloud, as I made the mistake of not finishing my dissertation prior to becoming "matched" for internship.

Speaking of the match process, it, too, was yet another experience that no one adequately prepares you for. Based on my lack of mentorship regarding the match process, I like to compare it to parents who avoid talking to their children about sexuality and where babies come from. It creates this phenomenon in which no one wants to go into grave details, as it seems rather taboo. Therefore, everyone tells you that it's a much-needed requirement, like the requirement for procreation in efforts to sustain mankind, but you never seem to get a step-by-step tutorial of the process. Unfortunately, it just kind of unfolds day by day, and you learn in a "trial by fire" kind of way as the process slowly unfolds. Each person develops their writing project to minimize these painful kinds of experiences. You would think that after all the chaos that I'd had enough tough experiences to tuck my tail between my legs and go home.

Home, no not me! Upon completion of graduation and all academic requirements, I decided to take the stress to an even higher level by joining on even more hierarchical organization called the US military. I found out that I had been matched at Brook Army Medical Center in San Antonio, Texas, and agreed to join the military on a full-time basis. Unfortunately, because I had not completed my dissertation prior to this selection process, completion of the dissertation became a grueling task. I faced the nightmare of trying to balance the vast responsibilities of clinical practice, which included extensive administrative tasks (note writing, assessment/reporting writing, and routine briefings,), adapting to the active duty military climate, office policies, adjusting to neurotic clinical supervisors, managing a sturdy caseload of trauma clients, and adding a nice balance of all-nighters two to three times per week to finalize the dissertation process.

You Are the "Elephant in the Room," So Get Used to It

There seems to always be the notion that you are the pink elephant in the room, because as a "Minority" or a person of color, this fact alone may lead itself towards your abilities being scrutinized. One question that is frequently raised for many individuals, who share a predominately Western worldview, is "Are you truly skilled at your profession?" or "Where you placed here by affirmative action?" Although we have made leaps and bounds about race relations in the United States of America, this thought process is commonly reflected in the minds of some majority professionals across the country. Despite the implementation affirmation action laws to facilitate equitable hiring practices and exposure to quality education, it does not forgo the qualifications necessary for selection in both academic and professional settings. As a young professional, I often felt the need to prove my abilities and skills within the professional environment. Regardless of the fact that I had earned three degrees (an associate, bachelor, and master's degree) prior to entering the doctoral program, I would still hear comments such as, "That was really a good speech; I didn't know you were so articulate," or "Wow, I'm shocked by your writing ability." It was almost as if the stereotypes and prejudgments were emphatically spoken, without regard to the psychological or emotional impact it could potentially have on the student. Therefore, thick skin is imperative within this area! If you don't have it, find a way to obtain it prior to engaging in the process of pursuing a doctoral degree.

We must know and understand that it is our primary responsibility to dispel, undermine, and obliterate every stereotype and prejudgment that is subjected all minority groups. Therefore, we must work diligently to cultivate an environment of ethical practice and professionalism through our words, deeds, and professional identities. We must keep the faith and not become weary in our professional well-doing!

Effective Clinical Supervision and Mentorship Is Imperative

I felt the need to prove my abilities to minimize embedded stereotypes, such as stereotypes which infer that African Americans are unprofessional (frequently called the "G"-word, ghetto) loud, intimating, abrasive, or unapproachable. Although I considered myself to be intellectually equal to my counterparts, deep inside of me there was still a twinge of insecurity, a voice questioning whether "I was good enough," even though my clinical skills and expertise seemed to speak for itself. I was constantly told by clients that they loved any style or felt a sense of improvement from our clinical work. This confirmed that I was just as good as, or even better than, some of my peers about clinical practice. However, the one thing that was lacking was reassurance, affirmation, and words of encouragement from authority figures, most importantly, those providing clinical supervision of my work. I learned that affirmation of competence and clinical autonomy. Thus, I began to seek out mentorship from other seasoned professionals and found solace through dialogue and reflection with like-minded individuals. I cultivated relationships with other students of diverse backgrounds who also experienced the same feelings, thoughts, emotions, and the similar insecurities related to professional growth and development; it wasn't until I began hearing the stories of others that I knew this was not an objective experience that I had to face alone. I knew that this was a concern often felt by many ethnic students in the professional world. These cohorts of professionals were the foundation of both my emotional and professional success.

Experiences As the "Lowly Student"

As an older student, it is difficult for people to understand that you are a student coming into the organizational setting with a vast array of life experiences that many young professionals starting out have not experienced. Coming to terms with this transition in roles requires a tremendous amount of humility on the part of the student. I found that, many times, supervisors did not know how to adjust their leadership style for students with intermediate skills, which resulted in a nebulous "one size fits all" attempt to train and lead. This approach most often resulted in ruptures, strains, and microaggressions that negatively impacted the process of clinical supervision in professional practice.

Having come to the military environment with seventeen years of experience one could be viewed as a seasoned professional. Thus, one becomes used to a certain level of autonomy. Considering my own clinical background and extensive training, it appeared that there were individual supervisors who were trying to marginalize my efforts for autonomy. It was uncommon to have students in the setting who were of more of an intermediate level. Therefore, they do not know how to adjust their style to provide an environment that was conducive to learning while allowing for sufficient autonomy. From this experience, I learned that once another professional develops a need for marginalization (regardless of whether they are a subordinate or peer), they have already questioned this professional's skills/abilities on a more covert level. Thus, a lot of supervisors tend to micromanage, which is an overt expression of their professional dismay as it relates to assessing competence. In hindsight,

I realized that these issues negatively impacted the therapeutic relationship between the supervisors and the employee. I found myself trying to avoid these microaggressions personally or allowing them to impact my overall self-esteem, as it related to clinical practice and professional growth. However, I realized that, over the long term, it negatively impacted my overall impression of the capacity for fairness, objectivity, and equity within the organizational setting.

Often, you will find yourself trying to "dumb" down your skills as a means of pacifying other professionals as well as being perceived as "trainable," or to protect against one being viewed as a "know it all" during the training experience; this, subsequently, creates an internal struggle with the interpersonal development of autonomy, comfort with exposing authentic weakness and employing—skills as a "seasoned" clinician. This is one of the many challenges that assisted in learning to adapt to various settings based on the idiosyncratic nature of the environment; simply put, I learned to become a professional chameleon. I also had a paradigm shift with regards to the sense of pride I had regarding the extensive clinical background I brought with me. I challenged myself to adapt to the current "student" role and embraced the fact that there was always room to learn new and exciting things, as well as expand my clinical knowledge. This mindset saved my life!

Your Professional Identity Is Your Prize Possession, Protect it At All Cost

We must protect our professional identities, as our name is oftentimes the one thing that precedes our presence into an organization or venue. Therefore, we must do our best to perform with excellence. Ethical practice and professionalism are paramount. The lack thereof can make or break you. Our supervisors are constantly watching us and formulating opinions. Many times, the opinions that are extracted are not always accurate ones. Nevertheless, as the colloquialism states that "first impressions are lasting impressions," it still stands whether it is skewed or not. Within each working environment, there is an "organizational culture." These organizational cultural projects are expected of you within families, sororities, or small towns. The cultural environmental often has unspoken rules which largely echo trends regarding what is expected and how one should behave. How you ascribe to and function per those rules determines whether one's reputation is viewed positively or negatively. Specific factors such as timelessness, overall professionalism, positive relationships, credibility with peers, social skills, professional knowledge, professional writing skills, and public speaking skills are all various skills that may be routinely assessed. These factors can highly affect how people interact with you and determine whether your opinion and/or ideas are deemed credible from authority figures within the organizational setting. Awareness regarding how you weigh-in on each of the factors is paramount to sustaining your professional name, credibility, and staying power within any organization.

Given various situations, you may feel the need to assert your voice to resolve a problem, gain respect, or share professional knowledge that other team members cannot offer. We must thoroughly assess whether our voice will be heard and validated. Within a hierarchical organization, I found that before we assert our voices to offer opinions, it is important to equally assess the power differential and ask ourselves one salient question. Do you hold the necessary power to effect substantial change within the hierarchical infrastructure of the organization? If not, this may not be the best time to offer feedback or an opinion. One may be better served by using their voices to protect themselves during time of slander, professional abuse, or to liberate and educate other following careful planning. It is very important to strategically determine when to empty one's voice and when to preserve one's voice, because timing is everything.

The primary thing to understand is that we must preserve our reputations at all cost. Therefore, be mindful of how body language, voice tone, and other non-verbal behaviors and actions are perceived by others, particularly those who do not share similar cultural or worldviews. It is very difficult to rebuild one's professional identify after instances of slander or misrepresentation. Unfortunately, negative reputations can make a significant impact on your future career endeavors, relationships, and goals. Therefore, we must remain diligent in preserving our professional identities. We can attempt to do so by taking on a defensive posture and implementing efforts to minimize negative perceptions and interactions in the workplace.

Triangular Communication to Avoid Confrontation

Triangular communication occurs when one person witnesses a mistake you've made or has a professional concern with regards to an unresolved issue that you may have been involved in. For example, a conflict has happened, but rather than discuss the matter at the lowest level, the supervisor decides to avoid implementing the necessary effective communication skills and relays the information to your supervisor without bringing it to your attention first. When people avoid confrontation, and incorporate passive aggressive or manipulative communication styles, they may attempt to avoid communication at the lowest level. Many times, try to find the person who has the most authority and communicates with them first, tries to sabotage or undermine their subordinate's capacity for effective communication or ability to impact change. However, there are exceptions to this pattern. There are also instances in which this behavior is not intended for sabotage, but to the contrary, it happens to be the person's primary communication style. Due to cultural differences and uncertainty about how they should employ effective problems solving and critical thinking skills in the face of conflict, rather than seek consultation to address and resolve matters, they simply use avoidance as a defense mechanism to compensate for the fear and discomfort that stems from the anxiety, provoking an event such as avoiding an opportunity to tell an employee/supervisee that their leave was not approved, despite the employee having already purchased tickets to Hawaii.

Moreover, considering my own personal experiences as an African American female working in professional environments with less than 2 percent African Americans, it appears that we do not share this same communication pattern that lends itself to exclude or avoid communication at the lowest level. The problem with triangular communication is that the primary issues at the root of the problem are never addressed. Consequently, it creates massive strains or ruptures across professional relationships.

A common trend frequently observed within various professional settings is that African American women who are assertive, goal-oriented, and are not fearful of conflict or confrontation are often categorized or labeled as overzealous, intimidating, or given the title of the "angry woman." Unfortunately, it occurs many times because our non-verbal communication, body language, and voice tone is drastically different and often misunderstood by non-minority leaders. As a corrective measure, we must self-reflect with an open mind and avoid knee-jerk responses that may be perceived by others as combative in nature or not functioning as a supportive team player organizational goals.

Unfortunately, measures to maintain a sense of collegial harmony can also lead to extreme efforts to alter our professional identity in ways that make others feel "more comfortable" but are no longer authentic or true to who we are as professional or individuals. We must keep in mind that our primary goal is to strike a nice balance between adapting to the environment is overall style of communication and organizational climate while sustaining a sense of personal authenticity.

Know Your Value and Self Worth

It is important to know your value, validation of skills, and celebration of intrinsic and external accomplishments. Be prepared to hear more about your weaknesses and the mistakes you have made versus your strengths. Create a network or professionals within your field that will be objective and tell you the truth regarding various clinical experiences to include your shortcomings, strengths, weaknesses. This is essential for sound emotional wellbeing. Seek out peer groups, consultation, and feedback on a regular basis. It is when you least expect to hear criticism about your abilities that makes it hard to maintain a positive outlook. However, if you look for feedback regarding self-improvement and ways to increase your knowledge within your profession, then you will experience a true sense of professional growth and development. Furthermore, it is important to hold onto your values, beliefs, and morals and not lose sight of yourself while trying to transition into your new now role as "the doctor." Some safeguards include:

1. Create a cohort of professional support among other minorities for ethical dialogue and consultation.
2. Rely on your family and friends for love, support, and encouragement.

• • •

CHAPTER 10

Dr. Doshie Piper

Professor and Researcher, University of the Incarnate Word

BIOGRAPHY

Dr. Doshie Piper is an assistant professor of criminal justice at the *University of the Incarnate Word.* (UIW) She is from Houston, Texas. She is a feminist and community criminologist. Dr. Piper is an expert on gender and crime. Her teaching experience includes several courses taught within the department of *Sociology and Criminal Justice* at the UIW: *Introduction to Criminal Justice; Drugs and Crime in Society; Issues in Contemporary Criminal Justice; Juvenile Justice; Criminology; Probation, Parole and Community Corrections, and Senior Seminar.* She has done work with the *Bexar County Detention Center.*

She has appeared in numerous media outlets as an expert on gender and crime. She has appeared on *KROV 91.7FM2, KDRY 1100 AM,* and has been featured on *KABB Fox San Antonio, San Antonio Observer*, and many others. She has published articles in *Contemporary Ethical Issues in the Criminal Justice System, Customer Service - The Reason Some HBCUs are Destined to Fail, and The Use and Abuse of Police Power in America.* She and Dr. Miles have presented on *Crime and Entrepreneurship* at the *Academy of Business Research Conference* in New Orleans, LA. She is a member of the *San Antonio Ladies-Talented Tenth* (SALTT).

CREDENTIALS:

- PhD in Juvenile Justice, *Prairie View A&M University*
- MS in Criminal Justice, *University of Cincinnati*
- BS in Criminal Justice, *University of Cincinnati*

"There's no people that need all benefits resulting from a well-directed education more than we do."
~ *Frances Ellen Watkins, Abolitionist, Poet*

"He who learns, teaches."
~ *Ethiopian Proverb*

***Disclaimer:** The stories in this chapter reflect the author's recollection of events. Some names, locations, and identifying characteristics have been changed to protect the privacy of those depicted. Dialogue has been re-created from the author's memory.

The Journey to My Doctorate

Introduction

Sometimes I do not believe it myself, I actually have a Doctor of Philosophy in justice studies. It all happened so fast, well, maybe not that fast, but it is still a blur. The time flew by, and despite the many obstacles, here I am, Dr. Doshie Piper. As stated in the acknowledgements section of my dissertation, my mother was the driving force behind this accomplishment. I remember, when I was in high school, a United States (US) Air Force recruiter came to my home to speak to my parents about me being a military nurse. The recruiter was explaining to my mother how the Air Force Reserve Officer Training Corp (ROTC) could pay for my undergraduate education, then I would commission as an Air Force nurse. My mother told that she asked the recruiter, "Why would my daughter want to be a nurse when she can be a doctor?" At the time, I did not know how profound that statement was, because I was a junior in high school. It was not until I heard my mother tell that story the second time that it would forever have an impact and change my life.

Personal Background

I have always lived in what the sociological and criminological literature calls a socially disorganized community. One plagued with crime and disorder, public alcohol, substance use, and broken homes. Including my home, as a child I did not realize that the home I was growing up in was broken, but according to traditional definitions, it was very much so. My father had been married twice before he met my mother. It is still unclear to me whether he was officially divorced when they started dating. You see, my father's second wife, Deborah, and my mother were pregnant at the same time. Now, do not get me wrong, it was not like they were both having their babies at the same time, but they were both pregnant at the same time. My brother Ruben (Deborah's son) was born July 19, 1978, and my brother Judah, was born March 22, 1979. There was about a month or two overlap.

Given my father's infidelities and relational problems with multiple women and children, that never prevented him from showing me the love, care, and consideration that I needed. Clearly, problems existed in the home. However, somehow, we were shielded from the negativity of being a blended family. It was normal at Christmastime for my parents to purchase gifts for Deborah. This was done whether she was spending Christmas at our home or not. Those were good times. It would not be until I went to college that I would realize that this practice of civility was viewed as odd and rejected by the larger society. Society has an expectation that divorce is ugly, volatile, and vicious. It may be, but childhood memories of my father and his ex-wife's interactions were not.

Of course, this is a one-sided account of the story that has very many versions. I know my brothers Judah and Ruben have childhood stories that are very different. However, I grew up in a home with both of my parents. We moved a lot the first ten years of my life. Then in the early 90s, we settled in Houston. It was my father's hometown. My mother's home was New Orleans. My parents met through my Aunt Linda, my father's sister, who went to college with my mother. I completed my fifth grade year of school at Highland Heights Elementary. I went on to M. C. Williams Middle School, finished from there in 1994, and began high school. There are many statistics and assumptions associated with children who come from mixed or blended families. However, I believe that my family composition is what has given me the ability for defy the odds and not become a statistic.

I graduated from Booker T. Washington High School in Houston, Texas, in 1998. Coming from the inner city of Houston, with working parents whose income barely covered the cost of overhead bills, federal financial aid and scholarships were the only options I had when I began college. Therefore, I tapped into the only resources available to me. My journey to complete my bachelor's degree in 2003 and master's degree in 2006 from the University of Cincinnati was a challenge without the assistance of family financial support. Relying solely on funding available through the state and federal governments and institutional funding was another challenge. Transitioning from Texas to Ohio was an expensive task in addition to the cost of out-of-state fees.

Family Educational Background

I came from an educated family. My mother and most of her siblings have at least a bachelor's level education. My father did not have a college education, but two of his three sisters have master's degrees and one of the two has a doctorate degree. So, it was understood that I was going to college. "I came from smart people." I am not sure where that saying came from, but I constantly heard people say it. I heard that phrase all the time. I believed it. I internalized this saying as I embraced my family's legacy of education.

My cousin Leah, my mother's sister, Ruth's oldest daughter, was the first person in my family I remember graduating from college. No, I am lying; my Uncle Benjamin was my first memory of a college graduation. Benjamin was my mother's youngest brother. Even though I do not remember the exact year, I remember this event being important in the 80s. Then my cousin Leah graduated from Smith College in Massachusetts. This was another big deal because Leah was like me, in a sense. I grew up with Leah, even though she was about ten years older; we were both from the inner city, working-class households. Our mothers were sisters, and I trust they both wanted similar goals for their children. This was a very proud event for my family. Even though I was not able to travel to the graduation, I remember all the chatter and planning.

Her sister, Sarah, graduated from Smith around 1998. I could be wrong, but 1998 stays in my memory, as there was a scheduling conflict between her college graduation and my high school graduation. A few years passed, and she obtained her master's degree. My cousin Leah had received a master's degree and was behind the scenes promoting higher education and other educational opportunities. I was not aware of what was going on when I was a high school student, and my mother kept talking about the future. The only thing on my mind was band and my friends. I had a time of disconnect during the 80s and 90s. There were things occurring in the 80s that seemed old to me. I did not consider Leah old, but she did graduate from college in the 80s. I could relate to Sarah, because she and I graduated at the same time. I looked up to her and her sister Rebekah. I wanted to be like both. I idealized Sarah for her intellect and hard work. I liked Rebekah's drive and determination.

My father's sister, Naomi, completed her doctorate in 2006. By this time, I had my bachelor's and master's degrees and had an idea of how hard it was complete a doctoral program. I was so very proud that I had a PhD in my immediate family. I had medical doctors in my extended family who were my grandparent's nieces but not in my immediate family. I was ecstatic. Sarah finished her PhD two years later. This was interesting because I had been applying to graduate schools for the past two years. At that point, I knew it was attainable and still had not imagined being a PhD, even though I was applying and had two family members who had their PhD.

I know it is sounding like I was destined to be a PhD, but I still did not believe it. Life was happening all around me, and I was not very good at making selections. I was having problems in my personal relationships. These problems were trying to take me off course. Additionally, I am from an inner-city neighborhood, and although I had left my childhood environment, the environment did not leave me. At times, it felt like I was living multiple lives and I could not, or did not, know how to be educated and cool at the same time. So, I would act one way around a certain group of people and another way around another group. I never was into drugs, or alcohol, for that matter, but I did enjoy going out. The club scene caused some problems. My attitude at the nightclub caused me a lot of problems.

But, "Praise be to God," I had people who believed in me when I did not believe in myself. I am thankful for my father Joseph and my Aunt Ruth, who are no longer with me, for teaching me how to be strong and to "fight the good fight." I am especially thankful for my mother, Mary, for teaching me how to make wise decisions and how to be faithful. My mother was an active part in this entire process; praying for me throughout the journey was important. I must give thanks to my sister, Tamar, and brothers, Judah and Ruben, who are both my inspiration. Their decisions inspired me to want to do something about a system that is designed to see young and brow boys and girls fail. I must acknowledge my cousin Rebekah, who has been constantly on my mind during this process.

College Educational Experiences

Undergraduate

I believe that my first roadblock was in the first semester of my freshman year at Stephen F Austin (SFA) State University in Nacogdoches, Texas. I wanted to attend Jackson State University in Jackson, Mississippi, but my mother forbade me from attending. I remember her saying very distinctively that she would never subject her children to the racism in Mississippi. I was disappointed because I had a band scholarship to go to school in Mississippi. I am not sure if the fact of not attending Jackson State contributed to my drinking in Griffin Residence Hall with about five or six other female students. The reality of drinking alcohol was bad, but the marijuana smoking was worse. If I had not acknowledged the seriousness of what was happening to me and being pointed in a different direction, I would not be where I am today.

During the second semester of my freshmen year, my school bill came, I gave it to my mother. I had been in school for a semester and had not received a bill. When my mother received the bill, she immediately scheduled an appointment for us to meet with a financial aid counselor. At that point, I was introduced to student loans. During this time, after my first semester, I decided not to pursue chemistry as a major and had become an undecided major. So, the Welch Foundation Scholarship in Chemistry that I had when I first began college was no longer available because I changed majors. One of my consistent life struggles has been a lack of financial resources. During this time, I was not aware of the financial burden of college and my family's lack of financial resources. I graduated in the top 25 percent of my high school class. I did not realize my parents, my high school teachers, and counselors always promoted college but did not focus on getting financial assistance. The idea of college was always attainable. The conversation of cost never came up. All the college talks, without the cost discussion, led me to believe that I could afford it. I do believe that student loans were the sole reason that I could stay at SFA the spring of 1999, but at nineteen years of age, I did not understand how destructive educational loans could be.

When I began SFA August of 1998, I was on two scholarships: a freshmen leadership scholarship and a Welch Foundation Scholarship. I was well acquainted with the dean of Student Services, because a requirement of my leadership scholarship was to meet with the dean on a regular basis and discuss leadership-related issues. Of course, when the dean received notification from the campus police about the marijuana and alcohol, he knew exactly who I was. This behavior was so contradictory to what the leadership program was about. Yes, I was terribly embarrassed and humiliated but was spared; I received thirty days disciplinary probation for my campus drinking. I attended summer school at SFA but transferred to Texas Southern University (TSU) for my sophomore year of college. I think that it was important to state explicitly what led to my transfer. My transfer from SFA to TSU was not linked to the drinking incident, but it was due to my family's inability to pay the out-of-pocket expenses I was incurring at SFA.

When I began school at TSU after having a not one but two less-than-desirable experiences at SFA, I was a much more focused student. The two experiences I am referring to is one, the loss of my scholarship and needing to take out loans; and the other was my father had become ill. Initially, I thought my parents' insistent demand for me to return to Houston for college was due to bad decision making while away from home. Later to find out that the reason for my return was two-fold. The first reason was financial. The amount of money I was getting in scholarships, grants, and loans at SFA while still needing my parent's financial assistance was more than enough money at TSU. I did not have to live at home with my parents even though we were living in the same city. I did not have a vehicle in Nacogdoches, but I could have a car in Houston. I think the idea of having transportation was appealing. Plus, I was almost arrested more than one time in East Texas. My mother had a constant fear that something was going to happen to me in East Texas. I would always bring up Mississippi and her not allowing me to attend school there. I arrived at SFA in Nacogdoches in August 1998, three months after James Byrd Jr. had been slain less than seventy miles away in Jasper, Texas.

Racism in East Texas

The Black community was upset and wanted justice, but Black people in East Texas were injured because this was their community. The New Black Panther Party, the Nation of Islam, and other Black Nationalist, civil and human rights organizations were demonstrating. There was a need to send a message of intolerance for hate crimes to the larger public. The two perpetrators were apprehended and being prosecuted, but there was a need to have a public show of solidarity for the Byrd family and any other families who were victims of racist violence. There were also supremacy groups rallying in Nacogdoches. I had naively thought the Ku Klux Klan (KKK) had all died off. How misinformed I was. There were hooded and unhooded Klansmen, most unhooded. I had not witnessed such a public spectacle before in life. It was amazing, although there was this artificial fear present, based on what I had known from stories and history lessons about the KKK. When I told my mother about what I was witnessing, her advice was "Stay indoors; I do not want to have to kill one of them for messing with my child." I obeyed her and looked from my third-floor window at the demonstrators who occupied the streets and commercial parking lots of businesses in Nacogdoches.

Despite all the racial tension that were high in East Texas in 1998, that was not one of the reasons why I left SFA. As stated previously, I left East Texas was because my father was ill. I understood after I returned home that his health was his responsibility and there was nothing that I could say or do to make him make his physical health better. I could support him mentally but not physically. My father's wish was for me was to finish college, and he knew that being in Houston was a distraction, because it is home, and I could always find something else to do at home.

First Undergraduate Transfer – Texas Southern University

My father had his first massive stroke in September of 1999. I had just started my second year of college at TSU, and although I had been in school for year already, I was not considered a freshman because I had nine hours that did not transfer my freshmen leadership course, freshman orientation, and a developmental math was not accepted. I was not deterred or dismayed; I pressed on. My first semester, I took Biology and Political Science and tried to get my required courses out of the way. I had declared pre-pharmacy as a major, because this major I know is one TSU is known for. I excelled in both memberships, I decided against being a member of any sorority. I can remember vividly two Biology and Political Science classes and was asked to be a political science tutor. My biology professor took an interest in me and wanted me to join her sorority. I was, however, flattered by her offer and did go the interest meeting. After listening to the entire requirements, the Greek organizations were expressing interest in me, again, I declined both because I never considered myself a joiner.

Academics were easy for me at TSU. I am not sure if it was because of the Black educational agenda at TSU, my decision to get serious about school, or my parent's prayers that I get it together; I believe that it was these. One mistake that I made while at TSU and doing much better academically than I had while at SFA, I became involved in the nightclub life. When I was at SFA, I would go out to a club once or twice a month. I was poor and could not afford to go out. I was still poor at TSU, but I was getting a financial aid refund check that made me believe otherwise. My once or twice a month going out turned into four to five nights a week going. Several factors contributed to this besides the fact that I had the finances to go out. The main factor was there being way more opportunities to go out in Houston than in Nacogdoches. With my increased going out came increased drinking, underage drinking at that. I was not twenty-one in 1999. Bartenders did not care, I do not even think, that I was going to eighteen-and-up clubs. I was attracted to the twenty-one-and-up clubs. This was at a point in time when a female was not asking to provide identification to get into some clubs. I only went to clubs I knew I could get into.

From time to time, I would drive home drunk. I would always try to have a designated driver. Most of the time this was a roommate who was not a college student but a friend from high school. However, when she drank, I would have to drive us home. We would say stupid things like, "I am going to watch the yellow line, and you watch the curb, and we will get home in one piece"; as if running off the road was our only concern. I am so grateful that nothing ever happened to us and I am alive and free to tell my story. I stayed at TSU for one semester. My mother was not fond of the partying.

Military Exposure

My mother had a brother, Levi, who was in the military. He received a transfer from his duty station in Fort Sill, Oklahoma, as a master sergeant over a field artillery unit to a Reserve Officers' Training Corps (ROTC) instructor position at the University of Cincinnati (UC). When she found out where her brother was, I was on the first thing smoking to Ohio. My mother sat me down to have a conversation with me about moving to Ohio, and I was excited. The idea of moving out of the state was stimulating, and my thinking began to change about being away from home. I applied to UC, was accepted, but had to worry about paying out-of-state fees. My uncle, in all his wisdom, suggested that I join the Ohio National Guard to receive military scholarships to supplement my college costs. My mother did not like this idea. Her disdain was fueled by memories of conversations she had with my father about why he did not join the military and did not want his children to join. She adamantly opposed it. I knew that I needed to get out of Houston, so I decided to do it.

I flew to Ohio in December of 2000 to meet with an Army National Guard recruiter. I enlisted that day and was scheduled for basic training a few weeks later in January. My military occupational specialty (MOS) was a twelve Charlie a Bridge crewmember. I did not have a clue about what I was doing. I attended something called OSUT (One Station Unit Training). This is where the army combines basic training and job training into one single course. I thought this was going to be a great idea to complete twelve weeks of one training program opposed to ten weeks of basic and then complete four to six weeks of Advanced Individual Training (AIT), where I would learn the skills to perform my army job.

Until that, I was met with all kinds of adversity, the drill sergeants would be all over me for the littlest thing. If I looked a certain way, I mean that literally, if my eyes were a certain way, I was accused of having a bad attitude, and I had to do pushups. I struggled with the running portion of military training. I could run short distances, but I was not much of long-distance runner. The two-mile requirement was very difficult for me. I found myself in what they called the slow run group.

I would barely pass the physical fitness test. I told my mother about the difficulties and challenges that I was having, and she would always encourage me; she would send me Bible verses and pray for me. We would have extended talks about the disproportionate numbers of males to females in my platoon and the racial disparities. There were seven females max to fifty males. There were only three soldiers in the whole company. At one point, my battle buddy, Potiphar, decided to leave in the middle of the night, and I was blamed for that departure. I mean, we all had conversations about how much we hated the way that we were being treated and wanted to leave, but I never in a million years thought that she was planning her escape. I was so uninformed.

I made it through basic training, with the help of my First Sergeant. He kept the Drill Sergeants from being too hard on me. However, after Potiphar's AWOL, and the endless questioning, I grew tired and at one point I refused to answer any more questions. I mean if I am not going to be believed anyway then why keep talking. At that point, the Head Drill Sergeant said that my conduct was unbecoming of the Army way of life, and he was recycling me through basic training again. I refused to go through that process again and because I was enlisted in the National Guard. The state had authorized any extended stay, so they could not technically do that. I went to the National Guard Liaison who asked me a series of questions and requested that I take a physical fitness test, which I passed, and then she informed me that she was changing my enlisted status as a split option solider and I would be going home the next day.

Nothing had happened fast during my time in the army, but my release was swift, and before I knew it, I was on my way to Ohio. I still did not fully understand what had just occurred, but I knew someone who did. When I arrived in Ohio, I had a conversation with my uncle who explained to me what a split-option solider was. He explained that usually students elect this route to enter the military. They completed their basic training one summer, then the following summer they complete AIT. He went on to explain that I could avoid going back to complete AIT if I enrolled in ROTC in the Simultaneous Membership Program (SMP). Since I was already a member of the Army National Guard and enrolled at UC as a sophomore, I was eligible for ROTC and SMP. In the SMP, I would be a cadet serving in the Army National Guard and attend ROTC classes "simultaneously." That sounded good to me, anything to prevent me from going back to training.

Second Undergraduate Transfer – University of Cincinnati

I began my coursework as an undergraduate political science major. I had good experiences with lower-level political science courses, so I thought, *Why not, I would make a good attorney.* That was the only thing I thought I could do with a political science degree. Then I took a criminal law class that was offered by criminal justice professor, and that forever changed my mind. I fell in love with the idea of knowing more about crime, criminal behavior, and how society responds to this behavior. The criminal justice (CJ) department at the University of Cincinnati took the time to explain all the different occupations I could pursue with a CJ degree. I was provided information about the various law enforcement jobs, court workers, and correctional jobs.

I don't know if this was the first time this had ever happened or if this was the first time that I paid attention to what was happening. I attribute this moment of clarity to my military experience. Before going into the military, I knew racism was real, especially after what happened in East Texas. But experiencing discrimination because I am female, educated, and Black by employees of the United States military was an eye-opening experience. I did not want to believe the things that my mother and aunt told me that their father told to them about his sons and the military, but I lived it, and it is so very true. Now that I am member of the Ohio National Guard, I have state residency. I have a National Guard scholarship, an ROTC scholarship, and an academic scholarship, because I love criminal justice; I made the Dean's List every semester.

Good and Bad ROTC Experiences

However, I am still in a dimension of Hell. The ROTC faculty had the same attitude about me that their peers did. Despite doing well academically and fulfilling all the requirements of the ROTC and being in running for cadet leadership position based on my academic performance, the ROTC commander could not imagine me leading anything. This perception he had of me may have been influenced by my attire when it is not uniform day, or the way I put my hands on hip and point my finger when I am talking or because I asked questions about ROTC issues that did not make sense to me. One spring afternoon, on a non-uniform day, the ROTC commander, who was a lieutenant colonel, requested a meeting with me. I showed up for the meeting in my school clothes and not my military uniform, and he refused to meet with me because I was not dressed in uniform. At this point, I was becoming irritated, and I described that I was a college student and our meeting was not scheduled for an ROTC uniform day, so I would not be in uniform. The subsequent meeting was scheduled for a uniform day.

At the meeting, I was prepared because I had a bad feeling that the lieutenant colonel was up to no good. My uncle had been out of the office on official army business while these shenanigans were taking place. I was well prepared. He began the meeting with highlighting all my accomplishments and accolades over the past year or so. Then, he began to critique my physical performance on the two-mile run, which I never failed, but he pointed out that I barely made time. He went to criticize me in other personal ways that had nothing to do with my ROTC performance. Next, he followed with informing me that the department had ranked all the third-year students by overall academics, ROTC academics, physical fitness, and leadership capabilities, and I was at the top. And the way that it was looking, I had a good chance of being the cadet commander or the second-in-command. Finally, he concluded with a request that I take a physical fitness test to ensure that ranking was accurate. I agreed; he scheduled and administered the test himself. I took the test and beat any previous run time that I had previously.

At that point, despite passing and breaking my own record, I discovered I was fighting a losing battle. These people did not want me in the army, and I did not want to be there. I did some reflecting and understood that I was not losing, they were losing. I would no longer have the ROTC scholarship, but I was in the National Guard, and I still had my academic scholarships. I researched what I needed to do next to fulfill my National Guard split option requirement since I was about to resign from ROTC and would no longer be in the SMP program. That was when the heavens opened and poured down a blessing on me. I found out that the time requirement had expired for me to go back and complete AIT.

I called my mother first and told her the good news. She said that was great, but I needed to call my uncle first and let him know what I was about to do. I did and found out that the military had denied him E-9 rank as sergeant major. I was not surprised and felt bad for my uncle because he had given the army over twenty years of service. Ultimately, he supported my decision and told me he was only returning to Ohio to pack, because he decided that since he did not get promoted, he was retiring. His decision confirmed my decision to quit ROTC. I believe that our fate was tied, because the lieutenant colonel in the Military Science Department decided to meet when my uncle was away, and his evaluation as his commanding officer may have contributed to why he did not get the promotion. I graduated the following year with honors with a Bachelor of Science in criminal justice from the University of Cincinnati.

Graduate School

I had done so well the last two years of my undergraduate degree, my professor really encouraged me to go to graduate school, and that is what I did immediately following my first degree. I applied and accepted to UC's criminal justice master's degree program. A program that was designed to be a yearlong, it took me three years to finish the program. I started fall of 2003 and graduated spring of 2006. My first year was a real struggle. I had to work. I mean work; I was on a partial (80 percent) University Graduate Scholarship (UGS); this meant I had to take out financial aid for the other 20 percent and to live off. There was no way I could have worked any job and went to school. I was fortunate to be in a position where I did not have to punch a clock. Unfortunately, life interrupted my plans in other ways.

Life Struggles

My father received a terminal diagnosis in the spring of 2004. This disrupted my whole world. My thoughts were *Daddy, what do you mean you're dying?* I may have literally spoken those words and not just thought them when he told me that his doctors had given him two years to live. I decided and immediately returned to Houston. This time, the decision was not only affecting me, but I was engaged to be married and my fiancé, who was very supportive, was home in Ohio. We also had a dog. I had some novel idea about being a schoolteacher after seeing several promotions of the alternative teacher's certification program. It was a good idea in theory, but in practice, it did not work out as I had planned.

We arrived in Houston in August, and once we settled, I began the program. While I was enrolled in the certification program, I was technically a long-term substitute teacher, because I did not have the proper credentials to be a teacher. While I was in Houston, I was supposed to be assisting my mother with the care of my father. I was then assigned to a second-grade classroom in an elementary school. Because I was a second-grade teacher with a criminal justice background, behavior management was a concept I had mastered in my class. I had those second graders behaving better than fourth and fifth graders. Until a parent was displeased with the way that I was managing my classroom and requested a meeting with me and my principal. The outcome of meeting was in favor of the parent, and I was being transferred to a fourth-grade gifted and talented science classroom. I was pissed! I had worked with my students and now someone else was going to benefit from my hard work. Now I must learn a different group of students, and they had to teach me as well.

I began to research jobs and schools in Ohio. I reapplied for admission to UC's graduate school and applied to Northern Kentucky University (NKU). I decided that NKU was the quickest route to get me back to the Midwest.

NKU's Master of Public Administration program was an adult learner program, so most, if not all, of the classes were offered in the evening, and you could only take six hours a semester. I had the time and needed the money, so I found full-time employment. I found meaningful work working with adolescents. Ninety percent of my employment during my time at NKU and subsequent has been providing direct care, supervision, or therapeutic services to adolescents. I found this work to be especially rewarding with clients turning to me for leadership and help when I was not officially designated as their treatment provider. Seeing other treatment provider's clients, sometimes just to be a listening ear, had a very significant side effect when trying to pursue a graduate degree; precisely, I lost study time. Fortunately, budgeting time is one of my strengths. I was at the Children's Home forty hours a week; I provided services to a woman with Prader Willie Syndrome for fifteen hours a week; I stay enrolled in NKU and professional trainings, attended some Criminal Justice Society activities, and spent time with my family. With twenty-four hours in a day, six lost to sleep, and countless others lost to maintaining my household, aided by the needs of my significant other, this was no small task.

After living irrationally for eight months, I decided I needed some structure and some direction and followed up on the readmission request. I did not complete the program at NKU and left to return to UC. The graduate school granted me re-admissions and 60 percent scholarship in undergraduate studies (UGS), which meant that I still had to work two jobs. I changed jobs and supervised an adolescent residential independent living for two years while obtaining my master's degree from UC. There was some controversy surrounding my graduation. The Kentucky Cabinet for Health and Family Services, Child Protective Services Division, had an annual meeting for youth phasing out of the foster care system. At this meeting, youth were provided with information about education and vocation training, obtaining and maintaining employment, housing, and other self-sufficiency resources. This conference was taking place the weekend of my graduation, and my employer expected me to be present with our residents. My staff transported the residents there, and I attended the morning sessions for managers but left at lunch time. Word got back to my director, and I was once again having a meeting. The meeting did not go well. There was some conversations about how the administration knew I was graduating, also they knew about how I was to attend the entire annual meeting. I was faced with decision to leave this agency, so I left.

Work Experiences

I bounced back quickly. I had a master's and now two to three years of work experience. I had maintained two jobs. I held a position as a diversion therapist for the Children's Home of Northern Kentucky. I worked with a clinical team to provide comprehensive treatment to clients who were threatening out of home placement in the juvenile justice system through in-home education and therapy services on an individual and family basis. I provided direct care support to individuals with mental retardation or a developmental disability through the state of Ohio. My duties were supporting residents in living, learning, or working in their neighborhood and community while providing one-on-one support services to individuals living within their families. I was feeling like a work horse and unfulfilled. I grew homesick.

In January of 2007, my life changed but not my goals. I relocated to my native Houston, Texas, from Cincinnati, Ohio. I secured a six-month grant-funded position as a crisis counselor with Mental Health Mental Retardation Authority (MHMRA) of Harris County. I was responsible for providing mental health services and short-term interventions to individuals and groups experiencing psychological reactions to Hurricanes Katrina and Rita. I had these re-occurring feeings like I needed to make a difference in my current position. I was only helping people, and it was cool, but I was growing tired of doing for people what they could do for themselves. Once the grant ended, I spent the next five months preparing to return to school. That became the single most important activity in my life, and today, I am reminded of that; after considering attending graduate school for several months, I made the final decision to return to Ohio. I received a call about a clinical service provider position for the Talbert House Inc. and decided to work and put off going back to school once again. Since that decision, the doctorate school lose ends were constantly at the forefront of my mind.

I worked as a clinical service provider for about six months, then a clinical program grant coordinator position came available, and I had found joy again. As the grant coordinator, I led tasks relating to planning grant obligations for a collaborative of several female-servicing agencies. I spent time researching, organizing, and coordinating written communication and reports for internal and external review. I conducted literature reviews and needs analyses and devised implementation and sustainability plans for a gender-specific mentoring program and tracked outcomes. I was doing a job I enjoyed. I was inspired to return to school at that point; nothing was going to stop me from pursing my PhD. I had done a job for a year that was like what I'd be required to do as part of my dissertation requirements.

Doctoral Study

The transition to doctoral study made me realize my focus had primarily been on work and schooling experiences. However, what I think makes my story unique and interesting is the juxtaposition of my work, school experiences to my life experiences (familial and personal). It is the familial and personal experiences that influenced me to pursue my doctoral education. I am blessed to have women in my life that are risk takers, courageous, bold, and fearless, and these women do not let anything, or anyone, stop them from achieving their goals, especially not adversity. I have two very special women in family who already completed the PhD process, my aunt and my cousin, so they were role models and examples. But there are many others I could not have completed this process nor had any successes without the loving support, encouragement, and contributions of all my family members, specifically the women in my family.

University Choice

My mother's younger sister, Elizabeth, wrote me a letter of recommendation. I cannot believe I am admitting to this now. But when I was applying to graduate school, I applied to three schools the University of Cincinnati (UC), Sam Houston State University (SHSU), and Prairie View A&M (PV). All the schools had lengthy application processes, but the program I was applying to at PV was in the process of moving into their new building, and their mail kept getting lost, or that is what they told me. One of my professors from UC who had written me several letters of recommendation became frustrated with PV and told me that "it was not her fault that they keep losing them." She proceeded to tell me she would place five letters in my campus mailbox. This mailbox was in Ohio, and I was in Texas about to interview for the program at the time of the request. I began to worry, and I was having a conversation with my aunt, venting about my interview experience with PV, and she agreed to write as many letters as I needed or wanted. This act of kindness was admirable, and I know this is my mother's sister, and that is what families do; I chose to attend PV. I knew I wanted and needed to be near Houston. I had grown and matured in 2009 since I had last attended school in Houston ten years before, in 1999.

I began to see my mother's younger sister in a different light. I began to reflect on all our experiences and thought about how she was there for me during my first engagement. We had a lot of the long conversations about loss, lack, and perseverance. That dialogue was very therapeutic, and even though I knew I was on my way to doctoral school, I never realized until I sat down to write how all the little things I thought were trivial did matter and were working together for me to become a doctor of philosophy.

Experiences During Doctoral Work

Because I had entered the PhD program, my mind was made up to finish; failure was not an option. I had people praying for me when I was not able to pray for myself. I had already relocated to Houston three times. I heard somewhere that the third time was a charm. The beginning of the program was a culture shock. I had grown accustom to the UC and their way of educating. Campus life was a difficult process to adjust to. The way students conduct themselves on a Historically Black College and University (HBCU) campus was very different from the predominantly institution. The comradery the students shared was something that I was not familiar with. My cohort was very close, and I was apprehensive about their intentions and motivations. You see, I came from a place that was very competitive. Students were always competing for assistantships, scholarships, grant funding, and faculty mentorship.

I wanted to quit. I felt so different from the other students, and although I was learning, growing, and developing, I just did not feel like I fit in for the first six to eight weeks. I went home every day and told my mother (because I was living at home again), "Today was my last day; I am not going back tomorrow." She would ask me, "Well, if you are not going back to school tomorrow, why are you studying?" We both knew that I was not being honest with myself. The adjustment process made me uncomfortable, but I loved learning, and the more I more read and learned, the more I wanted to know. I particularly appreciated my experience as the grant coordinator at the Talbert House and what I learned about gender and females in criminal justice. Because females are met with opposition or looked at as helpless, I despised both perspectives and began to think about my female family members, friends, and, most importantly, myself and our experiences with the legal system and every paper I wrote for every class I took that required a paper was written for a gender-specific purpose. When I completed my course work, my dissertation proposal was almost complete. I had identified a problem, considered the theoretical implications of the issue, and knew exactly how I wanted to investigate the problem.

Another Financial Roadblock

I am at the end of PhD coursework and have already begun to work on my dissertation prospectus; I was once again faced with financial burdens of funding my own education. I made this discovery my last semester of coursework. I had one class left that was I was planning to take over the summer while I studied for my comprehensive exam. When I began the doctorate program in juvenile justice, I was awarded a graduate assistantship, which involved twenty hours of research duties or teaching duties. No other financial assistance was made available through the university, so I took out more federal financial aid loans to pay for my tuition. At that point, I had taken out a total of $152,195 in student loans.

I have almost reached the federal student aid maximum as shown above. The little financial assistance I received from PV from the graduate assistantship was ending once I completed my coursework. My fear was, if I did not get financial help, I was not going to be able to finish my PhD program. It was already difficult enough to try maintaining coursework obligations, research duties, teaching responsibilities, and service without any family support, school support, scholarships, or grants. And to think about attempting theses task while trying to work a job to pay for my education and bills was almost incomprehensible.

However, I had to do what I had to do. I first started working for The Change Institute Center as a contract program counselor. I was responsible for collecting information about the clients from referral sources, conducting interviews and assessments, and making treatment recommendations. Another aspect of my job was counseling clients, individually or in group sessions, to assist in overcoming dependencies, adjusting to life, and making changes. I found this work fulfilling, and because it was a contract position, I could work when I it was convenient for my academic schedule. Of course, I still had to make some real money, because having a job that you work at your convenience was not very lucrative.

I then pursued employment with Riverside General Hospital, Houston Recovery Campus (HRC) as the outpatient program lead counselor. While I was at HRC, I managed a hospital-based outpatient treatment program for substance abusing clients. I also developed a relationship with the adolescent program manager, and he agreed to support me with collecting my dissertation data. I could make money and pay my school bill.

Married Life While Pursuing my Dissertation

My marriage, which came at the very end of my PhD journey, was both a good and bad experience. It was only bad because the marriage ended. It was great because it gave me my wonderful daughter who has taught me so much about life. I had been out of a bad relationship for about five months when I met a man. I was not trying to meet a man, but nonetheless, I met a man. A tall man, a very charismatic man, who was passionate and said all the right things when he spoke. He was supposed to be dating one of my friends. I was dating someone else at the time we met. After we went on a double date, I liked him, and he liked me, so we pursued each other. Now, we did let the other individuals we were involved with know that we were no longer interested in them. When I think about it now, that relationship was doomed from the beginning, but I pursued it anyway.

My mother, in all her wisdom, would occasionally ask me questions like "What do you know about this man?" "Who are his people?" or "Where he is from?" I could answer these questions only on the surface or superficially, not in depth. I knew just enough about him to keep my mother wrath's off my relationship. I met my husband the last semester of PhD coursework. I would spend a lot of hours at school in and out of class. I burned the midnight oil almost daily. I would stay on campus most nights until 1 a.m. Since we were only dating, he did not voice his discomfort with my long school hours. After about a month of dating, he began to ask questions like "Don't you think being out after midnight is a little late for a single female?" I would always reply with my commitment to my academics and eventually agreed that I would shut things down at midnight and head home.

This was a huge sacrifice, because I was in another relationship when I started the PhD program, and he had concerns about my long hours. I would dismiss his concerns because I knew this was only a temporary obligation. Whenever I would have school-related travel, I would always take my mother or the person I was in a committed relationship with. When I was in a relationship, I would take my significant other. When I was out of a relationship, I would take my mother. My rationale was simple. I was thinking, at that time, I spent so much time at school working, and now I have school-related travel, let me show this person what all that hard work was for. I do not think they got the point. My mother, of course, she did, but those men, no way.

Eventually, Simon asked me to marry him, and I said yes. Shortly after the proposal, I found out I was pregnant. I was so happy to know I was having a baby with a man I loved and who loved me. My pregnancy was very difficult, and there was some contention about what I should and should not be doing while pregnant. Initially, we were planning an October wedding, but at some point, we decided to push the wedding up to June so that the baby would not be born out of wedlock (I guess having a baby will give you a sense of morals temporarily). We had a wedding in June, and the baby came the next month, in July.

I was supposed to defend my dissertation prospectus in August, a month after having the baby. I want you to understand that while I am growing a baby, planning a wedding, catering to my future husband's needs, I was still writing my dissertation proposal. However, I finished the process, and I give thanks and partial credit to my ex-husband for traveling the last leg of the PhD road with me. There were hills and valleys along the way, and he suffered in silence while I spent every spare moment studying or writing. He taught me a very important lesson, and that is to always be positive and smile in the face of adversity.

Motherhood

I had a difficult pregnancy and suffered a stroke a week after giving birth to my daughter, Jabez. However, I still completed my dissertation while recovering from a stroke, which was induced by perinatal hypertension." I had done the hard work first, completed the study, I just had to analyze the results. My child became my inspiration. I wanted to her to know that all that I went through to get her into this world was not in vain. I was not a quitter, although

I had quit other jobs and projects in the past. I defended my proposal six months after my stroke, and my dissertation defense was three months after that. I am proud of my dissertation, titled "Gendered pathways: An investigation of juvenile females' path to delinquency."

University Politics

Unfortunately, I missed the graduation application deadline due to the accelerated pace of my two defenses. I had to appeal to PV to allow me to graduate due to extenuating circumstances that prevented me from meeting the January 30th extended deadline. The department chair had informed me that I had missed that deadline when she did not see my name on the list for degree audits for students that she submits to the dean for approval. This list was only the students who made the graduation application deadline. I began my appeal plea. I informed PV of the reasons why they should grant my appeal for May graduation. I had documentation from Methodist Hospital, Herman Hospital Rehab, and I could have provided a letter from my neurologist if needed. They agreed, and I graduated with my PhD in juvenile justice from Prairie View A&M University.

• • •

CHAPTER 11

Dr. Wanda Goodnough

Government

Dr. Wanda Goodnough has worked for the government of the United States, located in Macomb County, Michigan. She been employed for nineteen years. Currently, she is the food service director and has worked in her field for forty years. Currently, she is retired and still working for the government, and actively looking for a new career.

CREDENTIALS:

- PhD in Organizational Management & Leadership, *Ashford University*
- MHA in Healthcare Administration, *Ashford University*
- BHA in Healthcare Administration, *Ashford University*
- AAD in Food Management, *Macomb Community College*

The function of education is to teach one to think intensively and to think critically. Intelligence plus character — that is the goal of true education.
~ *Martin Luther King, Jr.*

Education is our passport to the future, for tomorrow belongs to the people who prepare for it today.
~ *Malcolm X*

***Disclaimer:** The stories in this chapter reflect the author's recollection of events. Some names, locations, and identifying characteristics have been changed to protect the privacy of those depicted. Dialogue has been re-created from the author's memory.

My Journey Through the Ivory Tower

Growing Up and Family Background

I was born on 6 June 1966 in Mount Clemens, Michigan. Both my parents were nineteen-year-olds, and they had been married for about two years when they had my brother. Later, they divorced when I was two years old, and my brother was one year old. My mother moved to California, and my dad soon followed. After they left, my grandparents obtained custody of my brother and me.

My grandmother was working as a nurse for thirty years, and my grandfather was working in the foundry for thirty years. My grandparents were very kind to me: my grandfather spoiled me rotten, and my grandmother and great-grandmother taught me how to become a young lady. I think my brother and I experienced the perfect childhood, although there were only a few close friends to have much fun together. Please understand that my grandparents wanted us to stay focused on learning, and they paid much attention to our education. So, there was not much time for play.

On Sunday evenings, we usually attended a Sunday school at the church where we had a choir rehearsal. On Wednesdays, we had to sing in the choir with the youth group, and we just hated this day. However, my grandparents did not want to hear any excuses from us. Thus, we attended church every Sunday, and we had to sit next to a particular woman. I should say, she was the meanest lady I have ever met, and she would pinch my brother and me if we made a sound while there was a church service. If I told my grandmother about that lady, her response would be "Well, you should sit still during the service in the church." As a result, I just cringed every time that woman came near me. I thought the years would lighten that woman's demeanor, but it appeared as though it became even worse. Therefore, I was grateful when my grandmother stopped attending that church, but my grandfather continued to visit it. Now I am sure that my grandfather would spoil me to death, and my grandmother would pamper my brother. We had grandparents who loved us, cared for us, and made sure that we were always well-mannered toward our elders.

They had been married for about sixteen years when they decided to divorce, and my brother and I stayed with my grandmother. For the most part, things seemed to be useful, but my grandfather remarried, and my grandmother did not. Instead, she concentrated on education, and she had to find several jobs after the divorce. Recalling their careers, I should state that my grandmother loved to help others while working in the healthcare field. In his turn, my grandfather started to work right after high school. He tried to help anyone as long as he or she treated him with respect.

Furthermore, my grandmother always loved baking, sewing, and crocheting for others. Thus, my grandmother made the most beautiful blankets. If she liked you, she would ask you about your favorite color, and within a week, you would have a handmade quilt with all your favorite colors in it. I still have the one she made for me. My grandfather was an excellent cook, and he made the best biscuits in our town. Still, the topper was my grandmother's homemade rum cake. I should accentuate here that my grandparents meant, and mean, the world to me. My grandmother played a huge part in my life. She died in 2016, and I miss her dearly. Fortunately, my grandfather is still very much alive.

I must say a few more words about the women in my family. My grandmother was a force to be reckoned with, and she and my great-grandmother are the spiritual backbone of our family. My great-grandmother worked a lot in her life, but she never attended a college or even a school. As I understand, from many conversations with the grandmother, my great-grandmother's grandmother was a slave who always influenced the path of influential women in my family. In the situation of having no opportunities for African American people in the South, many of them migrated to the North to find jobs to support their families. So, Black families had no jobs, education, and money to help their close people.

I remember that when my dad came home from Vietnam, the federal government he served for did not provide help for African American veterans. So, my dad had to find any job, and I remember him telling me he had to clean ovens and cut grass, among other odd jobs. The period was in the 1960s, when the Vietnam War took its significant toll on many families, especially Black families. My dad told me he had to decide with his life, so he thought long and hard about what was needed for him to move forward. As a result, he enrolled in a community college along with my grandmother, but they had separate majors. I was so proud of both of them, and as a young girl, I observed how incredible people pushed to pass the status quo. Thus, my grandmother was one of the two African American women to graduate in her class. My dad had quite a few African American people in his graduating class, which was probably the result of the Vietnam War.

I have had such remarkable role models in my life, such as my grandparents. I should state, they provided my brother and me with all the tools we needed to excel in school. All we had to do was receive good grades, be respectful, and mind our manners. Nevertheless, at first, attending a school was somewhat challenging for me. Although my grandparents loved us and believed in our success, I still do not think I was smart enough to receive good grades.

Furthermore, I always thought I was not smart. I knew I could learn to do my best, but it was not enough to earn a degree. I saw how my grandmother and my dad worked hard, and I noticed that my grandmother received rather high grades. However, my dad told me he did not receive good grades. So, I thought that might be my case as well. However, I wanted my family to be proud of me. Thus, I was the first in my family to graduate from high school. I received a full-ride scholarship to Tennessee State University. I was so proud of myself, but I still had some strange feeling in my stomach. I understood that I was going to college, but what subject would be my major? I was clueless, and the only thing I could be good at was cooking. I picked that up from my family. Since I was very good at it, I thought I might obtain a degree in food administration. Besides, what else could I do? So, I had plans to attend college in the fall, but instead of furthering my education, I had my son. It took me forever to return to school. I had two jobs, and that made me exhausted, and the pay was not that great. I needed to return to school, and my son was eight years old by the time I made my decision. I was a nervous wreck: how could I do this with an eight-year-old child? However, I had a support system, and my grandmother and a few friends would help me with my son.

I was very proud to enroll in college, as I knew this was the only way I could take care of my son and myself. It took me six years to obtain my first degree; that was in food administration. The second degree in healthcare administration, BHA, was acquired in two years because I switched majors. The third degree in healthcare administration, MHA, took me one year. Moreover, my, probably, last degree, PhD, took me six years.

I have worked in the foodservice industry for over forty years, and nineteen of those years were associated with working for the government with little or no upward movement. Thus, I tried to obtain a new position in upper management. Still, it took me over eighteen years to earn a place in mid-level management. The result of the situation for me to receive a mid-level management position was in the fact that the previous director left the department. Nevertheless, Human Resources preferred to pay me less money in comparison to the former director. When I did receive an interview, I was praised for obtaining a few degrees but was not moved or promoted when working for the government.

Most members of the top management team were males, and the rest were white females. Accordingly, there is only 1 percent of African American women in upper management. My experience of working there , was nothing less than awful, and at times, it was downright painful to work there. Yes, it was my job, but I wanted to develop my career, and that was not going to happen when working for the government.

College Experience

As I stated earlier, I was the first in my family to receive a high school diploma and the first to attend college. My educational journey began in December 1996. My son was eight years old, and I liked the classes I took. Thus, once I knew that I was capable of learning, I understood that everything was possible.

After I had obtained my first degree, I could not land a job in management. So, I began my educational journey taking psychology courses, not knowing what I wanted to do with the classes. I loved helping people, but I was so confused about what I wanted to do with my life. I decided to go to the local college, which people chose when they did not know what they wanted to do with their lives. After I had obtained my first degree, I worked a lot, and I thought I liked my job, but it was not enough for me. I wanted to develop a real career that would help me take care of my son and myself. I wanted comparably high compensation that could be higher than the minimum wage.

After working for a long time in the healthcare industry, my boss asked me what I was going to do with my degree. I said I would prefer to work in management and not just middle management. I wanted to obtain a position in upper management. Well, I should say that never happened, at least in the healthcare industry. I tried to apply for several jobs to receive management experience, and no one would give me the chance. So, I continued my educational journey, and once, I thought I wanted to be a social worker.

I had a conversation with my dad, and he said, "My little girl, are you going to pursue those kinds of degree? You need to work on your PhD." When I asked why, he told me, "Well, an average person has a bachelor's degree. So, this degree is just the same as an associate degree." I thought, *Oh, no! Not this girl! That was a way too much work.* My dad said that it was the only way I was going to be able to move around. At that time, my classmates were addressing me as Dr. Goodnough. I just smiled and laughed. I thought, *Could I obtain a PhD in my life? Was I up enough for the challenge?*

So, I continued my educational journey with social work classes, keeping the idea about a PhD degree in the back of my mind. My grades were ending, and I thought if I became a social worker, I would gain a new career to equate to my degree. Yes, I wanted to earn more money.

After searching for information about social workers' salary, I switched my degree path. I changed it to healthcare while thinking I would surely be able to obtain an upper management position. After receiving my BHA and MHA, I knew I was ready for a perfect career. Thus, I put on my "job search hat" and began applying for jobs; I also had my resume professionally written several times. Now I was prepared to go. So, I started to apply for jobs in 2010, eleven years later.

I was still working for the government with no lateral movement toward my dream career. I applied for quite a few jobs with some interviews within the government or anyone else. After working for the government for nineteen years, which feels hopeless, but not discouraged, I understand I need to be related to someone or know someone to move into upper management. I have just completed for a fourth degree my (PhD), and I am applying for jobs like crazy to start a new career.

Doctoral Studies

In 2013 I first thought about obtaining my PhD degree. I had applied for many positions, and I still had no interviews. So, I decided to enter the University of Rockies (now Ashford University). They offered the online form or education, and I obtained my bachelor, masters, and, currently, my PhD studying online. The courses were set up for seven days a week, and students had to log in every Tuesday before midnight. Also, we had to respond to two of our classmates and their posts and write papers.

When I began to study at an online university, it was a different experience for me. I was not ready for that process, but over time, I became well versed in an online setting. I knew when this journey started that I would need a person of color on my side. I wanted to make sure that I understood the process from the beginning to the end. The university I attended was a predominantly institution. Thus, I tried to find like-minded people and participated in the Black Doctoral Networking Conference held in Atlanta, Georgia. The conference was organized to inform people of color, men and women, scholars, educators, and all newcomers.

I did not have a mentor for my dissertation process. At least, not at the beginning of the dissertation courses. However, in the end, I asked my professor to become my chair for the committee. I asked him to help me earlier during our coursework at the beginning of the program. I did not receive a response until we had only two classes left for the program. So, I asked again, and he finally said he would be my dissertation chair.

I was happy about the process that was going to take place. I was ready for what would come. I had my research questions, interview questions, and the population I wanted to interview. I thought my topic was tremendous and could add to theory, research, and practice.

During one of the sessions, I attended with a new associate, we came across a scholar in his own right, Dr. Miles. The new associate made some comments about this scholar's professionalism, so I decided to use my chance and went over and introduced myself. I thought he would say no. I explained to him that I needed a mentor and asked if he would be interested in working on my committee. Still, he politely responded yes, stating that he likes to help women of color become successful.

My project was six years long, and Dr. Miles helped me with every step of that way. My chair dropped in every once in a while. He was assisting several women in obtaining their degree. With his help, I was ahead of my classmates, and I was thrilled working on this project. I worked hard, and I cannot tell you how many revisions there were from the beginning to the end.

Moving forward, I graduated in October 2019. I honestly thought that when I had this degree, employers would come knocking at my door. This experience has been truly amazing, and I believe I would repeat it all over again. Still, the hardest part is, with all this education, no one wants to hire you if you are Brown or Black.

I stated earlier that the interviewing process is always enjoyable. Human Resource managers review my resume and all my education degrees and experience, and they interview me to find out I can speak well. I am hardworking, organized, and I am an aforethought thinker. Nevertheless, that appears not to be enough when being interviewed for a new career. Overall, this process has taught me a few things: demonstrate patience, listen, and read as you have never read before!

Trying to gain a new career is extremely challenging. I have had a few interviews, and my current employer does not promote Black people to top management positions. The majority of the lower-level jobs are given to or black people. All the upper management positions are delegated Caucasian people with less education or no education. I know it is time for me to move on.

Post-Graduation Reflections

There are no employers who are enthusiastic about hiring me. I am very confident with all my degrees, knowledge, and skills that someone will want to employ me. Indeed, after receiving a PhD degree, I should be employable. Therefore, these aspects will not become barriers to developing my career in the future. The problem is that many other obstacles can prevent me from obtaining managerial positions. I think there will be more situations when I will need to prove my skills because of the color of my skin.

I understand I have done almost everything possible to develop the career of my dream and make my family proud of my success as a professional. I believe that now I am on the right path in my life, and I am looking forward to positive changes in my career. Furthermore, I am sure that all this experience with obtaining my doctorate is not in vain. Further, I take directions by the Creator, and I will receive my chance to realize my potential in the nearest future.

• • •

CHAPTER 12

Dr. D. Anthony Miles

CEO and Founder, Miles Development Industries Corporation

BIOGRAPHY

Dr. D. Anthony Miles is a serial entrepreneur, award-winning researcher, award-winning professor, statistician, legal expert witness, business expert and best-selling author. Dr. Miles is a nationally known startup and marketing expert and forensic marketing expert. He is CEO and founder of Miles Development Industries Corporation, a consulting practice and venture capital acquisition firm. He is also host and executive producer of a nationally syndicated radio podcast show, *Game On Business Talk*. He has presented his research at conferences around the country. Most notably, he has presented at Stanford University. He was invited to Harvard University by the Harvard Business School.

Dr. Miles has been a business subject matter expert who has been featured on nationally syndicated media such as ABC News, CBS News, Fox News, NBC News, and CNN, as well as in *Huffington Post, Forbes*, and *Reader's Digest* and on Bloomberg Radio, BlogTalkRadio, WGN radio in Chicago, iHeart Radio, AM/FM radio, and numerous others. He is an author and researcher who is well published in numerous academic journals. He is a best-selling author of three books, including *Risk Factors and Business Models* and *Entrepreneurship and Risk*. His latest book, *How to Get Away with Murder in Marketing: Forensic Marketing*, is creating a buzz and set to be another bestseller.

He has won numerous awards for his applied statistics research in marketing and economics. He is a twenty-one-time winner of the Academy of Business Research Conference's *Award for Best Paper* in Marketing and Economics. He was inducted into *Marquis Who's Who in America* and is a member of the American Statistical Association. In 2010, he won the Teaching Excellence Award from the Texas A&M University System Board of Regents, as one of the top 25 percent of participating faculty in eleven universities in the A&M system. In 2009, he won a United States Association of Small Business and Entrepreneurship Doctoral Consortium fellowship for his doctoral research.

He was selected as one of seventeen distinguished doctoral researchers nationwide in the field of entrepreneurship. In 2002, he was inducted into the Delta Mu Delta National Business Honor Society and Fraternity.

CREDENTIALS:

- PhD in Entrepreneurship and Business, *University of the Incarnate Word*
- MBA in International Business and Marketing, *Our Lady of the Lake University*
- BBA in Marketing, *University of Texas at San Antonio*

"You can't break me 'cuz you didn't make me."
~ Ruben "Hurricane" Carter

***Disclaimer:** The stories in this chapter reflect the author's recollection of events. Some names, locations, and identifying characteristics have been changed to protect the privacy of those depicted. Dialogue has been re-created from the author's memory.

Journey Through the Ivory Tower

Growing Up and Family Background

I was born and reared in San Antonio, Texas. I am the oldest of four children. My mother is Bettye Miles, and my father is Winston Miles. My father did not live with us, but I saw my father nearly every day. I grew up in a middle-class family. I grew up in a traditional family and had a normal childhood. I had four siblings (two girls and two boys) in our family. I was the oldest male in the family. We were neither affluent nor wealthy by any means. My mother was a purchasing agent for an automobile manufacturer. My father was an assistant principal at a middle school. My father graduated with a bachelor's degree from St. Mary's University and a master's degree from Prairie View University. My mother graduated with an associate degree in business from St. Philip's College.

My upbringing was strict. My father was a strong disciplinarian. So was my mother, maybe too strict. Reflecting on my childhood, I think my parents may have been too hard on me. They were harder on me than the rest of my younger siblings because I was the oldest.

My parents were good parents but, again, sometimes too strict. I remember getting spankings for everything. My mother was a loving mother but not touchy-feely. My mother did not cry easily, hug, or kiss. She was somewhat aloof. If I got hurt, my mother would not hug and kiss me; she'd say, "Stop crying about it and take care of it." That is just the way she was, I guess. My mother was like a tomboy to me. She is very competitive.

I remember being closer to my mother's side of the family. My mother's family was female dominated. All of the women on my mother's side of the family were Alpha Females. The women pretty much ran the family. All of the women in my mother's family were strong Black women. I think their strength caused them many marital problems. My grandmother was a strong woman. She was the alpha female matriarch that led my mother's side of the family. I think she passed many of her traits to my mother. The women in my mother's family were all divorced and by themselves or had a male friend. For some reason, I thought that was odd when I was a kid. My Uncle Julian (my grandmother's brother) was literally the only man in family. Also, my Uncle Sam (my grandmother's son) was the only male in the family on my mother's side of the family. My Uncle Sam (aka Sammy Joe) took care of my grandmother until she passed away. His role was to take care of her which he took seriously. I am forever thankful to him.

On the other hand, my father's side of the family was the complete opposite. My father's side of the family was male dominated. The men on my father's side were all Alpha Males. My grandfather was a former Negro League baseball player, John "Mule" Miles. He was the alpha male patriarch that led my father's side of the family. He was also an aircraft mechanic with the famous Tuskegee Airmen. Although my grandfather did not graduate from college, he made sure that three of his sons earned a degree. My grandfather was a kind, funny, laidback, and smart man. I was actually close to my grandfather until he passed away. He was like my buddy. My memory of my grandmother is that she was a happy and cheerful woman. I remember her smiling all the time, particularly when she saw me. I do not remember much else about her. She passed away when I was about five or six years old. On one particular visit, I remember going over to my grandparents' house and watching the *Ed Sullivan Show*. During another visit, the movie *A Hard Day's Night*, starring the Beatles, came on TV. I freaked out at who they were. It is funny, you should never underestimate the recollection of a child.

The Red Squirrel

I had some touching moments as a child, but I also had some tragic ones as well. I remember, while in the second grade, my teacher thought that I was a bit too slow for her class. The teacher passed out this paper with an illustration of a squirrel. We had to color the picture of the squirrel. Now, we all know that squirrels are brown. However, on this particular day, there were not any brown crayons in the crayon box. I could not find a single brown crayon to be found in the classroom. I think the rest of class took the brown crayons. So, just to finish the assignment, I colored the squirrel with a red crayon. This teacher asked me why I chose that color. I told her there were no more brown crayons. Due to my response, and maybe because of some other things, she assumed I had a learning disability. Next thing I knew, they put me in a slow class while I was in the second grade. In my opinion, she should not have been allowed to assess a student's cognitive abilities until that student was properly certified by an educational diagnostician. While I was growing up, in the 1970s, there were a lot of White teachers that did those kinds of things. The tragedy here is that it was a black teacher that did this to me. As a result, Black children, especially Black boys, were routinely and needlessly placed in special education courses.

During that time, there were always teachers who believed it was their duty to place Black boys in slow classes. Reflecting on this, I was not slow; I just had a different style of learning. This incident caused my self-esteem to suffer. As a result, I think this contributed to me being an average student and not doing my best in school. I was an average student in elementary school because I began to get bored with school. The rote method of teaching and learning did not resonate with me. My learning style did not match with the teaching style primarily used in elementary school, so I was just average. School was just boring to me. My genius as a child was not captured in elementary school, middle school or high school. Many years later, I researched this phenomenon during my doctoral studies and post-doctoral studies. I read three groundbreaking books I read on this topic. The first book was Dr. Howard Gardner's *Frames of the Mind: The Theory of Multiple Intelligences.* The second book was Dr. Robert Sternberg's *Successful Intelligence*. The last book was Dr. Craig Wrights' *The Hidden Habits of Genius: Beyond Talent, IQ, and Grit - Unlocking the Secrets of Greatness*. We have a significant number of teachers who overemphasize academic and analytical intelligence but do not stress enough of creative intelligence. Intelligence is complex, and it is difficult to make an assessment about a child's cognitive abilities based on examining one dimension of intelligence. Often, schools have the tendency to measure only analytical intelligence. This is supported by television shows for children when I was growing up. That is why some children like the PBS television show, *Sesame Street*, while other children prefer the other PBS show, *Mr. Rodgers Neighborhood.*

During my formative school years (K-12), I developed an interest in sports. This interest came from my father's side of the family. My father's side of the family were athletes. My father was a standout basketball player in both high school and college. He was a basketball star at the old Wheatley High School in San Antonio, Texas. It was a predominately Black high school. My father received an athletic scholarship to St. Mary's University and played with the legendary Buddy Meyer. He used to tell us about the athletes he played against in college. Some of them included Elgin Baylor, Zelmo Beatty, and others who ended up playing in the National Basketball Association. I found out later that my father actually turned down contracts with the Boston Celtics and Philadelphia 76ers in order to care for my grandmother, who, at the time, was very sick and dying. My father and grandfather were both great athletes. However, I did not have their talent. I was an average athlete. It put a lot of pressure on me in school, as I was always being compared to my father. It was very discouraging for me. To follow in your father's footsteps is difficult. It got so bad, I eventually quit playing sports. One of the many things my father used to tell me was that he preferred I be a scholar rather than an athlete. I never quite understood why he frequently repeated that message. Recently, St. Mary's university retired my father's number and put him in the hall of fame at the university. Myself and my grandfather had to accept the award and honor for my father at halftime during a game at the university. It was a great honor for our family.

While in kindergarten, I remembered the day Dr. Martin Luther King died. I will never forget that day as long as I live. That was in 1968. It was a strange time. I remember the day of the funeral. It was an odd day at school, and it was cloudy. I remember there was just something wrong in the atmosphere at school. It was something that I will never forget. It was like time stood still. My parents always preached education. My dad was a coach, teacher, and administrator. He was always on my case about studying and grades because he was employed with San Antonio Independent School District. He would get our grades before we did. That, too, was hard for me, because I was an average student.

Bad Advice from a Black High School Counselor

I went to an all-Black high school. I never wanted to go to college because I did not think I was good enough. This thought was reinforced by a Black academic counselor who told me I was not college material. The worse part of this experience was this counselor was actually a friend of my father. I never told my parents about this incident. Since my father was a middle school principal, he knew all of the other principals and administrators around the school district. I knew if I told my parents, they would have been angry and confronted this counselor. Luckily, in spite of this counselor's dire warnings, my father made me go to college. One day, he picked me up and took me to St. Philip's College, a community college. Once there, he told me to register. If it were not for my father, I would have never gone to college. While my parents wanted us to go to college, they could not afford to pay tuition for all of us. At that time, there were four of us starting college. My father told me I would have to pay my own tuition. Fortunately, I had a job at a local large grocery store chain in the San Antonio area. So, my salary paid for my tuition and books. Also, I was able to live at home since my mother told me as long as I was going to college, she would not charge me any rent. Thus, I sent myself to college. It was a very hard time.

I will be forever grateful to my father for that day at St. Philip's. He used to tell me I could do anything if I put my mind to it. He said he had paved the way for me. Also, he shared his experiences at St. Mary's University. He talked a lot about the racism he experienced while at the private, Catholic university. Once he told me about a White professor who had accused him of cheating on an exam because he got the highest grade in the class. This professor told him point-blank, "Negros don't make A's in my class." Then the professor made him retake the exam! My father was so furious. So, he retook the exam and got a higher grade than he did on the first test.

He used to tell me I did not have the right to be average or mediocre. He said he always had to be smarter, because many White professors believed that Black males, and especially Black athletes, were dumb. That story resonated with me for a long time. He said that you always have to be the BEST! My father's stories of what he went through at St. Mary's University were riveting. He always talked about being treated differently because he was Black. He never wanted those experiences to happen to his children. My father was the first in the Miles family to graduate from college. Then he was also the first to get a master's degree. In fact, he had two graduate degrees. My father always told us we could do anything if we worked and studied hard.

Character-Building Time: Putting Myself through College

While attending St. Philip's College, I worked at grocery store. It is a large grocery chain based in Texas. I started as a bag boy and worked my way up to general merchandise, grocery, and produce. I worked in nearly every department at the store level. While working at the grocery story, I experienced a considerable amount of racial prejudice. Since my background before then was restricted to my life experiences in the African American community, this was a rude awakening. I encountered many managers had either never worked with Blacks or had limited contact with them. White males, by far, were the worst. It seemed there was something in their sociological development that affected their mental dynamics and caused them to display racist behavioral characteristics. Their interaction with people of color at the grocery store was historically racial and condescending. At that time, it was a common pattern at the store to promote a new White manager and place them in a store in a low-income community. First, these young White managers would automatically harass Black employees. This happened to me on many occasions. It happened so many times. Racist behaviors were also displayed by Hispanic managers. It was as though they were trying to make a point with Black employees. These behaviors reminded me of how a slave master treated his slaves, as in *I will show them who's in charge*. I saw this often in my career. New bosses immediately confront black employees to let them know who's boss.

While there were many incidents that gave me a wake-up call, one incident in particular, resonated with me vividly. I used to work in the produce department while I was working at the grocery store. A new White male store director was assigned to the store. His name was James Hall, and I disliked him immediately. He exhibited a similar pattern of harassment by picking on me and letting me know that he was in charge. He always had something critical or negative to say to me in every encounter I had with him. It always seemed that he interacted differently with Black and non-Black employees. He was always picking on me for trivial things, and there was nothing I could do about it because I needed this job to pay my way through college. There were many days I wanted to quit. It was one of the worst times in my life.

Black History and Watermelons: Dealing with Racism at the Workplace

One day, while I was working, James Hall was in my area talking with my manager Hector Morales. When I walked by, Hall told my manager that I was a "connoisseur of watermelons." I guess he was trying to be funny by making a joke. My manager neither smiled nor laughed. I just looked at him. I wanted to kill that SOB. His racial wisecracks were frequent. During another incident, Hall told my manager to tell me if I had made a mistake or screwed up on a transfer order that was done with another store, he was "going to make Black history out of me."

I hated this SOB beyond infinity. If he were comfortable saying such things to my face, what do you think he was saying behind my back? It seemed like life stood still during that time. I think I left my body. I wanted to beat him senseless. The company had the temerity to put a moron like this at a store in a predominantly Black community. I feel a lot of suppressed anger and hatred when having to relive these experiences. These are but a couple of examples that were typical of my experiences and development of dealing with White men and racism. I had to take all kinds of crap not only from employees but also from belligerent customers. I had to tolerate several things to pay my tuition and fees. I have to say that my experiences while working at this grocery store, overall, were not good, but I had to do what I had to do. Sometimes, life is not fair, but I learned from these experiences. I was eighteen years old when this happened to me, and it was a lesson I will never forget.

Attending the University of Texas at San Antonio

I decided to attend the University of Texas at San Antonio. This was after I attended community college at St. Philip's, a historically black college and university. I have a lot of history with the institution because my grandfather attended the school there. I quickly learned this was a huge university. On reflection, I had no idea why I chose UTSA. I probably should have attended a smaller Catholic university. The experience was overwhelming. I remember when I was eight or nine years old, riding in my grandfather's camper and truck. We passed by UTSA on the expressway. My grandfather pointed at the university and said to me, "Someday, you will be going to school there." I looked at him, but I couldn't fully conceptualize myself going there. I had no idea that my grandfather's words would be so prophetic. I ended up attending there and graduated.

My experiences at UTSA were more of a culture shock. UTSA was a predominately White university. Coming from a predominately Black high school and community college, this was a big adjustment. I remember taking my business classes; I had no idea how unprepared I was for university work. It was there that my academic performance and study habits had to change. This was a big-time university in the UT University System. I was not ready for university work. I remember taking my business law class. There were two hundred students in my class! It was such an overwhelming experience. I struggled at UTSA. The school was a place you had to really study and stay on top of your game. UTSA has a reputation and culture of being elitist.

My Mentors at the University

I can say this reflecting on my life, you can never have too many mentors in your life. I had some really great mentors that really helped in my life. My experiences at the university confirmed those thoughts. While at UTSA, its College of Business program was one of the best in Texas. At the time, the university was trying to get Tier 1 status. So, they put students through academic rigor above most other universities. It was there I crafted my business mindset. I met two mentors that had a profound influence on me as a student. They were Dr. William Mitchell, professor of marketing, and Dr. Luisa Urdaneta, professor of anthropology. Dr. Mitchell had a majestic voice and demeanor. He was from Chicago and had a wealth of retail experience. When he spoke, he commanded your attention. I had him for six marketing classes. Dr. Mitchell always pushed me to be my best. His classes were extremely tough. For some reason, I could not get a grade higher than a C. That grade in his classes was an A at another university. His classes were that hard! This professor showed me how to eat, sleep, think, and breathe marketing. I remember the first class I had from him, I actually flunked! I want to thank him till this day for pushing me to understand the science of marketing and developing my marketing philosophy. About ten years ago, I visited him at his office at UTSA. He was very happy to see me. At the time, I was completing my MBA. I did not think he remembered me, but he did. During his class, I had longer hair with a Jheri curl and played in a rock and roll, heavy metal band. He reminded me that he knew I was a smart student, but I was uninspired. So, he was hard on me. Now he wanted to know what I was up to and what I did after graduating from the university. It was one of the most memorable times in my life, to gain the approval of my mentor and professor.

My second mentor was Dr. Luisa Urdaneta. She was another tough professor, and I believe she was an archaeologist as well. She demanded excellence from her students. Her tests were so hard! As a student, I did not take her class seriously, because anthropology was not my major, so I thought I could wing it. What I am about to share with you is a life-changing moment. One day I showed up to class and she stared at me saying, "Mr. Miles, I would like to see you in my office. Please make an appointment. I would like to talk with you." I was scared. I had no idea why she wanted to see me. When I arrived at her office, she told me that she wanted me to go the university bookstore and purchase a book called *How to Study in College* by Walter Pauk. Dr. Pauk was a professor at Columbia University. He developed a study system called the "Cornell Study Method" for college students. I told her thank you, then I went to the bookstore and bought the book.

Reading this book opened my eyes. Studying is a system. I was astonished at what I did not know about how to develop proper study habits. After I read this book, my grades, behavior, and in-class motivation improved tremendously. It finally resonated with me that my college grades and performance were attributed to my lack of knowledge of how to properly study in college.

This information changed me as a student. Before, when I would show up to classes, I would just show up unprepared and listen to the lecture and scribble down some notes. Now, I would show up to class with a plan of attack. That book was my bible to learning in college. Dr. Urdaneta touched my soul. She saw a student that needed help and reached out to that student. I cannot thank her enough for touching my life as a student.

Recently, after graduating with honors from Our Lady of the Lake University, I went back to UTSA to thank her. I had been inducted into the Delta Mu Delta National Business Honor Society and Fraternity and I had one of highest GPAs in the MBA program. I wanted to thank her for coming into my life and blessing me with guidance and tough love. I am indebted to her for turning my life around.

The story actually gets better! Dr. Urdaneta wrote a letter of recommendation for my application to the doctoral program at the University of the Incarnate Word. Dr. Urdaneta subsequently attended my public dissertation defense. She got the opportunity to meet my mother. They were kindred spirits. It was such an honor to see my mentor at my public defense. She was also my voice of reason while I was having problems during my doctoral program. I am so blessed I crossed paths with Dr. Mitchell and Dr. Urdaneta.

Almost Famous: We All Have to Grow Up Some Day Because Life Happens

Around 1981, after I graduated from high school, I wanted to be a musician. I always wanted to be a musician. However, everybody in my family were athletes. My grandfather played pro baseball, and my father was a standout basketball legend at St. Mary's University. Athletic ability runs in the family. However, being a musician did not. One day, my cousin and I visited a friend's house. He was helping me put a stereo in my car. We went to his room, and I noticed that he had an electric guitar lying on his bed. I saw him pick it up and strum it. I thought that was cool. This reinvigorated me to start playing an instrument. This was a longtime coming for me. I wanted to be a musician since I was six years old. I wanted to be a drummer.

When I was a kid, I asked my mother if she would buy me a drum set. She said no. I was crushed. I have always had something inside of me that was dying to come out as a musician. I cannot explain it. It did not seem like enough to just listen to music. I had to play an instrument. I guess it was just my musical demons trying to come out. When I was around twelve years old, I messed around with the piano. One day, while I was at the Boys' Club, there was this old piano in an activity room. I sat down and started playing with it. A guy heard and said that I sounded good and asked how long I had played piano. I told him I did not really know how to play. He told me that I should consider taking lessons; because I was into sports, I did not pursue it.

At eighteen years old, I had never played guitar before in my life. I went to a pawn shop and bought a guitar. It was an inexpensive guitar. I paid around twenty dollars for it. I started practicing on it. I did not know how to tune it or anything. Then I bought some Mel Bay books and learned the basic structure of the guitar. I cannot believe I did this to this day. I did not have a tuner or anything. Talk about green and inexperienced. I learned basic scales and chords. I learned open chords and barre chords. I was learning the best way I could. I practiced until my fingers actually bled. It hurt like hell, but I kept practicing.

My little brother told our dad I had bought a guitar. My father immediately criticized me. He stated that I did not do anything but waste my money and time. Then he said that I never showed an interest in music, so why all of the sudden did I want to learn music now? That actually pissed me off. I said if I wanted to play guitar, that it was my decision as long as I did not ask him to pay for the guitar. Then that was it. I was more determined than before.

After making some sense out of the instrument, I learned how to play it. I took studying the instrument very seriously. Something inside of me just made me want to keep playing the instrument. I could not put it down. I would practice for hours. Eventually, my mother would ask me to put it away, because she was tired of hearing it. Those days were tough.

I started practicing two hours every day. I originally learned pentatonic and Blues scales. As I was practicing, I became impatient. I was not happy with my development. So, I went to a music store in Windsor Park Mall called Richard's. It was a cool place. All of the cool musicians hung out there. I ran into several guitar players. Some of those guys were really way ahead of me, technique-wise. To be honest, it was very intimidating. These guys were playing "Crazy Train" by Ozzy Osbourne, "Ain't Talking about Love" by Van Halen, "Stairway to Heaven" by Led Zeppelin, "Looks That Kill" by Mötley Crüe, "Purple Rain" by Prince as well as other popular rock and heavy metal songs out at the time. There is a funny scene in the movie *Wayne's World* about guys playing "Stairway to Heaven" in a music store is so true! Many people know how to play that song and did it, ad nauseum, at the music store. I actually hate playing that song!

I signed up for guitar lessons by a teacher named Mark Stover. Mark was really nice. He had a lot of patience with me. For my first lesson, he wanted me to show him what I knew, just really basic chords and not a lot of scales. When I started playing, he stopped me and told me my guitar was out of tune. He showed me how to tune my guitar. Then he showed me things like basic barre chords. He showed me some blues, rock and roll riffs, and other things. Mark totally deconstructed the guitar for me. He put me on a practice schedule. For the next lesson, he had me practice on pentatonic and blues scales and barre chords. I went home and practiced what I learned. Then Mark asked if there was any music I wanted to learn. I started bringing things that I found were interesting to learn. Mark would listen to a few bars of the song and then stop the cassette and show me how to play it. I just that thought that was so cool! To hear something and then start playing it on the guitar was magical to me. The assignment and song Mark gave me was to study and learn was "Sunday Bloody Sunday" by U2. I thought it was the hardest thing because my fingers were not coordinated.

As I became more comfortable with the guitar, I started getting more confident in my abilities. For some reason, it was not hard for me to pick up a guitar and play it, but I was not a natural; I had to work at it. I did this while attending college and working part-time. Till this day, I am still not sure how I did all of this.

Jheri Curl Days and Music

While practicing my instrument, I dreamed about becoming a rock star, starting my own band, and touring. Then, I started seeing guys with a Jheri curl, and I wanted my hair to look the same way. So, I let my hair grow long and had it done in that style. At last, I looked like a rock star musician. At UTSA, I took a classical guitar class as an elective. Michael Richter was the professor, and he was a wonderful instructor. He was very patient with me as I learned how to read music and perform pieces from our textbook. While I took this class, I learned how to read music. I also learned how to fingerpick with my right hand. This elevated my guitar playing technique to another level. It was such a good class that I earned an A. As part of the class, I attended a classical music recital by a classical guitarist. It was a very good performance and increased my interest in classical music.

As I progressed on the guitar, I started listening to a lot of rock and heavy metal guitar and several different types of music. I saw the music I was listening to as training material for me to learn my instrument. I started transcribing songs and deconstructing them. I studied harmonic minor scales, major scales, diminished minor scales, Hungarian scales, Oriental scales, jazz melodic scales, exotic scales, and other scales. I studied all types of music and learned chord progressions. I learned ear-training and listened to minor and major chord notes. For some reason, I thought the best guitar players were not in R&B music, in particular, but in the blues. Blues players like Johnny "Guitar" Watson, John Lee Hooker, Ike Turner, Guitar Slim, Magic Sam, Muddy Waters,

Howlin' Wolf, Chuck Berry, and Bo Diddley were the ones I listened to frequently. Then I started really listening to the music of Prince. He was a game changer because he played every instrument on his records. I remember seeing him on the television shows *American Bandstand* and the *Midnight Special.* That was a trip. Then I started listening to rock. This was around the time, the cable channel, *MTV* (music television) came out. Then I saw the artist, Aldo Nova on *MTV* channel. They used to show his video for his song, "Fantasy." I loved that song. That was the first rock album that I purchased. I loved his guitar playing on the album.

Then I started listening to more rock guitarists and music like Jimi Hendrix, Tony Iommi (Black Sabbath), Eddie Van Halen (Van Halen), Randy Rhoads (Ozzy Osbourne), Steve Vai, Joe Satriani, Eric Johnson, Brad Gillis and Jeff Watson (Night Ranger), Stevie Ray Vaughan, Tony MacAlpine, Vinnie Moore, and Yngwie Malmsteen. Jimi Hendrix was on another level during his time. He did not sound like another other guitarist from that era. The *Band of Gypsys* album was on a different level.

After Jimi Hendrix and Van Halen, I thought Yngwie Malmsteen was the one pivotal guitar player that did it for me. He was from Stockholm, Sweden. He played the guitar like a violin. It was like a lightning bolt to hear him. When I first saw his album cover, it actually scared the heck out of me! So, I was really disconnected from R&B music at the time. I had a bit of a time learning some of his stuff, like Black Star and others. He was a technically proficient guitarist. Yngwie introduced me to classical music, so I started listening to classical composers. I started listening to classical and flamenco musicians, like Paco Peña and Carlos Montoya. I started listening to Andrés Segovia and Eliot Fisk. I started listing to Baroque music. I was listening to Mozart, Chopin, Bach, Paganini, Strauss, Wagner, Tchaikovsky, Vivaldi, Schubert, Handel, Mendelssohn, Schumann, and other classical composers.

Then I started listening to jazz and its guitarists, like Django Reinhardt. My musical tastes were becoming so complex. It was then that I started thinking that R&B and pop music were just too simplistic for me, because my musical taste had expanded so much. Then I started listening to jazz musicians, like Art Tatum, Wes Montgomery, Thelonius Monk, Miles Davis, Duke Ellington, Stanley Clarke, George Duke, Earl Klugh, Dave Brubeck, Joe Pass, Kenny Burrell, and numerous others. One jazz guitarist who blew me away was Stanley Jordan. The way he played the guitar was groundbreaking. He played the guitar with two hands, like a piano. He played the guitar polyphonically. My musician buddy, Preston, and I saw him at the Travis Park Jazz Festival one year. He blew everybody away! It like nothing I have ever seen. Then he played the unthinkable. He did an encore performance of Led Zeppelin's "Stairway to Heaven" and brought down the house. It was magical to see such musicianship. My appetite for learning and listening to different types of music influenced my guitar playing and technique. Sometimes what you listen to comes out in your playing. I thought it was strange, but it's true. Out of the hardest music to play and learn, I found jazz to be the hardest.

While I was learning all of this music, I met a guy named Antonio. He was a musician. I am not sure where we met, maybe at a music store or something. I was still learning my instrument. We talked, and he asked me if I would like to play in a band with him. I said that I was not sure; I was still learning. He said it was okay, that we were all still learning. He said there was an event he wanted to play and needed to put a band together. I said okay, let me know when and where. So, we exchanged numbers and hooked up. Again, I was a little nervous to be part of a band. I had never been in a band before.

When we got together, we practiced at his house. He wanted me to be the lead guitarist. I should have thought about this because I did not know any Black R&B songs whatsoever. I came from a blues and rock background. So, it was weird to start off. His band was an R&B band, with keyboards, bass, drums, and singers. It was intimidating, because learning an instrument is one thing, then you have to learn orchestration. I was learning all of this. And while you are learning that, then you have to learning stage presence, when you are playing in front of an audience. Many musicians are great players but lack stage presence. Again, this was a challenge because I never played in a band before. When we formed, Antonio was going to be the leader. I had to learn ALL of these R&B songs. The guys in the band were looking at me strangely because they thought it was odd that I was Black and did not know any Black music. It was really awkward. I just had different influences. I had a blues background as opposed to R&B. Antonio started giving me the list of songs we were going to play at this event. I found out later the event was called "Take Pride in the Eastside." This was going to be a show at Pittman Sullivan Park. So, Antonio assembled the band.

We started going over the songs for our set. I swear I did not know anything! Antonio had to show me a lot of stuff. I had to learn R&B music. We were playing a lot of Prince and Minneapolis stuff. We were also playing music by the Time, André Cymone, Mazarati, Alexander O'Neal, Cherrelle, SOS Band, and other popular stuff from the 1980s R&B music scene. Antonio named the band "First Class." I thought the name was odd, but oh well, it wasn't my band. We practiced every day, or as much as we could. I learned a lot from Antonio, but he had a really big ego. He could play all of the instruments in the band.

At the time, Antonio was much more accomplished as a musician than I was, but he was not a good lead player. He was a much more accomplished R&B rhythm guitarist than I was. He had a good ear and good sense of musical pitch. He did not have a perfect pitch, but he had a good amount of relative pitch. He could listen to a song and figure out how to play it by ear. At the time, my ear was not fully developed yet because I was still learning my way around the guitar. We bumped heads a lot of times. We had to take promo pictures for the event. I was not there because we'd gotten into an argument. Antonio, to me, was a street dude who was manipulative. My picture was not in the promo. I had a long Jheri curl. I thought I was really fly back then. I used to put that gel on my sides so my sides would not frizz up. We had to get outfits, so we looked halfway decent on stage. We wore black and white. I used to have black boots that came up to my calf. I loved those boots!

I guess there is a silver lining after this. After this embarrassing gig, I went on to play in other bands. One band I was playing with was trying to secure a record deal, but it just did not happen. There were further embarrassing moments on stage playing in a band, but I was much more experienced about it. For some reason, the lead singers and guitarists tend to be a-holes in a band. Now, I am not saying that I'm one, but I know all about it. Musicians just have big egos. If a girl out in the audience screams for one musician, then the others will get mad because she did not scream for them. I have seen women throwing their panties at us. I've seen women try and screw every guy in the band. I ain't trying to get with that! I think that the majority of guys who start playing music do it to get women. That is my honest opinion, and I see it all the time.

I got tired of dealing with egos and arrogant musicians. So, I bought me a little Sony four-track analogy recorder and started composing my own music. I really started getting into composing and recording my own music. I played all the instruments. I did that for about nine years. I ended up recording eight or nine instrumental albums of original music. My music is the avant-garde type of music. Because of my musical influences, it is really different. I listened to it every now and then. I don't know if this is typical of other musicians, but it is hard for me to listen to my music because I am so self-critical of it. I wish I could just listen to it like everyone else. One day I might put it on iTunes or something. By now I was an accomplished guitarist/musician/composer, but I had to grow up and cut out my Jheri curl. That was tough.

Later, I found a gig that I played with a band on an old VHS tape. I took it to place and had it converted to DVD. I recently showed my two daughters. They were on the floor laughing! That really hurt my feelings. They were really laughing at my Jheri curl. I guess I was not as fly as I thought I was. That really hurt my feelings!

Just think, I was almost famous!

Racism 101: The First Job I Got after Graduating from College

The joy of graduating from college was an experience that cannot be described in words. This was May of 1992. I just graduated with my BBA in marketing from the University of Texas at San Antonio. UTSA was a tough school. Their College of Business program valued their reputation. UTSA had the one of the best business programs in the state and their accounting program was one of the top programs in the nation. It was truly an honor to have graduated from there.

After graduating from UTSA, life was wide open for me. I was in my late twenties. I was both bright-eyed and bushy tailed. However, there is something I learned after graduating from school. Racism always rears its ugly head. After I graduated from college, I got recruited into a management training program. It was truly an accomplishment. I was blessed and just damn lucky. I was recruited by the firm and was one of eighteen trainees from around the country. This was in the financial services industry. I was hired October 21, 1992.

After I made the cut, I was flown to Baltimore, Maryland, with the other candidates. It was all so mind-blowing. The company flew us there for the orientation and the training program. I met some really interesting and smart people from around the country. It was a great experience for a young twenty-something! We spent about four days in Baltimore. Traveling to the East Coast was a new experience for me. After the orientation and training, I was told that my training site would be in San Marcos, Texas. I had to commute every day, back and forth, from San Antonio to San Marcos. Commuting like that can put much wear and tear on your vehicle.

I was excited about my first job with the new company that recruited my right out of college. It was invigorating. On my first day, I arrived early before everyone else. I had to wait outside in my car until the staff came in and opened up the office. When I got entry into the office, I introduced myself to the staff and met everyone. Everyone was very nice to me, but nothing could have prepared me for what was going to happen next.

I met the branch manager, Tom Scott. He was a tall, older White male. He reminded me of the actor John Wayne, with his personality and demeanor. He seemed nice. After we met and introduced ourselves, he then told me that he would like to talk with me in his office. We went to his office, and he waited for me to sit down. First, he told me that my college degree got me into the door and that I still had to learn this business. Next, he told me that we would probably view Martin Luther King differently. I had a puzzled look on my face. I was thinking, "Why is he bringing this up to me?" Then he went on to say that Martin Luther King did not do all of the great things that everybody says he did. I still had a puzzled look on my face as to why he was telling me this. At this point I was speechless. Obviously, this was a good ol' boy. I was not sure if he was saying this to get under my skin or test me, but I played it cool. Then, to patronize me, he said he felt the same way about former President John F. Kennedy. I knew this man was a racist by even stooping so low to say something inappropriate such as that.

I was in shock hearing this on my first day on my new job. This was definitely a message that was sent to me: no matter how educated you are as an African American, racism trumps everything. After he told me this, then he talked about how much of a Christian he was. I saw him as a complete hypocrite. I guess Christians can be racists, too! It was also at this moment I began to see that a White person can harbor racist views, but they can still claim they are a Christian. This was my first day on this job, and I was dealing with a White supremacist. This was Racism 101.

While working with Tom Scott, I witnessed him making numerous racist remarks about our customers in the office. I remember one particular incident. We had a Black female customer who had an account with us. She worked at the U.S. Post Office. She wanted to borrow some additional funds. He asked me to review the application, and I reviewed her credit report. I did my review and turned over the application to him. He reviewed her application, then remarked that this lady made a very good salary at her job with the post office, but she still wanted to live in the ghetto! I was shocked that he made a remark like that. I was equally shocked that he made that remark in front of me. That was typical Tom Scott, a man of many prejudices. Another time, he made a remark about another customer, calling him a "Crazy Mexican." I doubt seriously the company knew he was making remarks like that in front of the staff about our customers.

One time, I found out that the uncle of a friend of mine, Dr. Earl Wright, was a dean of a department at San Antonio College (SAC). He actually knew Tom Scott. I asked Tom if he knew Earl Wright. I believe they both played sports over at St. Mary's University. I did not tell him anything about my knowing who Dr. Wright was. Tom Scott immediately went into this tirade and started criticizing him, stating how dumb and stupid he was. He went on to say that he was never going to amount to anything. I was stunned. After his tirade, I said, "You know, Dr. Wright is a dean over at SAC." He looked at me and got completely quiet for a moment. Then, he continued his tirade and asked how Dr. Wright ever got a job like that, because he was a dummy. I just looked at him and went about my way. After a while, he no longer surprised me with his racist behavior. I knew the person I was dealing with.

This goes to show you that racism in the workplace is real. If Tom Scott said these types of things in my presence, then what do you think he said when I was not around? He constantly made these types of remarks in the office. Nothing could have prepared me for this experience. I might have just graduated with my college degree, but I still had to get an education in the jungle. Racism 101 is alive and well. That was my first experience after graduating from college. Nothing that I learned in school could have ever prepared me for that. When I reflect on my career and experiences, I see how I have grown and evolved from this. If someone I encountered pulled this again, I would act completely differently. I would not tolerate this whatsoever.

Life can be such an irony. Tom was eventually forced to resign, or risk being fired. It was discovered he was manipulating the collection and delinquency numbers. He was padding his figures on his monthly reports. He was also caught doing illegal and other unethical stuff, like having an employee work overtime without paying him. The employee reported him to human resources, and Tom Scott got in serious trouble. He was indeed lucky he was allowed to resign. They were going to fire him. Tom Scott left the company in shame. He went back to selling cars. I will never forget how Tom Scott taught me the lesson of Racism 101.

Some of the Best Advice I Ever Received Early in My Career

In one of our beginning training workshops with the company that recruited me after I graduated, the company got the previous year's recruits who completed the program to chat with us. They sat together on a panel and discussed their experiences in the training program. They discussed their struggles while completing the program. They were very interesting to listen to. As we were new management trainees, they offered valuable advice on completing the program. I was particularly interested in one of the trainees on the panel who had completed his MBA. He was a bit older than the other panelists. He seemed more mature and more seasoned.

When we had our first break in the panel discussion, I approached him and introduced myself. He was very nice and friendly. I asked him if I could ask him a question. I asked him, "I noticed that you completed your MBA. I have been strongly considering getting my MBA. I wanted to ask you if think it is advisable for me pursue it right now." He told me that before I considered going back to school, I should get some industry experience. He said that it would be more valuable to do get that experience first as opposed to running out and getting an MBA. After getting about four years of experience, then I could consider going back and getting my MBA. He said that would be the best thing to do. I thanked him for his valuable advice.

I actually followed his advice. I ended up spending nine years in the financial services and banking industry. I went back to school in 2001 and pursued my MBA while I was working at Wells Fargo Bank as a marketing analyst. What he told me was the best advice that I ever got. I was a much better student at this point, and I was a more seasoned individual. I forgot his name. If I could look him up and thank him, I surely would. Thank you!

Experiences Entering My Doctoral Program and My Journey

Let's fast forward to me working in the industry and starting on my doctoral program. After getting downsized, after being married, divorced, and having two beautiful daughters along the way, I was thinking about pursuing a doctorate at this point in my life. It was actually my second choice. To be honest, I originally wanted to attend law school and study corporate law. I had no intentions of pursuing a doctorate. As a warrior in life, and I had some battle scars, it was a good time for me to consider this. I was completing my MBA program at Our Lady of the Lake University when I began considering pursuing a doctorate. At OLLU, I did extremely well in the program. I had a strong study regiment, because I just craved knowledge for some reason and kept reading many business books. This developed my business philosophy. For some reason, I could not get enough education. I hungered for more. I considered pursing a doctorate.

I made an appointment to meet with one of my professors at OLLU. It had a doctoral program, but I wanted to attend another university. It is just my thought that you don't get all of your degrees from the same university. My professor recommended that I stay at OLLU and go through their doctoral program. But it did not offer a program that was of interest to me. I think the doctoral specialization was in Leadership and it was the only one they offered, so I was not interested. It just did not appeal to me. I narrowed my choices down to three schools: University of Texas at San Antonio, University of the Incarnate Word, and OLLU. I did not have the means to attend school out of town, state, or country. I did not want to go to an online university either. I thought about pursuing a degree online. Pursuing a doctorate at an online university, was a big risk to me. Those schools do heavy advertising to recruit students, and In the future, I ended up, conducting research on online universities while I was in my doctoral program.

So, I made the decision to attend UIW. UTSA's doctoral program was very difficult to get into. I remember attending one of their information sessions on their doctoral program. It was okay, but I didn't care for what I saw there. There were a bunch of twenty-year-olds at the session. They were still finishing their bachelors. They had no work experience or industry background. Only three of us out of the group that attended had industry experience. Also, they wanted you to quit your day job and accept a stipend of seventeen thousand dollars a year. For some of us, that amount would not work. Also, you would be employed as a graduate assistant. That definitely did not appeal to me. Last, I had already got my BBA from UTSA, so it would have broken my rule on getting another degree from the same university. So, I made UIW my final choice by default. It was logistically accessible. I could get there in fifteen minutes or less. Also, the university had a brilliant and flamboyant president: the one and only Dr. Lou Agnese. That is the reason why I wanted to attend the university.

I had a very interesting experience at the university when I first inquired about the program. This was to be a foreshadowing of what was to come. One day, I made a phone call to university's doctoral department. I asked the operator to connect me to the doctoral program or director. The operator connected me to a person named Dr. Paige Wetherhold. She got on the phone, and I said, "Hi, I'm interested in your doctoral program. I would like to get some information and apply." She then retorted, "Excuse me, sir, I'm busy and don't have time to talk to you." Then she hung up the phone on me! I was shocked. This was the person they have leading their doctoral program? This was the first of many negative encounters with Paige Wetherhold. She is an older, Jewish White woman with red hair and dark-rimmed glasses. She was about seventy-two or seventy-three years old and very condescending. I immediately picked up bad vibes from her.

I didn't let that encounter stop me. I went to the enrollment center across the street from the university. I filled out the application and got letters of recommendation from two of my MBA professors at OLLU: the late Dr. Bill Schrank and Dr. John Swiger. They were both good professors and very helpful. Last, I asked Dr. Luisa Urdaneta, my anthropology professor from UTSA, for a letter. It was such an honor that she did that for me. It was like a mentor seeing their student progress to the next level. She was honored as well.

However, not everyone I asked helped me. One person I asked did not help me nor would call or take my calls. I finally got the application filled out and got the letters of recommendation completed. I received the call for an interview from the university. But I still had to take the GRE. I was prepared and did something that many prospective doctoral students do not; I brought a portfolio of my best work from my MBA program. The portfolio included copies of my past projects, business plans, cases, and marketing plans. I wanted to showcase the caliber of work I produced.

The Interview to Enter the Doctoral Program

Three people interviewed me: Dr. Paige Wetherhold, Dr. Fletcher Bekele, and Dr. Ryan Gershowitz. They asked me all sorts of questions. Dr. Wetherhold and Dr. Gershowitz would be two sorry individuals I would have to deal with in the future. Dr. Gershowitz mentioned my undergraduate grades in contrast to my graduate grades. He wanted to know the reason why my GPA was low compared to my graduate GPA. I explained to him that during my undergraduate years, I'd had a job and put myself through college and played in a rock and roll band.

Then the strangest thing happened. Dr. Wetherhold asked me why I wanted to pursue a doctorate and then she tried to discourage me from pursuing it! She said that I would never get a job with the degree and I would never make money with it. Mind you, this is the director of the doctoral program! That seemed odd to me. This woman was obviously a racist pig and I immediately got bad vibes about her. I did not care for her.

After that, I was handed a writing examination. I had to think of something to write but was having a terrible bout of writer's block. Ultimately, I pulled it together. After the exam, the panel returned to discuss what I had written.

Immediately, Dr. Wetherhold started criticizing my essay. She asked me more questions like "Why did you write or answer the question that way?" Then she asked me what my definition of entrepreneurship was. I gave a generic answer. So, she then said my definition was wrong. Then she stated that entrepreneurship is not putting a McDonald's franchise in a foreign country. That is not entrepreneurship. I would find out years later that she did not know a anything about entrepreneurship.

Again, this is one of many recollections and negative encounters with Paige Wetherhold. I always felt a racist vibe from her. While I was taking courses in this doctoral program, I subsequently found out the depth of her incompetence. She was the kind of person who made sly racial remarks and then patronized you to convince you she wasn't racist. I have zero respect for this woman. I also found out how she would manipulate and threaten foreign students if they did not do what she wanted. At the time, she was also head of the university's International Conference Center (ICC), which dealt with foreign students who wanted to attend the university and domestic students who wanted to study abroad. She was one of most difficult professors I have ever encountered at the university. She was also the most incompetent professor I had the displeasure of meeting. I will discuss that later in the chapter.

Experiences in the Doctoral Program

My experiences at the University of the Incarnate Word's doctoral program was interesting, to say the least. I have to say, there were some things that occurred at the university that I could not believe till this day. Let me share my experiences with you.

Great Professors in the Doctoral Program

My first two classes were with the late Dr. Reese Taylor. I really connected with him and miss him dearly. He was a great teacher and mentor. I was so blessed to cross paths with him and have the privilege of being one of his students. I took a class in entrepreneurship and one in international organizations from him. His class was very laid-back. Dr. Taylor earned his PhD in mathematics. It was inspiring to listen to him speak.

The next doctoral courses I took were with other professors in the program. While I will not discuss each one of them, I will discuss my experiences with the ones that were important to my story. Another great professor was Dr. Jason Dietrich. He was a professor in university's College of Business' MBA program. Dr. Dietrich brought a wealth of knowledge and experience to his lectures. I took his class on human resources. It was one of the best courses I ever had at the university. His class was always interesting. This was the class where I learned how to survey mentors. I asked him to be a member of my dissertation committee. He was so honored that I asked him, he accepted. For some reason, I preferred the professors in the MBA program rather than the professors in the College of Education. One reason was, while most of the doctoral program faculty had backgrounds in education, some of them were among the worst professors at the university. For this group, in addition to lacking critical thinking skills, some were simply poor teachers who frequently displayed acts of blatant favoritism with students and grades.

To be fair, some other excellent professors I had at the university were Dr. Bekele, from the College of Education, and Dr. Patrice Bateman and Dr. Nastassja Živkovi from the College of Business. The first time I had Dr. Bekele for a class, I actually thought about quitting school. He was a very, very hard professor. When he graded your papers, he left red marks all over your paper. I had never had my papers ripped apart like that. Another incident happened with my presentation in his class. I made a mistake of doing the same chapter analysis as another student. I notified him, and he looked irritated. I tried to talk with him before class when I made the discovery. He was very dismissive and told me to just do the presentation. I felt his wrath after my mistake. He gave me an F for the assignment. I was so shocked. I made an appointment with him and wanted to make sure that I did not flunk the class. That was first time I was going to quit my doctoral program.

To Sir with Love: My Visiting Professor Experience in Mexico

As part of my doctoral program, I had to complete a foreign internship. I did my internship in Mexico City, Mexico, as a visiting professor. It was a very big challenge. I had to leave my family, business, and job to do this endeavor. But it was an enlightening cultural adventure. I was able to set this up with the university because it had foreign sister campuses in different countries. For some reason, I had a lot of trouble trying to nail down an international internship. It seemed like every country I was interested in had either a terrorist attack or some other disturbance. I selected England, then it had a bombing. Next, I picked Greece, and the same thing happened. I picked four other countries, and each had terrorist bombings shortly thereafter. So, I decided to pick Mexico. First, it was close to Texas. Second, the university had a sister campus there. That made Mexico the best option.

What I Have I Gotten Myself Into?

The first week in Mexico was a true cultural and learning experience. Through the first week, I was making adjustments and getting acclimated to the country and culture. As I arrived at the airport, I realized that I was in a very different country. One of the most notable observations was that I did not see anything at the airport that was written in or translated into English. So, I literally had to learn and translate what the Spanish words meant. I was a little nervous. Miguel, my liaison for this internship, arrived at the Aeropuerto Internacional de la Ciudad de México to pick me up. Miguel is the director of Centro Universitario Incarnate Word. He was very gracious and showed me around the campus and the surrounding community. He took me to the local grocery store chain, MEGA, for groceries and things for the apartment where I would live.

The university's administrative staff gave me a birthday party on that Friday. Later, Miguel, the director of the university in Mexico City. He took me to a nice restaurant after work, and we had dinner that night. That Saturday, we dined at another charming restaurant, where I was introduced to his wife and daughter. The restaurant provided a show during our meal. If that was not interesting enough, the restaurant had another interesting element for which I was not prepared. It had a bullfighting ring! I thought that was very odd. From what I read about bullfights, the bullfighter dances and entices the bull. Then he stabs the bull with these sharp stakes and tries to get a brain shot. After the bull is killed, it is then eaten! I never understood bullfights until I got older. Later, I traveled to the shopping mall with Miguel and his family. I could not believe how crowded the atmosphere of the mall was. It was very crammed. We were constantly bumping into people. It was very difficult to move around freely due to the congestion. We went to a Starbucks-type of restaurant and had coffee and ice cream. My Spanish was becoming more developed as I observed and interacted with people. I had a wonderful time.

There's a Ghost in My Apartment

When I moved my belongings into the apartment, there were some strange things I heard at night. Miguel told me there was a rumor about a ghost in the apartment. He said it was a bunch of talk and started laughing about it. I thought it was just a joke. However, it was not. He told me the university used to be an elementary school that had a swimming pool. One day, an accident happened. A little girl drowned in the pool. After that, the school closed the pool and filled it with dirt. There are certain times when the little girl's ghost would still walk around the area where the pool was to protect people from walking there. Her ghost would come out at 11:00 p.m. on certain nights. My apartment was at the back of the university, and it was pitch-black back there. We had security guards at night, and they were even afraid to go back there. They would not go back there at all!

I would walk to the back of the school at night into the dark to my apartment. It was so dark, I did not see anything like the ghost of the little girl, but I felt a presence in my apartment. Every night, around 11:00 p.m. or 11:30 p.m., there were these weird noises. The door handles on my apartment doors would jiggle and make noise like somebody was trying to get in! This happened EVERY night the whole time I stayed at my campus apartment. I wish I was making this up. Then I would hear other unexplained noises. I used to sleep with the lamp on every night! To be honest, after a while, I got used to it. I would go back to the office and tell Miguel and the staff. They would just laugh at me! That was a scary experience.

The Martin Luther King Statue at the Park in Downtown Mexico City

One weekend I hung out with my colleague Adriana and her husband. We drove around different places in downtown Mexico City. We stopped at this park that had a very big pond with people racing small, remote-controlled boats. It was really fun. While we were visiting this park, I noticed something that completely freaked me out. At the park, there was a huge statue of Dr. Martin Luther King. A statue of Dr. King? I was thinking, *Why do they have a statue of him here in Mexico?* Wow, that really surprised me. I guess that statue was a good thing. What Dr. King stood up for obviously resonated with people beyond the United States. It was very inspiring to see and heartbreaking at the same time. That experience is why is it so good to travel, because you learn something.

Frida Kahlo and Diego Rivera

I was always invited to hang out with my new friends at the university. My friend and university administrative staff member, Yanina invited me to spend some time with her and her husband one weekend. It was a three-day weekend to celebrate the national holiday Revolution Day. So, there were no classes on that coming Monday. I got a chance to see the famous artist Frida Kahlo's house in downtown Mexico City. It is a museum, very colorful and full of her artwork. Diego Rivera's artwork was all over the house as well. It was really interesting to see. The night before visiting the museum, we watched the movie, *Frida*, starring Selma Hayek. In the movie, there were several scenes that were filmed on location in Mexico City. I got a chance to see a lot of those places. It was really strange to see a movie about Kahlo, then go to her house the next day. It was very avant-garde.

To Sir with Love

Just like what happened in the 1967 classic movie, *To Sir with Love* with Sidney Poitier, I had a very similar experience after completing my foreign internship. As a going away party for me, Miguel and the staff hosted a Christmas lunch for me. The cafeteria employees prepared a delicious meal with many traditional Mexican dishes. It was also a going away party for my colleague Adriana. Her last day would be that coming Friday. She had accepted a job with an advertising agency. It was a great dinner for the entire office staff, yet it was sad, because I would be leaving to return to the US that Thursday.

Leaving Mexico and Preparing to Return Home

Instructors always have to be careful dealing with students, whether they are either male or female. Nothing was certainly truer when dealing with students in international environments. All cultures are different. It was so sad leaving my students. Two of my students came to thank me for what they learned in my classes. One of my students who performed well in my advertising class gave me a Christmas present. That was very nice. Other students I hadn't taught asked if I was going to be back the next semester, because they heard that I was a good teacher. They were very interested in taking a class with me. It turned out to be a very good experience for me at CIW. When I left, three of the staff members hugged me with tears in their eyes. It was sad that I had to leave. But my assignment came to an end. I was definitely not the same person I was when I first arrived. I was definitely a better person for the experience living in Mexico. There were many days in which I constantly questioned my decision about performing this internship. After some time, I became totally acclimated with Mexico and its culture and I found a way to expand my socialization and embraced the people and the culture. It was an incredible experience I will always remember. Mexico became my second home. I did not want to leave. I fell in love with Mexico.

The Dissertation Experience: The Torture, the Hell, and the Politics

One of the most difficult endeavors I ever embarked on was completing a dissertation. You have to know what you are trying to study, or you will be doing it for a long time. Many are called, but few are chosen to finish. The dissertation is not necessarily hard; it's the incompetent professors that make it harder than what it is. It is like a hazing ritual. It is as if some professors are hell-bent on trying to make the dissertation process harder than what it already is for students. Some of them take joy in watching students struggle and have a nervous breakdown with their antics. Some of the antics that I have witnessed with professors in doctoral program have just been absolutely disgusting. I have no respect for any professor who engages in this type of behavior. The objective should be to develop scholars, not hazing them. Some of their antics are just plain unnecessary. They do this because they can, not because it is necessary. Not to mention, there are several bad dissertation committee chairs who actually do a lot of damage to doctoral students. They do a disservice to these students with their antics.

Some professors want to move up the ladder in the ivory tower and make students do some of the most ridiculous tasks to complete a dissertation. This will be the most difficult task you will ever face. Some professors are just flat-out failures in life. If they weren't teaching at the universities, they would be selling tickets to the circus or something else. Some of them are the most miserable people I have ever seen. The craft of teaching should be taken seriously. Instead, they act out their miscreant behavior and torment doctoral students, who are trying to do good work and graduate. They like to play many psychological games with doctoral students. The dissertation process is 80 percent politics and 20 percent research. Some of the things that have happened to me I will carry for the rest of my life. Let me share my story with you.

Enter the First Dissertation Committee and the First Chair

When I began to put together my dissertation committee, I had no idea what I was doing. If I had known then what I know now, I would've done several things completely different. The person I picked for the dissertation chair was Dr. Paige Wetherhold. This is the same woman who tried to discourage me from pursuing the doctorate when I was applying for the doctoral program at the university. I found out what kind of person she was. The reason I first approached her to be my dissertation chair was because my advisor, Dr. Bekele, recommended her. When I met with her, she asked me why I did not ask Dr. Bekele to be my dissertation chair, because she thought I was close to him. Really what she was saying was "Why didn't you pick Dr. Bekele? He is Black and you are Black." This was another observation of these little racial comments and microaggressions that I had to deal with from her. .

I found out a lot about Dr. Wetherhold. I don't go around accusing people of being a racist. That gets old. But this woman was quite comfortable in her racism. I didn't know that much about her other than she was buddies with president of the university. Sometimes, I judge a person by the people they have around them. Also, what surprised me was I found out she was disliked by many of the faculty members and foreign students at the university. I was told she was notorious for abusing her power at the university. She struck me as the kind of person who smiles in your face, then stabs you in the back. She constantly threw her power around and had an out-of-control ego. She did that to me on a few occasions and I did not like it whatsoever. She often misused her power when she felt a need to let you know who she was and what she was capable of. She was so vain, she used to dye her hair a bright color, trying to hide her gray hair color.

While I was there, one of the major problems that was prevalent at the university was the amount of nepotism that existed at the university. Many of the faculty members and employees who were hired at the university were hired through nepotism. They either were friends with someone or related to someone who worked there. It was really bad at the university. The faculty was practically Lily White. So, when I see a university that loves to boast how much of an international school they are but maintains an all- White faculty with one or no persons of color, their credibility is suspect.

Dumb and Dumber: The Dynamic Duo of the Dissertation Committee

When I was establishing the committee, Dr. Wetherhold told me who she wanted on the committee. I was taken back. She told me she wanted Dr. Ryan Gershowitz, an incompetent, racist, and overly sensitive, emotional professor. I did not want him on the committee because of my prior bad experiences with him as a professor. He was one of the worst professors I had at the university.

In the classes that I had with him; he was one of the laziest professors that I ever had. He would just show up to class and do minimal teaching. Till this day I cannot remember anything that he taught me. Now I had the worst professor at the university as a chair and the second worst professor at the university on my dissertation committee. What an A-Team! Now I know why the Asian students used to call them "Dumb and Dumber." When I asked that Dr. Jason Dietrich be a committee member, Dr. Wetherhold looked at me for a moment; she then scolded me for not asking her first! That was not a good sign. What I did not know was that Dr. Dietrich was denied tenure at the university. It was unfair what they did to him. So, then she told me that she needed to make a phone call to look into his status. That really pissed me off. I should have known some dirty stuff was going on.

We started the dissertation proposal meeting. It was then when I found out the depth of Dr. Wetherhold's incompetence. My dissertation study was about measuring business risk with startup and current small to medium-sized business enterprises. I remember, while I was trying to explain my topic to her, for some strange reason, she had an inability to understand it. I found out that she had no business background whatsoever. Every time we would meet to go over my dissertation proposal, Dr. Wetherhold was completely lost. If her backside weren't attached to her body, she would lose it. That was very problematic. She had an inability to understand basic business concepts. This was also evident to Dr. Dietrich, who pulled me aside and brought this to my attention.

Most of the faculty in the doctoral program seemed to show a lack of critical thinking skills, so they taught classes that reflected that . My major in the doctoral program at the university was international education and entrepreneurship. We did not have enough competent faculty to teach entrepreneurship classes in the doctoral program. They should have gotten professors from the MBA program to teach it. International education and entrepreneurship are an odd pairing. Entrepreneurship is a business discipline, not an education discipline. Dr. Wetherhold actually *taught* entrepreneurship. This was unbelievable. If she could not understand simple business concepts, then how in the hell was she teaching entrepreneurship? This woman was so inept it was embarrassing, and I could not believe it. I was thinking she had no business being the chair of my committee.

Every meeting I had with her was like trying to teach Algebra to a caveman. I constantly had to explain simple business concepts to her. However, there was yet another problem I found out while meeting with her. She did not understand statistics. I discovered all of this over the course of a year. She wasted my time and money for over the course of a year due to her incompetence. This put me behind from progressing through the doctoral program.

The Coup Attempt: The First Chair Is Up to Her Antics

Still there were other problems that surfaced. I began to notice that Dr. Gershowitz did not like Dr. Dietrich. Both of them would collude to do immature and sneaky things, such as intentionally not invite him to the committee meetings or not send him an email to keep up him up to speed on the dissertation progress. Dr. Dietrich tried to be a good sport about it, but both Dumb and Dumber kept pulling these dirty tricks. This really bothered me to see this. It bothered me so badly to see my mentor treated in that manner. Since Dr. Gershowitz immediately disliked Dr. Dietrich, he was very instrumental in influencing Dr. Wetherhold to remove him from the committee. After our first full meeting with everyone present, Dr. Wetherhold wanted to talk to me privately afterward. She told me that she was considering removing Dr. Dietrich from the committee. She said that she would be observing him, and if he did anything that she did not like, he would be removed. She did not think he was competent enough to serve on the committee. This was coming from a woman who was so inept, she could not comprehend basic business concepts. Dr. Dietrich has a PhD in management. Dr. Wetherhold had an EdD in education. I said to myself, "You really want to judge someone's incompetence?" That really hurt me. I had to sit in meetings with my mentor knowing all of this, and I could not tell him. I felt really bad with how they humiliated him. She actually made a threat to me that I better not discuss the situation with him. She also threatened me by stating there would repercussions if I ever told him. It was at this moment I should have fired Dr. Wetherhold as my dissertation chair. That was when I lost any modicum of respect for herWetherhold.

I remember I had private discussions with Dr. Dietrich about Wetherhold and Gershowitz. I asked him what he thought of them, without telling him what was going on. He told me that Wetherhold was way out of her league, had a huge ego, and was not knowledgeable about either business or statistics whatsoever. He said that Gershowitz was equally lacking in knowledge, and he was the weakest link on the committee. He was not only a weak researcher, but a weak committee member and very petty. He had no business being on my committee.

Want to Finish the Dissertation? Teach Yourself!

It was at this time I began seeking outside help with my dissertation proposal. I also began teaching myself. In our meetings, every time I would present my proposal, Wetherhold would mark it up like an English teacher in grade school. After a while, I hired an editor. I followed the editor's advice, and Wetherhold would still mark it up with stupid comments that amounted to nothing. She had no idea I hired an editor, so I knew there was nothing wrong with the drafts. Then it finally hit me: she only focused on editing rather than the content because she did not know anything else! The thing about English is that it is very subjective. Unless you have grammar issues, writing is very subjective. You cannot grade writing style. That is what several professors do to screw around with doctoral students. They use revisions as a device to stall your dissertation progress. With mathematics, something is either right or wrong; however, English can be subjective. So, I bought books on how to complete a dissertation. I had to teach myself because the inept chair did not know what to do. I began to restructure my proposal and make it better. I reviewed and downloaded sample dissertations from students at other universities across the county: Harvard, Yale, Princeton, UT Austin, Stanford, New York University, Arizona State University, University of Pennsylvania, several others. I wanted to know what constituted a stellar proposal, and by proxy, I taught myself how to develop my dissertation.

The First Chair Makes an Accusation

One day, before my meeting with Wetherhold, I was waiting in the lobby in the ICC building. Suddenly, she approached me and demands I come to her office. She tells me she wanted to speak to me. On arrival, she asks if I had someone write my dissertation for me. I replied, "What? Are you serious?" Then she accused me of having someone write my dissertation proposal. Again, then she threatened me again that if I didn't confess to her, she would take action through the university and I would be kicked out of the doctoral program if she found out otherwise. She did not think that I wrote my proposal draft. She then tells me that it was too good and I just had to have someone write it for me. I looked at here for a few seconds. I wanted to strangle her, but I had to keep my cool. However, I could not resist laughing in her face. I told her I had hired an editor, but no one wrote anything for me. At that point, she stated that she had no problem with an editor, but she had a problem with me getting help to write my dissertation proposal. So, I told her how did she know that I didn't review dissertations from other students as a model and patterned my work after theirs? I wanted to strangle this fool! I literally had to count to ten because I was going to do something drastic if I had not. What she was really saying was "Negro, you are not that smart. You are incapable of doing work this good." Then she repeated her threat and told me that she had her suspicions, and if she ever found out otherwise, I would be in a lot of trouble. Here was this incompetent, racist excuse of a woman making a baseless accusation. Then she had the audacity to threaten me. Again, I should have removed her as the chair of my committee.

The First Chair Brings in Her Man from Harvard

Over the course of a year, I was getting further and further behind with Wetherhold and the committee. At many of our meetings, she arrived unprepared. Not only would she forget to bring her copies of the proposal, but she would also forget things we discussed from the previous meeting. Additionally, she would misplace other items related to the dissertation. She did not know what she was doing as a chair. During one meeting, she suggested letting one of her colleagues look at my survey instrument. His name was Sergio Martinez. He taught in the MBA program and had a business background. Sergio Martinez was a graduate of Harvard with an MA in government and public policy. However, there was one problem: he did not have a background in the course area of my dissertation research on entrepreneurial risk. She asked him to review my dissertation and instrument I had developed. He came to the next meeting with her.

To be honest, he did not understand what I was trying to do either. I became frustrated and confronted him. I should have not acted in that manner. After that incident, he left; then Wetherhold threatened me again that if ever I acted like that again, she would walk off the committee as the chair. Oh, I was so scared…not at all. I wanted her to disappear. She also requested I apologize to Martinez in an email. At this point, I had enough of her, so I emailed him with a non-apology apology. Maybe it was foolish pride or something else, but I did not want to send even that message, but I had to do something just to appease this woman. I did not take kindly to being threatened, again. That was the second time she actually made a threat to me. Concerning this situation, I was wrong, and it was not his fault, but he was put in a difficult position by Wetherhold , because she was an incompetent chair.

While all of this was going on, I started noticing something else about Wetherhold. She relied on Gershowitz for everything. He was like the committee co-chair. Every time we would meet and agree on something, the next meeting she would completely reverse course. This happened several times and brought forth another boiling point for me. I finally figured out that, after we would meet, she discussed it with Dr. Gershowitz. Then he would tell her what was correct and incorrect with what she told me in the meeting. Thus, at the next meeting, she would completely change was she told me. I had had enough.

The First Chair Quits

I emailed her and requested a meeting. I think that she sensed I was going to remove her as committee chair. When I arrived for the meeting, I discovered that Dr. Keith Verhoeven, the dean of Graduate Studies and Research was in attendance, as well as Dr. Gershowitz. However, Dr. Dietrich was not there. She had made it customary practice not to invite him to any of the committee meetings. I wondered why the Graduate Studies dean was at the meeting. Wetherhold talked about how she wanted me to change my study's methodology. She did not think a factor analysis, a multivariate statistical design methodology was appropriate. Immediately, I refused, stating that I was going to conduct my study the way I had planned, since that was the best methodology for the project. That was when I found out that she did not understand what a factor analysis was and what it was designed to achieve. She wanted me to convert the study to a qualitative methodology. For some reason, I had my book *Applied Factor Analysis*, by Rummel (1970), with me at the meeting. I got mad and threw the book on the table. Then I asked her if she knew better than the author of this book. It got really quiet for a moment. Wetherhold got incensed and then turned red. At this point, I did not give a damn! Mind you, I did this in front of the dean of Graduate Studies! She got up and excused herself from the meeting, then left the room. When she returned, she informed everyone that she was stepping down and that I would need to find another chair. Of course, this happened after she wasted a year of my time with her incompetence. I will give her credit for being smart about one thing: quitting before I fired her.

Two of my friends were not as lucky and ended up with Wetherhold as their chair. She did the same with them, except she wasted two years of their lives. To compound her idiocy, she retired while they were still trying to complete their dissertations. She screwed them pretty bad. The university is still allowing this woman to teach entrepreneurship courses! I believe they were afraid to stop her because she was the president's buddy, so they treaded carefully with her. It is a travesty that they allow this woman to serve as a professor in any doctoral program. I have never in my life met a more incompetent professor than Dr. Paige Wetherhold. I hope the university does not erect a building in her honor. That would be an insult. The university is across the street from the San Antonio Zoo. They couldn't give her a job at the airport sniffing luggage or something? It was at this time I started questioning faculty at universities. They will hire an incompetent White professor who can't tie their shoelaces and chew gum at the same time, but will not hire qualified Black faculty. Racism in higher education is very rampant.

Enter the Second Committee and the Second Chair

After that meeting debacle with Wetherhold, I had to find a new dissertation committee chair. I asked Dr. Jason Dietrich whom he would recommend. I was very cautious this time. He recommended Dr. Jeanette Brannigan. I was very apprehensive at first, because of the crap she pulled with my advisor when I dropped her class, but I emailed her and requested a meeting. I was in bad shape. I was discouraged and pondering my future. I just wasted a year dealing with an incompetent chair, and I was trying not to make the same mistake twice. When we finally met at her office, I was willing to let bygones be bygones.

We talked about my dissertation and the process for selecting new committee members. I told her who I wanted this time. I wanted all the committee to be from the MBA program. I did not want anybody from the College of Education. I did not want any more incompetent committee members. I only wanted people from the School of Business. The new committee consisted of Dietrich, Vernon, and Živkovi , all from the School of Business. Then, out of nowhere, Brannigan tells me that I am required to have someone from the INEE field, because that was my major. Then she says that Dr. Ryan Gershowitz has to be on the committee because he is one of the INEE professors. I hesitated, then I said okay. I should have said something then. I had no idea what was in store for me. I hope he didn't start anything. After reflecting on this now, I think that was not true. I strategically stacked the committee with strong business professors and statisticians. That way, Gershowitz couldn't create any problems. I could not have been more wrong. For some odd reason, The university forces doctoral students to keep troublesome professors on their committee. When that same professor is a member of the new committee, they continue to cause the problems. They actually get worse because it's like payback. It is like a serious conflict of interest.

Then she tells me that Wetherhold wanted to be on the reformed committee. I said, "What?" She tells me that Wetherhold had previously discussed it with me. That never happened. Why on Earth would I want that incompetent, racist woman on my new dissertation committee? I told her that I did not know anything about that conversation. With this problem, I created another problem. Her buddy, Gershowitz, was on the committee. Little did I know, since I did not want his buddy, Wetherhold, on the new committee, he was going to create problems for me on the new committee.

I did not want Gershowitz on my committee for three reasons: (a) he was one of the worst professors at the university, and he is unfair and biased with his grading; (b) the previous bad experiences with him on the first committee and what he did to Dr. Dietrich; and lastly, (c) he was incompetent in business and statistics. On a personal note, I'm sorry, but I have a problem with anyone who is overly sensitive about everything. He is extremely nitpicky about unimportant things. He is a fussy, little man.

When I was a student, for some reason, I never liked him as a professor or as a person. Something always bothered me about him. He always seemed arrogant and condescending, like he thought was better than everybody or something. I never wanted him on my committee. I just did not care for him at all. I had run-ins with him before because he seemed to look down on students of color. I just didn't want to have to deal with him. He rubbed me the wrong way.

Everything was going okay until I started having problems with Dr. Brannigan. I believe she did not want Dr. Dietrich on the committee. I also think she was lying about not being able to get a hold of him. She kept telling me that she could not reach him. I found that be odd. I called Dr. Dietrich myself. When I talked to him, he indicated to me that she has never tried to contact him. Brannigan basically told me a bold-face lie; she had no intentions of allowing Dr. Dietrich to be on the committee. I lost a lot of respect for her after that. She was playing politics. It was also at this time I got smarter and started recording all of my meetings. There were not going to be any problems; I got permission first. I wanted to make sure if something happened, I had a recording of all the meetings.

I also had the capability to download the recordings and store them on my home computer as MP3 files. I wanted to make sure I CYA (Covered Your Assets), because I was determined to finish school. This was a master stroke in my plans because I almost had to hire an attorney. More about that later.

What disturbed me about the second committee and this chair was that they made me start over. Why should I have to re-accomplish what I had completed over a year ago? I paid money for tuition for a year and had my time wasted. That is the type of crap they will pull. The point is, there is a profit motive. To complete your dissertation, you have to take dissertation hours, which is like tuition for a class. Every semester you sign up to do dissertation hours, the chair and committee get compensated. The dissertation chair gets the most, something around a one thousand dollars a semester. Now, consider the increase in that amount for a chair that serves on over five to six dissertation committees. Get the picture? I'm not sure of the compensation for the rest of the committee, but everyone receives something monetarily. That is the reason dissertation chairs keep students working on a project for as long as they can. It is very unethical. Then they provide incomplete guidance, so it takes even longer to complete. So, if a doctoral student gets lost in the process, they eventually have to figure it out on their own. However, they don't want you figure it out. They want you to take as long as you like. They want to drag it out as long as possible. After all of that, when they can't make any more money on you, then they finally let you graduate. Personally, and professionally, I have a big problem with the dissertation process.

Then there is the dirty part of it. Some students pay to get through the dissertation. I was told by one of my Asian friends that two professors at the university allegedly got paid by two Asian students to get them out of school quickly. For legal reasons, I cannot tell you their names. Allegedly, one Asian student bought a professor a car. Another student, allegedy bought a professor a round-trip ticket to anywhere in world he or she wanted to travel. Most of the time, their parents, in their home country, paid their tuition to attend school. That is because most of the Asian students at the university came from affluent families. I had no idea this kind of stuff occurred. From my experiences with dissertation committee members, they are going to make you pay upfront or later by dragging out the dissertation to make a profit. That is the kind of crap that goes on. Also, some female students will provide sexual favors to a male dissertation chair and cut the process in half. I know of one whom I'm not going to mention her name. Other professors like students to provide lunch and food for them at every dissertation meeting. This can be very expensive. That might get you out of school quicker. It is all political. That is why you have some dreadful dissertations out there. They sure don't tell you this in the university's Doctoral Student Handbook! These practices lack ethics and totally undermine the entire dissertation process as well as the production of scholarly work.

As before with Wetherhold, I started having problems with Dr. Brannigan. She, too, was overly meticulous about trivial things. The items in the study that required her attention were not the things on which she focused. When I got to a point of presenting my proposal to the committee, they kept requesting changes to my instrument. To be honest, they totally ruined my instrument. My mistake was selecting another person, as chair, who did not have a business background. However, she was very astute in multivariate statistics.

The Second Chair Lets the Committee Member Take Over

Another problem I had with Brannigan was she allowed Gershowitz to direct the committee. This happened on many occasions. I swear she lacked leadership skills. She was another incompetent chair and was almost as bad as Wetherhold. Later, I learned that she was notorious for allegedly making Black doctoral students stay in school longer while demanding additional and unnecessary work. Two other Black doctoral students told me this in confidence. Another situation that was reminiscent of the suffering I endured due to Wetherhold. Brannigan did not have a business background either, so I had to correct her, constantly, on the appropriate use of business terminology and concepts. She had no idea about accounting, management, marketing, finance, or entrepreneurship. Other than her knowledge of statistics, she was almost as bad as Wetherhold.

Once again, I noticed I was not progressing forward fast enough with Dr. Brannigan. My literature review was done. She reviewed it, suggesting that I delete a bunch of researchers from the literature review. These were seminal entrepreneurship researchers. One day I just got tired of her, because I did not agree with her, and she did not know what the hell she was talking about. So, I went over page by page, and I wanted to know why this author needed to be deleted from the dissertation. I made her give me a reason for each one, and I was going to decide whether it was going to be deleted. She did not like that one bit. I really did not care. I wasn't going to let her screw up my work.

The next meeting with her, I just snapped. I told her that Dr. Živkovi should be helping me with literature review, because she had a PhD in economics. She did not understand business and had should not be editing my literature review. I just got tired of her. She kept trying to have me delete major researchers/research from the literature review. She got quiet, and then I left. She did not like me confronting her. I emailed Dr. Živkovi and asked her if she could review chapter two. Dr. Živkovi reviewed it and emailed me her opinion. Although there was some overlap in the content areas, she thought that my literature review was excellent. She even made the recommendation that I make it longer! I know this infuriated Brannigan. Živkovi said something totally opposite of her. She did not like that one bit. That is what happens when you get a professor with an education background trying to review a business dissertation.

As previously mentioned, Brannigan lacked leadership skills as the dissertation chair. It was like she was submissive to Gershowitz. I was not going to stand for it. I sensed that she treaded carefully because Gershowitz was good friends with the university president, so she feared him. That was why I kept recording our meetings, because I felt some funny business was going on. This man obtained his PhD in special education. What the hell does he know about entrepreneurship and statistics? I started complaining to her about him. She started telling me to just do what he says. I refused and would not do what he said. I hated him so much, I wanted to slap him because he's so stupid. I believe he knew I couldn't stand him and did things to antagonize me. I also believe that she would forward my emails to him in which I complained about him and his incompetence.

The Second Chair Strikes Again

They started pulling dirty things on me. For example, they made me do three pre-defenses. That is not the norm for a doctoral candidate. One is usually the norm. Two is uncommon. Three is extremely rare. I started noticing in the meetings that Dr. Gershowitz was asserting more power. He was the most vocal and the most critical of my work. Again, I did not like him trying to run the dissertation. Dr. Brannigan was like the cowardly lion from the movie, *Wizard of Oz*. Brannigan was a spineless powder puff. I cannot believe she let Gershowitz influence her. She was also the chair of my friend Simon's committee. She let a committee member embarrass him at this public defense. That seemed to be her typical pattern. Dr. Brannigan only knows how to get tough with students, not other committee members. Dr. Gershowitz was doing this crap because I did not want his buddy, Wetherhold, on the new committee; and Brannigan let him get away with such behavior. She had as much backbone as a marshmallow. Politics as usual.

One day I just had enough of Brannigan, so I snapped again. I got tired of her redundant and stupid revisions. She asked me to revise something one day, then asked me to change it back to way it to the original version. Then she would forget her instructions from the last revisions. So, I snapped. I told her that every time I gave her something, she gave me something back. I was tired of this BS. I told her I should have gone to law school. She got quiet. Then I asked if she were going to remain on as the chair. She told me she would let me know. "Whatever" was my reply. So, I left her office and went straight to the dean of Graduate Studies office. I told him what happened and showed him the ridiculous revisions she was having me do. I told him she was still reviewing chapters she already approved three or four months ago. He could not believe she was still reviewing chapter two. After we talked, he told me that he was going to talk to her. At that point, things were starting to get worse. Now I had two enemies: Dr. Ryan Gershowitz and Dr. Jeanette Brannigan. I'm quite sure she did not like that I went to see the dean of Graduate Studies. I had to get her attention.

After this incident, I was told that I would have only email correspondence with Dr. Brannigan. She refused to meet with me in person. Then, after that, she started requesting that I use the university's email account instead of my yahoo account. I thought this was extremely odd to ask me to use a different email address after years of working on my dissertation committee. I found out later that she was trying to protect herself from any legal action. If I used the university's email system, the email records could not be subpoenaed in a court case because the university is a private university.

If either my attorney or I wanted to access the email system, then the university's IT department could lock me out, and I then would have no access to any of the messages. If it were a public university, then all emails could be subpoenaed. I tried to use the university's email system. It was horrible and unreliable. So, I sent Brannigan an email, and I copied the dean of Graduate Studies requesting that they use my personal email account for any future correspondence. I also stated it was the second time I requested she use my personal email address. I came to the realization that Brannigan and Gershowitz were not going to allow me to graduate from the university.

Almost Quitting the Doctoral Program

After this incident, I had had enough. I made the decision to quit the doctoral program. I sent Dr. Brannigan an email that I was quitting the doctoral program. I had gotten tired of the racial stuff I had to go through. I did not tell anybody because I did not want to hear it. I called my mother and told her I was dropping out of the doctoral program. My mother got really upset with me. She told me I had gone too far to quit. I said I had enough and did not need this crap. My mother called my uncle in Washington, DC, and told him to call me and convince me not to quit. My uncle called and convinced me not to quit. We talked for a long time. He told me stories about what my father had to go through in the 1960s at another Catholic institution. My uncle pleaded with me not to quit. He said it was not only important for me to finish what I started, but I would be the first person in the Miles family to earn a PhD. My mother told me I could not quit. After I cooled off, I made the decision to stick it out. I emailed Brannigan and told her to please disregard the previous email; I was not quitting the doctoral program.

I also found out that my friend from Taiwan, who also had Brannigan as her dissertation chair, was conducting a study similar to mine. I also discovered that Brannigan was having me do a plethora of extra work that she was not requiring of my friend. My friend used to leave her revisions in the doctoral room, so one day I looked at them. Brannigan hardly wrote anything on her drafts. Contrast that with markings on mine. She was extremely nitpicky and citing me for anything she could that would stall my dissertation progress. I thought this was very odd considering that English was my friend's second language. That really pissed me off. This woman, like Wetherhold, was a real piece of work, just a different type.

After a year of this, as I was nearly doing my dissertation defense, I requested a reasonable date for my final defense. Brannigan refused to give me a reasonable timeframe for a public defense. She would reply with obscure statements like "If you do the work, we will have the public defense soon." That was unacceptable to me. She was intentionally making vague statements that did not give me a firm dissertation defense date. When I talked to my friend, she told me Dr. Brannigan had given her confirmation date for her defense.

The Second Chair Makes an Accusation

One day I sent her an email requesting that I did not want my dissertation published through ProQuest. I also stated that she had an inability to understand business concepts or terminology and that this issue had been a prevailing problem. Furthermore, I expressed frustration with her refusal to listen to me regarding the fact that I did not want my dissertation published. The revisions she requested were incorrect, and that meant the content was incorrect, and rather than be embarrassed, I requested my dissertation not be published. The revisions did not represent my work, ideas, or input. That must have really pissed her off. She forwarded my email directly to the dean of Graduate Studies. I was not prepared for what was going to happen next. This woman lied on me and said I threatened her! She put it that "she felt threatened by me." She literally played the race card. Any time you fall out of favor with a White person, especially an incompetent White woman, they will play the race card. Since she did not have anything on me, she lied and implied that I had threatened her. I could not believe this. Yeah, I threatened her all right; that's why she wrote a letter of recommendation for me to get a fellowship for USASBE Symposium for doctoral candidates in the field of entrepreneurship. I was ready to take legal action.

The dean of Graduate Studies emailed me and requested that I meet with him. It was an urgent matter. He then emailed me a formal letter with the university's letterhead stating that I was treading close to getting kicked out of the doctoral program. He cited university policy from the student handbook concerning conduct of a doctoral student. I got really angry. I got so angry that I called the provost, Dr. Deborah Hoyle, and told her about the situation. She told me that no one believed that I threatened Dr. Brannigan and not to worry about it. The provost used to see me waiting in the hallway outside of Brannigan's office nearly every time I had a meeting with her. She would always speak to me. She and everybody knew that I would never threaten Brannigan. I had been attending the university for seven years. I did not have a history of threatening professors. Dr. Brannigan totally fabricated this allegation to try and get the graduate dean to take action against me. I guess she couldn't handle me, so she had to run and tell "Daddy." What a loser professor and dissertation chair.

Uh Oh, I'm in Trouble: The Graduate Dean Wants to Meet with Me

I believe the provost and dean of Graduate Studies had enough of Dr. Brannigan. Before the meeting with the dean of Graduate Studies, I was advised that I should not meet with Brannigan alone. I wanted to meet with her, the dean of the department, and the provost. I stated, "Why should Dr. Brannigan be the only one to tell her side of the story?" Dr. Verhoeven informed me that such a meeting was not going to happen. He reiterated that I was not to communicate with Brannigan or any of my committee members. He urged me to meet with him the following Monday. I told him in the email that I was not confident in his abilities to rectify the situation. I felt he was only doing damage control. I told him that I'd had problems with Brannigan four months ago and he did nothing. So, he replied that he would handle the situation and implored me to meet with him to discuss the situation. Reluctantly, I agreed to meet with Dr. Verhoeven in spite of my reservations.

I met with Dr. Verhoeven, and he told me during our meeting that he had to send me that letter because Brannigan turned the situation into a threat. He explained he had to take action because the situation was getting out of control. He said, "I know you as a student, and you do not have a reputation of making threats against professors." I explained to him all the things that had been going on. I told him how incompetent Dr. Gershowitz was and the problems I had with Brannigan. I also told him of my problems in the doctoral program and how Wetherhold had threatened me, what they did to Dr. Dietrich, and how Brannigan mocked me in the dissertation committee meetings. He said that he was sorry for all the things that happened to me at the university. He told me the university had been having consistent problems with Dr. Brannigan and that I was not the first student to complain about her. I was still on guard. I did not know if he was playing with me or what. I let him know I had digital recordings of all of my meetings with her and the committee. I let him know I was prepared to take legal action if necessary.

He told me that he had a game plan for me to complete the doctoral program and graduate. He outlined them in the formal document he emailed me prior to our meeting. He informed me that Dr. Brannigan had stepped down at the dissertation chair. She was no longer my chair, and Dr. Starks was now the interim chair of the committee until I graduated. I do not believe she quit. I believe the provost, dean of Graduate Studies, and the dean of the department removed Brannigan as committee chair because they were worried about a forthcoming lawsuit.

The graduate dean strongly advised me to avoid entering the building where Brannigan's office was located. He feared that she might use to situation to claim I was stalking her. Additionally, I was warned not to speak to her or contact her in any what way shape or form because she might exaggerate it and say that I assaulted her. He also told me that I would have to be an idiot to screw up at my private defense to not pass it. He stated that he was going to be present. He did not say that my passing was guaranteed, but he did not see any reason why I would not pass my third private defense. It really was money in the bank. I knew my statistics in my sleep, so I had nothing to worry about. He told me that I did not need to use PowerPoint or any computer at the private defense. I just needed to show up, talk about my study, and answer the questions. To me, it was just a formality. I had already done two pre-defenses and was denied advancement, because of Gershowitz and Brannigan. Verhoeven knew Dr. Victim and Dr. Dumber were the problem and not me.

Enough Is Enough: The Second Chair Quits

This is the reason why I do not believe that she stepped down as chair. I believe they removed her, because they got tired of her antics that stalled my defense and graduation. They told me she quit, to save face and not tarnish her reputation with the students. How would it look to have the director of the doctoral program removed as chair from a dissertation committee? She had to be removed for another reason because she was focusing on retaliating against me rather than trying to get the dissertation completed so I could graduate. She made it personal. How long was this stuff going to go on without some type of intervention from the provost? I think when she lied and said I threatened her, they had enough. She had her power taken away. It was time for this entire show to end. She did not like it that I asked her questions and questioned her directives. That is what irked her the most. She could not misuse her authority and retaliate against a student who wasn't taking any of her stuff. There is a Mexican proverb that goes something like this, "I'd rather die on my feet than live on my knees." That was definitely indicative of my attitude toward her. Lastly, why would she quit if she was getting paid? If she quit, she would have to pay that money back, if I'm not mistaken.

Also, I was invited to attend my foreign friend's public defense. But since Brannigan was also her dissertation chair, that was going to be a problem. I decided not to go. I emailed Dr. Verhoeven and asked permission to attend her public defense. However, since Brannigan was going to be present, Verhoeven had to email Brannigan and ask if it was okay for me to attend or if campus police needed to be present. Brannigan emailed him back, and he informed me that is was okay with her if I attended my friend's public defense. That really pissed me off. I made the decision not to go. I could no longer be in the same room with this woman who was a liar. She was carrying out this lie pretty far. I just decided that I was not going to take any chances. If she lied about something trivial like being threatened, she was capable of anything.

The Dean of Graduate Studies helped me complete my doctoral program at the university. He overruled the policy and extended the deadline for me to complete my public defense and graduate by fall 2010. I was told by my friends the dean would never make such accommodations for a student in the doctoral program at the university. The graduate dean also made copies of my dissertation for the committee members at the private defense.

The dean attended and supervised the private defense. During the defense, he let both, Gershowitz and Brannigan know this defense was a wrap with his presence and that I was going to graduate. In retaliation against me, both of them kept trying to find reasons to prolong the dissertation. Dr. Verhoeven put a stop to it. This is what they were trying to do. It was personal, not business. This is what doctoral students deal with these antics with committee members. They were neutralized since Dr. Starks was installed as the new committee chair. Had Dr. Verhoeven had not intervened, I would have been in school another two semesters because of these two buzzards. To be honest, I believe the only reason I graduated from the university was because they thought I was going to get legal counsel and sue them. They were determined to try and get me out of school before that happened. They knew that I never threatened her, and they were worried that I might get legal counsel. Furthermore, the committee, including those two buzzards, agreed that I had one of the best dissertations to come out of the university. Don't believe me? Subsequently, I published two books and ten journal articles from my doctoral work. Also, I won three awards for my research in entrepreneurship and economics, and I won a doctoral consortium fellowship. Also, I have numerous citations on Google Scholar for my doctoral research on entrepreneurial risk. I have published the most academic journal articles from a dissertation than any other doctoral student in the history of university. I got the last laugh!

The Last Laugh: The Other Side of the Rainbow

After I passed my private defense and was preparing for the public defense, Dr. Verhoeven informed me that Dr. Brannigan would not attend. Wow, she was really trying to hurt my feelings by not being there? That was music to me ears. Good riddance! Now she can go ruin somebody else's dissertation! On the day of my defense, I actually saw her sitting in her office. What a dreadful and petty woman. After she lied and said I threatened her, I still graduated. After all of her antics, I still graduated. Once she was removed as the chair, I graduated. I won and got the last laugh. Like I said before, if she had behaved like a chair, she would not have been removed as the committee chair.

After I graduated in the fall of 2010, the next semester, I went to school to drop off copies of my new book that was published from my dissertation research. I gave a copy to a few selected committee members but not Dr. Victim or Dr. Dumber. While on the way to a professor's office, I saw Brannigan in the hallway. She said hello to me as I was passing by. I ignored her and just kept walking as though I neither saw nor heard her. I had to admit, that felt SO good! After you've done the many dreadful and unfair things to me, now you have the audacity speak to me? Now I don't have to deal with this person any longer, much less see her. That was the end of my journey dealing with the politics, trials, and tribulations at the university. Now I am part of the academic brotherhood.

After graduation, one of my friends was told that Brannigan was doing the same things to her as a she did to me. A leopard never changes their spots. One of my other friends told me that they forced Brannigan to retire from the university. My friend told she was demoted as director of doctoral students and was replaced. I was also told they gave her a closet for an office. Lastly, they totally restricted her from teaching any doctoral courses but only easy non-technical courses, so she could not cause any damage to doctoral students.

It was apparent they were trying to make her quit. For her retirement party, I heard they gave Brannigan a crappy retirement gift. The university wanted to get rid of her really bad. It was time. That speaks volumes. Karma is a mother. They basically let her know they wanted her gone. For that to happen, she must have had problems with many doctoral students. They had enough of her, so she left the university in disgrace.

Post-Graduation: Reflections of Attaining the Doctorate

The pursuit of attaining a doctorate is one achievement that trumps everything in your life. Being Black and a scholar is an achievement within itself that you cannot put into words. You reached the zenith of your educational endeavors. By far, this is the highest achievement that I have accomplished. I have finally joined the 1 Percent Club (less than 1 percent of the population has a doctoral degree). That is no easy feat. Now having attained the doctorate, I guess the privileges have come slowly. To have students call you "Dr. Miles" is still weird to me. I feel like they're talking to someone else. Now that I have arrived professionally, there are costs I had not imagined.

You Better Put Some Respect on My Name!

I find it interesting how some students disrespect professors by not addressing them properly by not calling them doctor. I find this is especially common with White students and Black professors. I have experienced this firsthand. To some White students, they don't feel as though they should have to respect your credentials compared to a White professor. This is very common. One semester, when I was teaching at the university, I had two White students email me with some questions. In the email, the students started with "Mr. Miles," blah, blah, blah. In my email response, I politely corrected them: "My name is Dr. Miles, not Mr. Miles." A few students apologized, but there were some students who did not. One time I had a student call me by first name in an email! I do not think this is a mistake. Remember, you have to think about what you are writing in an email. Then they play dumb like they did not know they were being disrespectful. They are well aware of what they are doing.

After I corrected these particular students who addressed me as "Mr. Miles," these students then went to the department chair and complained that I asked them to call me "Dr. Miles." The chair of the department emailed me and requested that I meet with him to discuss this. At first, I thought this was a joke. They actually went to him and complained that I asked them to address me by my name. This made me angry. I wonder if I were a White professor that requested the same courtesy, would they have the same audacity to complain to the department chair? That really made me angry. This antic is like saying, "Negro, I don't have to respect you nor your credentials." I thought, if I were a department chair, I would not have let a student come to me over such a trivial matter.

First, I would have said is "And this is a problem because why?" It isn't as if I'm standing in line at Burger King ordering food and requesting the person behind the counter call me "Dr. Miles." After our meeting, I went back to my class and continued correcting students who did not address me the way I preferred to be addressed. I think a professor with a PhD should have the right to be addressed as "Dr." if it is his/her choice, despite the students getting upset about being corrected. Get a life and get over it! To me, the entitlement mentality of this generation is going to bring down the institution of higher learning. As I reflected on my years in undergraduate school, I have NEVER gone to a department chair to complain about a professor. This is the sign of the times of with this generation. This speaks volumes on the mentality of this generation. They think that somebody owes them something. I do not entertain this thought with my students. It is just a shame this is the generation that is coming up behind us. I have concerns.

Confessions of A PhD: Post Traumatic Doctorate Syndrome (PTDS)

I hope that my story touched you, made you laugh, cry, and go "Wow." If I did not have a sense of humor about all of this, I would probably be in prison right now from committing homicide. I hope that I can pass my experiences on to someone that can avoid the same mistakes I made. My story is not a screenplay, by any means, but it's *my* screenplay. First and foremost, I would like to give all praises due to God for allowing me the opportunity to reach my goals and share my journey. I thank God for blessing me through meeting great people in this journey of life. I would also like to thank all of the people who were my support system.

• • •